TRADITIONAL WATER MANAGEMENT SYSTEMS OF INDIA

TRADITIONAL WATER MANAGEMENT SYSTEMS OF INDIA

Editors

Kalyan Kumar Chakravarty
Gyani Lal Badam
Vijay Paranjpye

Indira Gandhi Rashtriya Manav Sangrahalaya
Bhopal

Aryan Books International
New Delhi

TRADITIONAL WATER MANAGEMENT SYSTEMS OF INDIA

The book is based on seminar proceedings on 'Traditional Water Management Systems' organised by the Indira Gandhi Rashtriya Manav Sangrahalaya, Bhopal and held in four components, at Bhopal (16-18th September 1997), Ahmedabad (19-21st January 1998), Pune (3-4th April 1998) and Bhandara (26-28th October 1998).

ISBN: 978-81-7305-315-3

Published in **2006** by :
INDIRA GANDHI RASHTRIYA MANAV SANGRAHALAYA
Shamla Hills, Bhopal - 462 013 (M.P.)
and
ARYAN BOOKS INTERNATIONAL
Pooja Apartments, 4B, Ansari Road, Darya Ganj, New Delhi - 110 002 (India)
Tel.: 23287589, 23255799; Fax: 91-11-23270385
E-mail: aryanbooks@gmail.com
www.aryanbooks.com

Computer Typeset and Printed in India at
ABI Prints & Publishing Co., New Delhi

FOREWORD

It is our immense pleasure that the volume 'Traditional Water Management Systems of India' edited by Dr. K.K. Chakravarty, Dr. G.L. Badam and Dr. Vijay Paranjpye is brought to light, jointly published by our Museum and Aryan Books International, New Delhi. There cannot be a more opportune moment for this publication at least for two reasons. First, in recent times, much emphasis has been put by UNESCO and the Govt. of India for documentation of traditional knowledge systems, sometime also known as intangible cultural heritage, since there is a steady loss of these forms of knowledge from the collective memory. Needless to say, our Museum has always been in the forefront in documenting, disseminating, conserving and revitalizing traditional knowledge systems as an important input in development strategies. This volume is yet another pointer in that direction. Second, in an age when the ground water level is steadily going down and deeper, when there is even talk of a Third World War – if it ever happens – on the issue of water, and when there are contrasting problems of water, flood on the one hand and drought on the other, there is no denying the fact that the traditional modes of water management, which have stood the test of time for centuries and generations, are to be emphasized and revitalized for better conservation and efficient management. This is a case where emphasizing the 'tradition' does not mean putting the clock back, but rather it is a means for sustainable development.

The present book is the result of workshops on Traditional Water management Systems, organized by our museum, as a part of the Golden Jubilee Celebration of India's independence in 1997, when Dr. K.K. Chakravarty was the Director and Dr. G.L. Badam, the Academic Advisor. I congratulate the editors for their painstaking work and the contributors for their cooperation. Publication of the volume jointly by our Museum and Aryan Books International, New Delhi – I convey my sincere thanks to the latter – is another example of the success story of our new publication policy in the form of public-private partnership.

I sincerely hope that the book would be found interesting by people at large, in particular, specialists in water management and conservation, historians, archaeologists, sociologists and anthropologists.

Kishor K. Basa
Director
IGRMS, Bhopal

PREFACE

Since the emergence of the humankind, water has played a major role in its survival. In the pre-historic past, human beings always preferred to live either on the river-banks or in places close to the water source, for sustenance and safety. Most of the pre-historic sites, ranging from Lower Palaeolithic to Neolithic, have been found on the banks of the rivers, in the vicinity of lakes or near the streams. An awareness regarding the proper management of water and its sources came about only in the Neolithic, with man exploiting water sources for cultivation, transportation and communication.

There is evidence that water management was one of the major aspects in town and country planning during the Harappan and Chalcolithic periods. Sites like Mohenjo-daro, Harappa and some of the Chalcolithic sites in the Deccan (for example, Inamgaon) have yielded important traces of irrigation and water supply. The evidence of ploughed field at the site of Kalibangan in Ganganagar district of Rajasthan points to the existence of irrigation system. Scarcity of water was one of the crucial factors that caused the decline of the great Harappan civilization. Similar was the case with the sites in the Ghaggar and Drisadhwati valleys (Rajasthan, Haryana), which were abandoned with the drying up of perennial rivers that supported them.

The majority of Early Historic sites witnessed the afflorescence of hydraulic civilizations. Sites like Ujjain, Vidisha and Taxila were not only well fortified but also protected by natural or artificial moats. The Early Historic site of Sisupalgarh (near Bhubaneswar), which was excavated in 1940s, is worth mentioning here. The Early Historic settlement at Asurgarh had a massive moat around it along with a proper water supply system.

A well-organized hydraulic system existed during the days of the Delhi Sultanate and Mughals. A well-planned water circulation system was a part of their exquisite gardens and air-conditioning facilities. Arrangements were also made to supply water to the forts on the hilltops with great difficulty. This very system became a contributory factor in the decline of the medieval forts. One of the strategies of capturing the forts was to cut off water supply to the forts. Akbar shifted his capital from Agra to Fatehpur Sikri and back to Agra because of acute water shortage during summer.

Traditional water harvesting and irrigation systems continue to be relevant till today, in places where rainfall is scarce, e.g., Gujarat and Rajasthan. In the Thar Desert, the local harvesting device is known as *Kundis* (huge concrete saucers), in which the rainwater gets accumulated. This water is utilized by both men and animals. The *Kundis* are both public and private and the private ones are kept locked in order to protect water from both public use and overflow. Another example of water management comes from Jodhpur (Rajasthan) which, in spite of being situated in an arid climatic zone, rarely faced water problems, thanks to its well-managed canal system. There are a number of Rajasthani folk-songs related to water management.

In Mizoram, there is a system of collecting rainwater from the rooftops. For this reason, rooftops are made of corrugated iron sheets. In Nagaland, channels are dug to divert stream water into paddy fields. The forests along the streams are not cut because that helps them in bringing irrigation water, containing nutrients for unfertile soils of the hills.

The workshops on the 'Traditional Water Management Systems' were held as part of the Golden Jubilee Celebration of India's freedom, autonomy and variety of Indian knowledge systems including water management against homogenizing technological solutions imported from the West. The meetings took place in the backdrop of an exhibition on the history of Indian Navigation Traditions mounted by the Indira Gandhi Rashtriya Manav Sangrahalaya, with the help of voluntary organizations. Meetings under this project were held in four components, the first one at IGRMS, Bhopal from 16-18 September 1997; the second one at Gujarat Vidyapeeth, Ahmedabad between 19-21st January 1998; the third one with Econet at Pune, 3-4th April 1998; and the fourth one with the help of Econet and Water Managers at Bhandara from 26-28th October 1998. The seminars were followed by several field initiatives, co-directed by communities, for celebration of the history, sanctity and utility of waters, all over the country. The main aim was to locate the managerial, legal or financial problems, which stood in the way of recycling of the local water harvesting structures. There was also the problem of understanding the need for establishing the validity and feasibility of these structures as eco-specific and cost-effective alternatives to mega structures. The Indira Gandhi Rashtriya Manav Sangrahalaya (IGRMS), Bhopal, wanted to build indoor and outdoor exhibitions with a mobile component, to expose the common man to hard facts of mega dams, and to promote the conservation of traditional water management systems as a national heritage. The above meetings helped inaugurate a long term phase of mutually reinforcive and fruitful collaboration between the participants and the IGRMS and added to the existing knowledge of water management from pre-historic to the present times.

On the whole, the deliberations revealed that the traditional water management systems were still useful and had an important role to play in day-to-day activities of the local people. The main task was to preserve, re-charge and revitalize these systems. For this, people's participation and involvement is of utmost importance. It was also emphasized that traditional wisdom and techniques had to be taken into consideration while making developmental plans. Now-a-days, population growth, deforestation and industrialization cause major problems and hence it is the need of the hour to upgrade traditional water harvesting systems within the location specific technological framework.

Organizing deliberations of this magnitude would not have been possible without the participation and active involvement of scholars, drawn from various Central and State Government agencies, Museums, Institutions and Non-Governmental Organizations. The papers presented in the deliberations were of high standard which were followed by useful discussions and suggestions.

We are grateful to the Ministry of Culture, Government of India and the IGRMS, Bhopal for a generous grant which contributed to the successful and smooth conduct of the several workshops, seminars and the field trips connected with the programme. We express our grateful thanks to the Central Groundwater Board, and to Dr. G.K. Dev Burman, Shri Vinayak Potnis, Shri N.K. Dighe, Dr. (Late) B.R. Sharma, Late Shri Jagdish Godbole and others for rendering their valuable co-operation and help during the seminar, and also during the various meetings, preceding the seminar. Prof. K. Karunakaran, Prof. K.C. Malhotra, Dr. Arun Sud, members of the IGRMS staff, contributed immensely to the success of the seminar, right from the stage of organization to that of conclusion. The curatorial and technical staff and the Director's Office of the IGRMS willingly helped at every stage during the conduct of the seminar and thereafter. Special mention may be made of Shri R.K. Shrivastava, Shri G. Jayaprakashan, Shri Manoj Kumar Jain, Shri Sudhir Shrivastava, Shri K. Seshadri, Shri H.B.S. Parihar, Shri Ravi Shivas, Shri Anand Tahenguria and several colleagues of the IGRMS. We are grateful to Prof. G.C. Tripathi (IGNCA) for having spared his valuable time and made several important suggestions with regard to the sanskrit words and their romanised transcriptions.

In course of editing various papers, meaningful help was rendered from time to time by Shri Balaram Tripathy, Ms. V. Shobha, Ms. Anjali Paranjpye and Jitu Mishra (Pune), Ms. Shampa Shah, Shri S.K. Pandey, Shri P.S. Rao (Bhopal) and Ms. Shailaja Srinivasan (Ahmedabad) for which we thank them whole heartedly.

We are extremely thankful to Shri S.B. Ota, the then Superintending Archaeologist, ASI, Bhopal, (who held an additional charge of the Director of IGRMS for sometime) and the present Director, IGRMS, Prof. K.K. Basa for their co-operation and help in getting this volume published. Indeed, without their interest and help it would not have been possible to bring out the proceedings of the series of seminars on Water Management in the present form.

As said above, the various symposia in connection with Water Management were organized in Bhopal, Ahmedabad, Pune and Bhandara from 1997-1998, when Dr. K.K. Chakravarty was the Director of IGRMS and G.L. Badam its Academic Advisor (though still attached to the Deccan Collage, Pune). However, because of the change of address of the editors, some delay was caused in the organization and publication of this volume which we regret very much.

Shri Vikas Arya of Aryan Books International, New Delhi did an excellent job in bringing out the publication meticulously and deserves special thanks. We would like to stress that the authors alone are responsible for the data presented and the opinions expressed in their contributions.

Kalyan Kumar Chakravarty
Gyani Lal Badam
Vijay Paranjpye

CONTENTS

SECTION I

TRADITIONAL WATER MANAGEMENT SYSTEMS

SECTION II

TRADITIONAL WATER MANAGEMENT SYSTEMS IN CONTEMPORARY TIMES

SECTION III

SHORT COMMUNICATIONS, SUGGESTIONS AND RECOMMENDATIONS

LIST OF ILLUSTRATIONS

FIGURES

LIST OF CONTRIBUTORS

A.P. Joshi, Himalayan Environmental Studies & Conservation Organization (HESCO), Gwar-Chauki, Gholtir, Chamoli (Garhwal).

Ajay Dixit, Nepal Water Conservation Foundation, Kathmandu, Nepal.

Ashwani Wanganeo, Department of Limnology, Barkatullah University, Bhopal (M.P.).

B.S. Gajul, Department of Archaeology, Deccan College, Pune - 411 006.

Baba Mishra, P.G. Department of History, Govt. College, Bhawanipatna, Orissa - 766 001.

G. Vasudeo, Nardep, Vivekananda Kendra, Kanyakumari.

Gyani Lal Badam, Indira Gandhi National Centre for the Arts, Janpath, New Delhi - 110 001.

J. Manuel, Archaeological Survey of India, G.T.B. Complex, T.T. Nagar, Bhopal - 462 003.

K.C.B. Raju, Vivekananda Research and Training Institute, Mandvi, Kuchch - 370 465.

K.K. Chakravarty, Indira Gandhi National Centre for the Arts, Janpath, New Delhi - 110 001.

Kamal Saxena, Institute for Socialist Education, Secular House, 9/1, Institutional Area, Aruna Asaf Ali Marg, New Delhi - 110 067.

Krishna Gandhi, Lokodyam Sanstha, 78 Mission Compound, Opp. PWD Godown, Jhansi - 284 003.

Lavesh Kansal, Vastu Kala Academy, Secular House, 9/1, Qutab Institutional Area, Aruna Asaf Ali Marg, New Delhi - 110 067.

M.K. Dhavalikar, 33, Navketan Society, Kothrud, Pune - 411 024.

M.S. Mate, 1896 Mate Path, Off Bajirao Road, Sadashiv Peth, Pune - 411 030.

Makarand Pendse, Dwarka Housing Society, Prabhu Lane, Sivaji Road, Panvel, Raigad - 745 770.

Manish Rajankar, ECONET, 509, Bhide Lane, Behind Nagpur Times, Old Ramdaspeth, Nagpur - 440 010.

Meera Dass, E-1, 154, Arera Colony, Bhopal - 462 016.

P.K. Ghanekar, Department of Botany, Garware College, Pune - 411 004.

P.P. Dandawate, Department of Archaeology, Deccan College, Pune - 411 006.

P.S. Joshi, c/o Department of Archaeology, Deccan College, Pune - 411 006.

Pradeep Mohanty, c/o Department of Archaeology, Deccan College, Pune - 411 006.

R. Sreenivasan, Tank Programme, PRADAN, Madurai, Tamil Nadu - 10.

R.G. Arya, F-8, Housing Board Colony, Straw Berry Hills, Shimla - 171 002.

R.K. Patil, Centre for Applied Systems Analysis in Development, Pune.

Raman Patel, Programme Organiser (Water Resource), Aga Khan Rural Support Programme, Netrang, Bharuch - 393 130 (Gujarat).

Rumita Gupta, Himalayan Environmental Studies & Conservation Organization (HESCO), Gwar-Chauki, Gholtir, Chamoli (Garhwal).

S. Ramanuja, Vastu Kala Academy, Secular House, 9/1 Qutab Institutional Area, Aruna Asaf Ali Road, New Delhi - 110 067.

S.N. Rajaguru, c/o Deccan College, Pune - 411 006.

S.S. Raghuwanshi, E-6/2, Arera Colony, Bhopal - 462 016.

Shobhana Gokhale, c/o Department of Archaeology, Deccan College, Pune - 411 006.

Shubhada Kamlapurkar, 31/9 Adarsh Nagar, Pune Satara Road, Pune - 411 037.

Sunanda Kirtane, Lokodyam Sanstha, 78 Mission Compound, Opp. PWD Godown, Jhansi - 284 003.

U.C. Pandey, 6/353, Kalawati Colony, Nawabi Road, Haldwani - 263 139, Dist. Nainital.

Vijay Kumar, Water Resource Division, Action for Food Production, 25/1A, Institutional Area, D Block, Pankha Road, Janak Puri, New Delhi - 110 058

Vijay Paranjpye, Durga Bungalow, 92/2 Gangote Path, Opp. Kamla Nehru Park, Erandwane, Pune.

Yogini Dolke, ECONET, 509, Bhide Lane, Behind Nagpur Times, Old Ramdaspeth, Nagpur - 440 010.

TOWARDS A SUSTAINABLE WATER POLICY

K.K. Chakravarty

THE GLOBAL PERSPECTIVE

A policy of sustainable water management in India has to respect traditional water management strategies. These were based on the instinctive knowledge of poverty in plenty in view of the inaccessible nature of most of the water sources. Though three quarters of the earth planet is shrouded in water, 97% of this water is saline, locked in ocean, and 77% of the water in the 3% land is frozen in polar ice caps. Only 1% of the remaining 23% ground water is accessible through lakes, rivers and streams, while 22% goes waste in the absence of proper rainwater harvesting approaches. Of the 200 largest river systems, 150 are shared by two nations, and 50 by 3 to 10 nations. Though India comes 5th after Canada, China, USSR and Brazil with 4.9% of the world's annual run off from rivers, the per capita availability of water in India hovers around 1/4th of the global average of 10 to 12 thousand cubic meters. 80% of India gets 80% or more of annual rainfall only during four monsoonal months. India's average annual rainfall of about 4000 billion cubic meters is unevenly distributed temporally and spatially, ranging from 11,000mm in Cherrapunji in Assam to 200mm in Jaisalmer in Rajasthan. Most of it being lost in evaporation and seepage, only about 630 BCM is utilized. 70% of the fresh water withdrawal is dedicated to agriculture, mainly irrigation, and globally, 22% of such withdrawal goes to industry. Safe and adequate supply of drinking water and water for domestic uses remains a priority, and this is still dependent, to a very large extent, on traditional water harvesting structures.

LOCAL WATER HARVESTING STRUCTURES

The traditional water harvesting strategies had effected an integration of storm and floodwater regulation, wastewater collection, drinking water supply and micro-irrigation. These were location specific, slope efficient, gravitation based, inexpensive and non extractive methods of harvesting the extremely limited fresh water supply, accessible to human use. Indian communities had perfected management of the natural watersheds of forests, hills and dales, using knowledge of the hydrological regimes and rhythms, water veins and aquifers, slope and lie of land, history and movement of rivers, and myriad aquatic channels.

ARCHAEOLOGICAL EVIDENCE

Archaeology provides numerous examples of hydraulic civilization in ancient times. The gradually narrowing terraces for conserving water in pre-Harappan sites, on the pattern of Zoroastrian gabarbands; sloping terraces between storm water channels, filling reservoirs, hugging the gradients of Dholavira (3rd millennium BC); the inlet channel, connecting a trapezoid dock, equipped with spillway and stone anchors, with the river at Lothal in Harappan civilization (3rd millennium BC); the feeder channel enclosed by an embankment wall, connecting a tank and a river at Inamgaon in Chalcolithic Jorwe culture; the inlet channels, enclosed between brick platforms, flanked by wooden anchor posts, connecting river Cauvery at Kaveripattinam (2nd c. AD); the underground drains, joining stepped, tortoise shaped tanks, with spill channels and soak pits, constructed by Iksvakus at Nagarjunakonda in Andhra Pradesh; the channels cut in riverbed at Sirkatti on Mahanadi river in Raipur district, Chhattisgarh, to berth boats or floating trade logs (c. 6th AD); the feeder canals (kaluvās), equipped with sluices (tumūs) and embankments, built by Kakatiyas at Ghanpur or Ramappa, provide a series of examples of diversionary channels, which provide alternatives to large dams. The ancient embankments were breached at various places for providing subsidiary channels for conducting the fish to the paddy fields, ponds and tanks, and, for offloading floodwaters and fertilizing silt to the land beside the river.

PHILOSOPHY

Indian thought, art and literature are permeated by water cosmology. These conceive the universe as being managed by a rotary cycle of subterranean waters, incited by the solar fire. The nadīdevīs, Gajalakṣmī, yakṣas, yakṣīs, apsarases, vrkṣakās (āmra, śāla or aśoka bhañjikās), nāgas, mithunas, kalpalatās, padmavaravedikās, padmas, pūrṇakalaśas, the puṣpa and patrabhaṅgīs (folial designs) on doorjambs, pillars and mouldings of Indian temples, and all floral and faunal elements in Indian art are animated, according to poetic conceits, by waters, such as rain and dew, flood and milk, semen and mead, honey and sap. The ascent and descent of waters is the theme in the mythology of Śiva as Agni, Paśupati, Vāstoṣpati. The agniṣomīya paśu lives through the interaction of fire and waters. Inside the body, the yogī purifies by tapas (penance) the poisonous waters of passion (retas) into ambrosial waters of life. Ablution in the symbolically represented rivers at the temple threshold, is a purification of consciousness before its immersion in the noumenon in the temple womb. All principles of fertility, bounty and creativity, generative and nutritive powers are derived from these representations of waters. Creation and procreation, preservation and destruction of life are based on the harnessing, channelization, purgation, release and regulation of waters in the microcosmic body and the macrocosmic universe. Hence, the enunciation in the *Taittirīya Upaniṣad* II:6:1: रसो वै सः : He is the sap of life, or, in the *Śvetāśvatara Upaniṣad* 6:15: एको हंसो भुवनस्यास्य मध्ये, सः एवाग्निः सलिले सन्निविष्टः He is the only Swan in this world, like fire, shrouded (or surrounded) by the waters.

ICONOGRAPHY AND RITUALS

Rituals and ceremonials, associated with the inauguration, desilting, measurement or release of waters from tanks, provide an iconography of their own. Conventionally, Varuna, the trinity of Brahma, Vishnu and Maheśvara, or their pantheon, are associated with tanks. In Central India, Ghatoiyā devatās are installed on bunds or tanks, and, snake, lotus, conch shell or wheel marks are engraved on measuring pillars, planted in the tanks. Wooden poles, crowned by pots, are stuck in the middle of the tanks to consecrate them or to celebrate their wedlock. A festival is dedicated at Kumbhakonam to Thoniāppār, the God of the boat, the Lord of Shiyāli. The sea waters are territorialized and assigned to sea goddesses like Gangāmmā, Mariāmmā and Pīrs, worshipped by Hindus, Muslims as well as Christians. The bāhā flower festival of Santhals, Hos, Kharias and Oraons in eastern India, the elaborate dance and ritual art programme of theyyam in Kerala and lāi harāobā of Manipur, and muk zik ding rum faat among the Lepcha nature worshippers of Darjeeling and Sikkim, continue to sanctify the sacred water and natural resource management practices in India. Since Shahjahan's time, the fragrance of the first drop of rain on parched earth, has been considered to be the hallmark of the best quality perfume or *ītar*.

LEGAL REGIME

Traditional management of waters has been sustained by a regime of systematic exploration and legal regulation, elaborated in *Atharvaveda*, Kautilya's *Arthaśāstra* and *Manusmṛti*. *Viśvavallabha* by Chakrapani in Vallabha Math Library, Nāthadwārā, Rajasthan describes floral and faunal signs and signals to locate subterranean aquifers and water veins up to 1200 feet below ground (calculated as 200 purūshas or man measures). The *Atharvaveda* invokes Mother Earth to yield life giving water to those of pure conduct and right means, and to punish water polluters in these words:

शुद्धा न आपस्तन्वे क्षरन्तु, यो नः सेदुरप्रिये तं नि दध्मः।
पवित्रेण पृथिवि मोत पुनामि। AV. 12.1.30

Arthaśāstra provides for takeover by state, of private tanks, neglected for five years by individuals or groups; prescribes reward and penalty, including tax exemption, compensation or fines, to ensure community participation in construction, repair and renovation of water bodies; makes defilement of or damage to irrigation works punishable, as crimes comparable to embryocide, by penalties as harsh as drowning with stone, hung around neck. Among Pali texts, measures of water husbandry (jal pālanaya) are prescribed in Mahāvamśa, and in Jalabindu, Jalavāhana, and Jaladeepikā volumes, preserved in City Library, Amsterdam. For structures like the qānāt in Burhanpur, there have been provisions like reserving land (hārim) around the canal in Islamic law. In neighbouring Afghanistan, under customary Sunni (Hanafite) water law, hārim is the restricted area near wells or kārezes (canals). Water bodies have been graded according to soil zonation, bedrock, surrounding vegetation, habitation, and the code of conduct, evolved transgenerationally by the community for their use.

CLUES TO HISTORY

The study of names associated with tanks and hinterland landscapes provides clues to village history and history of waters. Chhai āgar chhai kori (126 tanks) have been constructed all over Chhattisgarh, including medieval capitals of Malhar, Arang, Raipur, Deepadih. The Lākhā Bānjārā of Sagar in Madhya Pradesh recalls association with a caravan of pastoral cattle herding nomads. The Hā Hā Pānchkumāri tank near Monghyr, Bihar is dedicated to the self immolation of five princesses. Inscribed herostones, installed on the bank of Chhattisgarh tanks, tell us about community history. Gharsisar in Jaisalmer was constructed by Mahārāwal Gharsi in 1335 and linked by waste weir with nine tanks. Āsutāl is the tank of hope in Jaisalmer on the Pak border. Kāliāsoth of Bhopal tells us about 365 streams connected under Paramāra kings to construct a 250 sq km tank, associated locally with Kāliā Gond. It took the Khalji Sultan Hoshang Shah of Mandu in the 15th century three months to break this tank. The tank took three years to flow out, thirty years to dry, and yield marshy and arable land. In Rajasthan, words like hākro (ocean) and palak dariyāv (instantaneous flooding in the twinkle of an eye), evoke memory of desertification, conversion of an ocean of water into an ocean of sand, and express hope for its reversal.

CONTINUING TRADITIONS AND TECHNOLOGIES

Aside from archaeological examples, water harvesting structures continue to be maintained by endogenous communities all over the country. Groundwater continues to be drawn from aquifers or palaeo channels in Rajasthan through *bārdi* (shallow wells in depressions), *tankās, khādin* and *johad* (underground storage pits), *kunds* (cisterns in catchments), *beris* (wells on river beds). Water is still channelized from streams or rivers into diversion, inundation or overflow channels, occasionally interspersed with storage structures and outlets, like guhls and kuhls in Kashmir, zings in Ladakh, jhorās in Darjeeling, bāndhārās in Maharashtra, keres in Karnataka, and kānwās in the flood plains of West Bengal and Bihar. In Himachal Pradesh, the naulās are waterscapes, centered on medieval shrines. Terracing, mulching, strip cropping, combining vegetation, cattle yards, manure dumps and ponds, continue to be in vogue in the zabos of Nagaland. The principle of gravitation and flow across slopes is still used in split bamboo drip pipes, to conduct stream and spring water in Meghalaya; to store rain water in jackwells among Shompens and Jarawas in Andaman and Nicobar Islands; to carry underground water through the qānāt system, comprising underground gallery, with hollow masonry columns, vertical air shafts, wells, and tile or masonry pipes in Burhanpur, Madhya Pradesh. In the absence of perennial rivers (except Māhi in central Gujarat or Tāpi in South Gujarat), Gujarat has developed 500 types of vāvs (stepwells), ekmukhī to saptamukhī (with one to seven openings), to catch the water where it falls, to travel down to its level, to take advantage of the water conserving strata of lignite and meliolite, or of lakes, stabilized by sand dunes, and covered by vegetation. Virdās have been constructed in Gujarat to separate sweet from saline water. Houses have been built with tilted roofs in Rajasthan to collect and store rainwater. Suraṅgams or tunnels in North Malabar collect moisture seeping through the surrounding laterite hillocks. Rain fed irrigation systems have sustained numerous local land races of peas, kulthis, sorghum, millet, gram, pulses, tubers, mushrooms, vegetables, and low rain fed paddy varieties, equipped with qualities of drought resistance, water tolerance, medicinal value and protein content. Germ plasm of twenty thousand rain fed, nutritious paddy varieties has been preserved in the rice plasma bank of Raipur Agricultural University.

All these environment specific strategies of local water management continue to be of relevance. Thousands of tanks, constructed by Chandela, Bundela, Panduvamsi and Kakatiya kings and local communities, and by older rulers before the Christian era, in Madhya Pradesh and Chhattisgarh, are arranged serially across settlements and around mud forts. They are named according to shape, size, location, function, nature of water and gender. Access is given to different ghāts (named as chaugharā, tighrā, āthghāṭṭi pokhar according to the number of ghāts) of these tanks for different uses and classes in the village according to time hallowed customs.

A glossary of terms has been developed through centuries to explain principles of equity, efficiency and identity, specific to various geo-hydrological regimes. The waste weir has names like neshtā, chalkā, aparā, or obrā in Rajasthan, chādar chalnā in U.P., kālangal in South India. The rush of water has been contained at crucial point in pāls (bunds), in different shapes, according to the lie of the land, with diverse names such as kohni or elbow. The āgor (catchment) or pandhāl (water slide) has been intersected by slope efficient trunk and tributary canals, to ensure storage and distribution. Nāgayashti, lath, jalyantras (measuring pillars) have been planted at different depths in the water body to regulate use. Architecture with fine stone block work, burj (bastions), jhārokhās (balconied oriel windows), pols (gates) and sculpture of superb quality have come up in Gujarat and Rajasthan for storage and movement of water.

SURVIVING MANAGEMENT PRACTICES

Community management practices have been transmitted by local water managers from generation to generation. The Gajadhars of Rajasthan have used long iron yardsticks called gaj as mark of their profession. Jalsuṅghās (water diviners) detect water veins using a mango or jamun twig. Pāliwāl Brahmins of Rajasthan or Chitpāvan Brahmins of Maharasthra have been responsible for construction and maintenance of tanks. Marginalized demographic groups like Kols, Bheels, nomadic Māldhāris, Silāwats and Meenās of Gujarat and Rajasthan, Gonds and Bānjārās of Madhya Pradesh, Nāyaks, Sabariyās or Rāmnāmis of Chhattisgarh, Luniyās of Orissa, Neerghantis of Tamilnadu have been associated with digging, maintenance and desilting of tanks and irrigation channels. Among women, queens, courtesans (Tilon kā pol in Sindh) and Panihārins (Madhya Pradesh) have constructed and dedicated tanks to earn merit. Urahi and śramdān (voluntary labour) is undertaken by communities in Chhattisgarh at the Cherchere festival to desilt tanks and to fertilize fields with silt. In Rajasthan, this process used to be launched by the king of Jaisalmer in the community game of lhās, and chunkārs, silāwats, odhis (lime workers, stone cutters, masons) would engage in āmāni (voluntary labour) to construct tanks. Community managed funds, designated purahi in Bihar or community entrusted rent free mānyam land in the south, have been set up as institutional arrangements for such managers.

Moslems of Malabar and Konkan, Malmis of Lakshadweep, Kolis and Mangelas of West coast, Tandels and Kharwas of Kutch, Paravas and Marakayars of Tamilnadu, Voda Baliyas of Andhra Pradesh, Rajbanshis of West Bengal have been boat makers, fishermen, sailors and navigators. They have classified the sea into zones according to depth and distance; made row, bar and sail boats and fishing nets of different designs, shapes and sizes, according to the winds, waves and sea currents; built ports on sheltered estuaries, tidal creeks and islands; prepared manuals, sea charts, voyage schedules, compass cards, oriented to physical, cultural and stellar landmarks; and, protected geo or bio shields like sand dunes and coral reefs as essential to the protection of the habitats of the oceanic flora and fauna, and, therefore, to their own survival.

The pastoral land in Lapodia near Anasagar in Rajasthan has been divided by local farmers into sāntrās (earthen trenches), enclosed within chaukās (rectangular earthen bunds) to channelize the rapid and wasteful rush of surface run off, into a slow, meandering course, through rows of horizontal corridors, to store excess water in dundtālāis, restore moisture, generate vegetation, and stop erosion. A core, buffer, multiple use surround approach has been adapted by Gujjar communities, nestled among the Aravalli hills, to facilitate natural regeneration of the forest water sheds, by dividing these into kaṅkad banni (shade giving trees at village boundaries), rākhat banni (scarcity reserve), gavāine banni (nistār or community preserve), gochar, gaur and chārāgāh (pasture and fodder reserve).

Orāns, devbannis, kenkris, and shāmlāt dehs in semi arid areas of Rajasthan, protected by Bishnois and Gujjars, deorāis of Maharashtra, sārnās and jaherthāns of Chhattisgarh and Jharkhand, kāvus dedicated to Āyyāppan, Bhagavathi or Cheerumbā, protected by Nambudiris, tribals and Arayan fishermen of Kerala, kovil kādukkals, dedicated to Āyyānaar and sthala vṛkshas of Tamilnadu, the mādāicos protected by Dimasas of Assam, mauhak and Umanglāi bamboo groves and shrines, maintained by Gangte and Meitei tribals of Manipur, the ki law groves protected by Khasis of Meghalaya, devarākādus of Karnataka, thāns of West Bengal, hariyālis of Garhwal, machuyāl of Uttarakhand, khechupālri lake or gompā groves of Sikkim provide examples of diverse natural resource and water conservation practices. These sacred precincts are focii of festivals and rituals, taboos and prescriptions. As micro watersheds, these have contained the intensity and incidence of forest fires, and helped in the survival of relict climax communities, specially, of vanishing food and medicinal plants, conservation of keystone functions of ecosystems, maintenance of transpiration and carbon sequestration, nutrient and water cycles, biomass and micro organisms, genetic endemism and natural speciation.

THE CRISIS

The water table has been going down in many parts of India because of deforestation of watersheds. Springs have been disappearing, glaciers becoming smaller, lakes dwindling. Cultivation in steep, high rainfall zones has led to soil erosion in uplands, siltation and flooding down stream. Drawn down aquifers have been collapsing through overdraft by bore wells and motorized pumps. Problems of water contamination and water borne diseases, environmental degradation and pollution, are growing apace due to drainage of toxic pesticide, herbicide, fertilizer, dumping of untreated wastes and effluents, discharge of heavy metals, cadmium, aluminum, mercury, and the influx of human and animal waste, into the waters, with growing urbanization and industrialization. Mechanisation, standardization and homogenization of location specific navigational strategies, and destruction of coastal shields by mega mining projects have endangered survival of poor fisher folk and traders.

The local water harvesting structures, rituals and associated fairs and festivals provide a corpus of common property resource management practice, customary laws, taboos and directions, sanctified by the principle of lex loci rie sitae or prescriptive rights, conferred by traditional association and use. These have tended to be overridden by invasive standardized legislation, intrusion of input intensive agriculture, capital intensive bore wells, and location insensitive structures and dams. They should be regenerated with the participation of local bodies and the traditional institutional mechanisms languishing in various parts of the country. They should be mapped and upgraded with modern technology, adapted to local experience, with respect to hygiene, water quality and slope index.

PROBLEMS OF MEGA DAMS

Degradation of wetlands and water quality, siltation and water logging have been particularly accelerated by many big dams. The artificially regulated constant flows, generated by several big dams, have endangered the survival of fish and insects, which require natural fluctuations in temperature for bringing up their eggs and larvae. Such dams have obstructed sediment replacement, lowered the riverbed and eroded the sand beds, river banks and riparian zones, which support wild life and human life. In the highly seismic zone of the Himalayas, the dams are structural and strategic risks. Over the years, the area prone to serious flood damage has been increasing due to forest conversion, population explosion and the interruption of water flow by concrete behemoths. The local water harvesting structures offer viable alternatives to big dams for maintaining links between surface and ground water, inland and coastal water, for arresting desertification and environmental degradation in areas where such dams are not economically or environmentally viable.

Once massive capital intensive mega dam projects commence, conflicts of interest among the technocratic, bureaucratic and political constituencies, among states and communities, make any comprehensive and equitable solution for all concerned impossible to achieve. It is, therefore, vital to take into account, before undertaking construction of such dams, the silent constituencies of forest, aquatic bodies, sacred landscapes and precincts. It is necessary to make, in advance, a proper calculation of the net present value of the resources likely to be lost in submergence and the cultural and social rate of return of mega dam projects.

Countries like USSR, USA and China are moving away from large to medium and small dams. There is a growing appreciation that as against big dams, the small community water harvesting structures do not under estimate capital cost by under compensating oustees, or, by ignoring the external debt trap and public debt burden. Being dispersed, noncontiguous and labour intensive, they are more cost efficient in capital externalization and operating costs, lower evapotranspiration and distribution losses, greater user participation and better utilization. They do not, like big dams, degrade the environment by creating stagnant waterlogged puddles in command areas, through accumulation of excess subsoil water. Nor do they bring about eutrophication through growing aquatic vegetation as in large dams, or invite water borne diseases like malaria, filariasis, schistosomiasis, fluorosis, and gastro enteritis; cause salinization of estuaries; induce seismicity and floods through shock releases; or, accelerate industrial pollution and slum and squatter settlements in hinterlands. On the contrary, they enrich the microenvironment and enhance general well being by regenerating grasses, tubers, roots, legumes, vegetables and foodgrains rather than by catering to water intensive commercial crops, cultivated by big land holders. Big dams, when they are not accompanied by land reform or occupational rehabilitation, do not, like these smaller structures, always ensure equitable distribution of benefits. They often suffer from inbuilt inequities in intra basin distribution, and problems intrinsic to an exclusively engineering solution. Local water harvesting strategies are small, decentralized, based on community solidarity. They are independent of bureaucratic and political vagaries, as well as uncertainties of state financing or management. Above all, they are reversible, unlike mega dams.

ALTERNATIVE POLICIES

Regeneration of natural watersheds can be done using percolation tanks, check and nallah bunds in low rainfall areas, fortification of vegetative and vetiver grass barriers in areas with middle to high rainfall. Revitalization of participative community water conservation structures has been, therefore, stressed in national water policy statements and programmes as a concomitant approach for building up a healthy and bountiful water regime in India. The frugal and equitable local water harvesting strategies question the Western water laws, based on principles of 'First in Time, First in Right', or of 'Beneficial Use' for urban, industrial or agricultural consumption, developed by 19th century miners, ranchers and irrigators. These local strategies do not consider the water left in the stream, or, flowing down the river into sea, as wasted. There is a paramount need to strengthen the low technology, slow impact water harvesting strategies for preserving appropriate soil moisture, vegetation and land use regime.

It is necessary to recollect, replenish and promote participative local water harvesting traditions sustained by communities in coastal and tidal lands, marshes and bogs, flood plains, fens, swamps and ponds, and other diffuse, non point sources of water and wetlands. Afforestation of the micro watersheds, preserved by communities over the years, can restore wastelands, increase biomass and food production, and help in cultivation with higher cropping intensity.

The local water harvesting structures must be regenerated to ensure optimal water use and allocation for competing uses, discourage free riders, share system maintenance cost, ensure equitable distribution of water for crops, with varying needs of irrigation water, and for critically important phases of plant development. The water tariffs have to reflect the economy and cost of water for productive uses, and restore the free and abandunt nature of fresh water resource. Community water quality management practices must be understood and revived, in order to adopt human activities to the threshold limits of nature, to combat vectors of water related diseases, to preserve hydrological, biological and chemical functions of eco systems, and, to ensure supply of water not only as an industrial solvent, coolant, a medium, a cleaning agent and for waste disposal, but also for domestic uses, and to replenish bio diversity.

Micro-hydro, photo voltaic and geo-thermal applications, centered around such local water harvesting structures, should prove more viable in the Himalayas than large hydrothermal projects involving costly transmission and distribution mechanisms, land subsidence and pollution of aquatic bodies. The price signals and bilateral and multilateral agreements favouring centralised energy grids need to be revised for promoting these decentralised water management practices. These practices can, in turn, be supplemented by trickle, bubbler, and sprinkler irrigation, contour and furrow bunding, terracing and gully plugging. Plantation of kallar grass for waterlogged areas, of sea buckthorn in fragile, dry regions, jojoba in tropical arid lands, and mesquite in degraded, cold desert zones of the Himalayas needs to be considered, for reclamation of saline and desiccated mountain lands. The movement of water, soil, vegetation, weather and life is indivisibly connected across the Himalayas, transcending national boundaries. A diaspora of culture, ideas, arts and knowledge systems across the Himalayas is symbiotically linked with this movement. Hence, a minimum measure of agreement is required among the Himalayan nations to deal with shared problems by collaborative research and action. This will enable them to manage and regulate sharp variations of radiation, wind and moisture induced by altitudinal zonation over short distances in the vertical span, and, with uncompensated drain of water, silt, sediment, nutrients, germ plasm and timber to the plains.

ALTERNATIVE COMMUNITY INITIATIVES

Communities in different parts of India have made heroic efforts to preserve, revitalize and upgrade local water harvesting structures. Publications, suffused with empathy, compassion and knowledge, based on rigorous field research, have emerged from public purpose institutions like Gandhi Peace Foundation, Delhi, Centre for Science and Environment, Gurgaon, Tarun Bharat Sangh, Alwar, to invigorate such efforts. The remarkable effort of Tarun Bharat Sangh in coopting the Meena tribal people in reviving the johads of Alwar have brought rivers like Arāvari and Rupārel back to vitality and turned them into perennial sources for combating drought. The ridge valley approach of watershed development at Ralegan Siddhi in Nagar district, Maharashtra hark back to the traditions of water conservation, enunciated by Sants Dhyaneswar, Tukaram and Eknath, and have helped in arresting the decline of water table and restoration of ecological balance through cooperative water usage. The Vivekanand Memorial Trust, Kanyakumari, has built on the traditional *oorāni, kanmāi* and other traditional water management systems in Tamilnadu, for desiltation and purification of water. The Arthik Samata Mandal of Vijayawada has constructed tanks for storage and filtration inside the Kolleru Lake on the Godavari river basin, and purified the lake water, polluted by 1986 flood wastes. The villagers of Sukhomajri in the Siwalik hills near Chandigarh, have constructed rain water harvesting structures, backed up by water sharing, plantation and grazing free zones, in order to irrigate and desilt the Sukhna lake catchment, and ensure its greening. The Kerala Shastra Sahitya Parishad, concerned with popular science, has helped arrest the Silent Valley hydro-electric project on the Periyar river in the Palghat district, and protect the

Valley as a National Park through a movement, informed by multidisciplinary research. The invasive Koelkero dam project in Bihar was stopped due to the solidarity of the Sārnā Sārhul movement. The movement against the Tehri dam in Garhwal Himalayas and the Narmada valley project in Madhya Pradesh has been going for years. Small earthen dams, accompanied by plantation, with minimum submergence and maximum irrigation, have been built in Palamu, on the traditional technology of āhārs and pynes as an alternative to the proposed Auranga dams. Such initiatives have been valuable aids in accelerating rural water supply, preventing and controlling pollution, resolving water disputes, and, in dealing with drought.

The Himalayas, being one of the greatest water towers in the world, is a Vavilov centre of bio-diversity and endemism of species. In the Garhwal Himalayas, the Chipko (hug the tree) movement in Chamoli, has been steered by dāliyon ka dāghrā (friends of trees). They have defended the bugyāls (mountain pastures), dotted with kharaks (cattle sheds of trans humant communities), by protecting the bānj (oak), pāngār (horse chestnut), burāns (rhododendron), painyān (mountain cherry), deodār, and uttis (alder), against clear felling and mono cultural industrial plantations. This has helped conserve the water of chhoyās and gadherās (streams and drains) by anchoring soil, on a highly vulnerable and unstable surface, and by ensuring slow and gradual drainage through a dense vegetative cover. Similar protection has been offered to such rain absorbent historic species to shore up naulās of Uttarānchal. NGOs have taken initiative for regeneration of bāvris of Uttarakhand and naulās of Himachal Pradesh.

IGRMS INITIATIVES

Several workshops on traditional water management solutions were held by the IGRMS in different parts of the country as an R&D agency, to restore memories, nomenclatures, rituals, materials and techniques of local water harvesting management strategies, specific to rainfall regimes, soil types, vegetation covers, catchment size and patterns of water flow, distillation and filtration. The hurkiyā bol of Kumaon, sung impromptu by folk artists at paddy plantation, the solemn and ceremonial celebration of the opening of the Maletha guhl in Tehri-Garhwal, the Thala Cauvery festival near Igutappa temple on Cauvery, the festival on the sacred Khechupalri lake in Sikkim, the Narmada festival at Udaypur and Hoshangabad were recalled, visited or celebrated by IGRMS as examples of cultural rootedness of water resource management approaches. The IGRMS celebrated a festival of rivers, organized seminars on river valley cultures, and cross disciplinary expeditions along the Narmada, in order to recapitulate the history, movement and sharing of waters, and, to recollect the traditions of organic and inorganic communities, living with these waters, in co-evolutionary interdependence, in synergy rather than in competition.

This book emerges out of this IGRMS project, designed for recovery of our sense of communion with the living geo-hydrological habitats of our country, for a balanced water harvesting regime. It pleads for recognition of the principles of optimal utilization, minimal interference and maximal equity, enshrined in local water harvesting structures. It requests initiation and revitalization of microwatershed development projects in the interest of long term ecological balance, distributional equity and economic prudence.

SECTION I

TRADITIONAL WATER MANAGEMENT SYSTEMS

1

TRADITIONAL SYSTEMS OF WATER MANAGEMENT IN MAHARASHTRA

P.P. Dandawate, P.S. Joshi and B.S. Gajul

ABSTRACT

This article studies the water management system with respect to medieval temples in Western Maharashtra, especially of *Kundas*, locally known as *Puskarani*, at Loni Bapkar and Roti (Pune). The former is a medieval Siva temple whereas the latter is dedicated to Rotamalanath (a form of Siva) belonging to the Maratha Period. History of these temples, their architectural features and some legends associated with the temples are discussed. Both the temples are regarded as living shrines.

INTRODUCTION

Water is one of the most important necessities for survival. Since pre-historic times, man has tried to control water resources and minimize efforts for obtaining water. During the Stone Age man preferred to settle near perennial water sources like rivers, ponds, lakes and natural springs. In the Chalcolithic Period, deliberate attempts were made to control water course by raising structures, like the Great Bath at Mohenjo-daro (c. 2500 BC) and artificial irrigation channels at Inamgaon [c. 1400-1000 BC] (Dhavalikar *et al.*, 1988). In the Early Historic Period, water was harnessed and distributed on a large-scale through the construction of dams and canals. The Sudarshan Lake in Saurashtra which received continuous attention right from the Mauryan to the Gupta Period is a unique example. As far as religious establishments in rock-cut caves are concerned, water reservoirs were dug to store the natural spring water, for example the rock-cut caves at Nasik and Kanheri (Gokhale, 1991). In early medieval times the technology of water management advanced to a great extent. However, special efforts were made to store water close to religious establishments like temple complexes by constructing specific structures such as *kunda* (tank, well, step-well). Such structures, built during the reign of Chalukyas of Badami, are present at Mahakuta and Aihole. Those at Sirval were built during Rashtrakuta times (Jain-Neubauer, 1981).

The structures which were meant to store water for various rituals in religious establishments received special attention during the Medieval Period, especially in Gujarat,

Fig. 1.1 Shiva temple at Loni-Bhapkar, Taluk Purandar, Dist. Pune.

Rajasthan and Maharashtra. This concept of step-well continued even up to the Mughal Period and can still be seen at Delhi, Agra and Fatehpur Sikri (Jain-Neubauer, 1981).

A survey of temples at Phaltan, Sinnar, Pandeshwar, Loni-Bhapkar, Varasai, and Roti (all in Maharashtra) was undertaken recently. This paper focuses on the *kundas*, locally known as *pushkarani*, located in the temple complexes at Loni-Bhapkar and Roti.

Loni-Bhapkar is located in Taluka Purandar, in Pune district. The temple complex consists of a medieval Siva shrine (Fig. 1.1) and the temple devoted to Dattatreya. The *mandapa* in the front portion of this temple as well as the *pushkarani* have been renovated. The Siva temple is of the Nirandhar variety and stylistically it is of the Bhumija order. The temple has a *garbha griha* and a pillared *mandapa*. The walls, pillars, lintels and architrave of *mandapa* are decorated and carved with scenes from the epics and the *Puranas*. An image of Nandi is also seen at the entrance. A unique feature of this temple is the superstructure which is made of bricks.

The *pushkarani* which measures 15 m x 15 m is similar to step-wells found in Gujarat and Rajasthan. It has spiral steps arranged along lateral staircases which provide access to water. The *pushkarani* also has a parapet wall around it with 24 niches (*devkoshtas*) none of which has any image (Fig. 1.2). It is quite possible that these *devkoshtas* were meant to house the 24 forms of Vishnu, known as Chaturvishnumurti. The *mandapa* opposite the Dattatreya temple is situated inside the *pushkarani*, on the left side. The *mandapa* is at present empty but it is suggested that it was devoted to Varaha; the temple devoted

Fig. 1.2 *Pushkarani* with Mandapa and 24 *Devkoshtas*, Loni-Bhapkar.

Fig. 1.3 Temple dedicated to goddess Tukai, Roti, Taluk Daund, Dist. Pune.

now to Dattatreya was originally dedicated to Vishnu. An image of Yajna-Varaha, bigger than life-size, lies behind this temple. Also depicted are the *Dashawataras* of Vishnu in zoomorphic forms and stories from the *Ramayana*.

Both the temples are living shrines though the *pushkarani* is currently non-functional. But as per the tradition, when it was in use, devotees had to take a dip in it. Besides, the *pushkarani* also played, to some extent, the role of a shrine. The 24 *devkoshtas* on the walls of the *pushkarani* were housed with divinities which were worshipped.

Roti is located in Daund Taluka, district Pune, near Patas. The temple is dedicated to Rotamalanath, an incarnation of Siva and belongs to the Maratha Period. The temple is of Nirandhar variety, and stylistically, it was close to Bhumija order. The temple has been renovated recently. It has a *garbha griha* which is enshrined with modern images of Rotamalanath and Jogeshwari, a pillared *gudha mandapa* and a *sabha mandapa*. Original images, no more traceable, were immersed in the river by villagers as they were mutilated.

Fig. 1.4 *Kunda* with a well, Roti.

Close to this is another temple devoted to the goddess Tukai which is encircled with a strong compound wall (Fig. 1.3). Along this wall, on three sides, there is a corridor (*owari*). A unique feature of this temple is a big *pushkarani* which is square in shape and very close to the temple (Fig. 1.4). There is a staircase leading from the left side of the corridor up to the *pushkarani*. At present, it is blocked by a big stone slab and therefore not used. The *pushkarani* has water but it is not clean. The legend reveals that there was a passage (staircase) between the temple and the *pushkarani* which was in use in the past. Much later, a circular well was constructed within the *pushkarani* to get clean water. Villagers use this water for drinking and other purposes. There is an electric water pump fixed to the well to draw water.

Both the above temples are living shrines; the *pushkarani* is currently non-functional but the well inside it is the source of water for villagers.

CONCLUSION

The aim of this paper is to focus the attention of scholars on the art and architecture of step-wells of Maharashtra in general and of Loni-Bhapkar and Roti in particular. The above observations are preliminary in nature. It is suggested that a study of *pushkarani* may be undertaken in detail to learn more about the water management, art and architecture in relation to religious establishments.

NOTES AND REFERENCES

Dhavalikar, M.K., H.D. Sankalia and Z.D. Ansari, 1988, *Excavations at Inamgaon*, Vol. I, Pune, Deccan College.

Gokhale, Shobhana, 1991, *Kanheri Inscriptions*, Pune, Deccan College.

Jain-Neubauer, Jutta, 1981, *Step-wells of Gujarat in Art-Historical Perspective*, New Delhi, Abhinav Publication.

2

INAMGAON: THE PROTO-HISTORIC IRRIGATION SYSTEM

M.K. Dhavalikar

ABSTRACT

Inamgaon in Pune is an important site of the Chalcolithic Period which has revealed several facets of the lifestyle of the Chalcolithic inhabitants of Western Maharashtra. Apart from the cultural data, the most noteworthy is the evidence of artificial irrigation – the earliest and most convincing evidence of proto-historic irrigation in India. Inamgaon also provides a unique example of a hydraulic system where the flood water of the river was diverted and stored and excess water was siphoned off for irrigating fields. Excavation and geomorphological investigations suggest that there was a channel to the north of the embankment in the past which fell into disuse in the Late Jorwe Period and got silted up by the activity of the stream which fed it.

INTRODUCTION

The discovery of Chalcolithic cultures in India, more particularly in Maharashtra, is truly epoch-making because it has illumined the Dark Age – the period between the end of the Indus Civilization around 1800 BC and the beginning of the Historical Period in the 6th century BC. Intensive explorations in Maharashtra have so far brought to light over two hundred Chalcolithic settlements which are mostly located in Central Maharashtra. These were small, self-sufficient, farming communities whose mixed economy was based on subsistence agriculture, stock-raising and hunting-fishing. They lived during the second millennium BC and died out as poor rural cultures. Among the important excavated sites, mention may be made of Nevasa, Daimabad (both in Ahmednagar), Prakash (Dhulia) and Inamgaon (Pune).

Many new facets of the Chalcolithic lifestyle were brought to light at Inamgaon, among which the most noteworthy is the evidence of artificial irrigation. The site was excavated by the author on behalf of the Deccan College Postgraduate and Research Institute, Pune, for thirteen seasons (Dhavalikar *et al.*, 1988). The excavation revealed a three-fold sequence of cultures as follows:

Period I : Malwa Culture (c. 1700 - 1500 BC)
Period II : Early Jorwe Culture (c. 1500 - 1200 BC)
Period III : Late Jorwe Culture (c. 1200 - 900 BC)

Of the three cultural periods mentioned above, the second, i.e., the Early Jorwe Period was most prosperous in the history of habitation of the site. The reason for this appears to be congenial climatic conditions with adequate or more than average rainfall.

The prosperity of the Early Jorwe Period is reflected in the sturdy, brightly painted pottery; in a variety of ornaments including beads of semi-precious stones and gold; in tools, weapons and ornaments of copper; and in the rich agricultural economy. The quantity of charred seeds recovered from the excavation gives us a picture of the prosperous agriculture (Dhavalikar 1988: 28-31). The principal cereal was barley (*Hordeum vulgare*), but wheat (*Triticum dicoccym*), jowar (*Sorghum vulgare*) and rice (*Oryza sativa*) were also cultivated. Besides the four cereals, the Chalcolithic farmers of Inamgaon raised many other food crops. Among them were four pulses, viz., horse gram (*Dolichos biflorus* Linn.), hyacinth bean (*Dolichos lablab* Linn.), lentil (*Lens esculenta* Moench) and pea (*Pisum arvense* Linn.). Mention should also be made of grass pea (*Lathyrus sativas* Linn.) and green gram (*Phaselous aureas* Roxb.). Wild seeds collected include wild date (*Phoenix sylvestris* Roxb.), Indian jujube-ber (*Zizyphus jujuba* Lamk.), jambolan-jamun (*Sizygium cumini* Linn.) and beheda (*Terminalia belerica* Roxb.). The occurrence of jamun and beheda, which are characteristic of areas with higher rainfall, indicates a wetter climate, but the possibility of their coming from other regions by way of trade can also not be ruled out.

Of the four cereals, barley, the main crop, was present in all the levels, but wheat occurred only in the second cultural period, i.e., the Early Jorwe. It was conspicuously absent in the Malwa (Period I) and also in the Late Jorwe (Period III). It is not a matter of coincidence, but only indicative of a wetter climate. Maharashtra does not get winter rains which is essential for growing wheat, a winter crop. Even today, wheat is grown in those parts of Maharashtra where the facility of artificial irrigation – either canal or well irrigation – is available. The presence, therefore, indirectly suggests the possibility of artificial irrigation at Inamgaon.

The ancient site at Inamgaon (INM) is represented by five mounds. To the west of INM-V were found heaps of stones roughly in a southeast-northwest alignment. When the area was cleared and partially excavated, it was noticed that the heaps actually formed a massive wall of stone rubble set in mud mortar. Only eight courses of this wall had survived. It is likely that the upper part of the wall was earthen. The existing wall was 240 m in length and its average width was 3 m. It ran roughly in a northeast-southwest direction for 120 m and then took a gradual turn towards the west. Even after exposure, it was difficult to offer any opinion about the possible function of the wall. From the study of the geomorphological features of the surrounding area, it became clear that it was relatively a low lying area which, even at present, is cut by the headway erosion of a stream just north-west of it.

The most noteworthy feature of the area where the wall was located, is the broad zone of unconsolidated dark brown soil, about 4 m wide. The dark green colour of the vegetation in this zone made it distinct from the surrounding region. The green patch represented a channel and the stone wall, its embankment, or in engineering parlance, a guidebund. A trench across the channel revealed that it was cut up to the rock bottom, and in section resembled a trough. Its width was about 8 m and the maximum depth in the centre was about 4 m. The channel contained hard, compact and sticky black clay that could easily be distinguished from the strata. It appears that the channel, after it fell into disuse in the Late Jorwe Period, got silted up by the activity of the stream which fed it. However, because of the moisture in the silt, the vegetation grew over it throughout the year. The earth dug out from the channel was used for building the upper part of the embankment. The water channel ran almost parallel to the embankment upto a distance of about 120 m; from this point, the water was diverted in the south-western direction where there is a natural slope that ends in a stream in the west. Here is a large tract (75 ha) of black cotton soil which is presently owned by the village chief.

THE MECHANISM OF THE IRRIGATION SYSTEM

The stream, which is situated to the north of the embankment, must have been there even in the ancient past. It is 30.5 m away from the northern end of the wall. The ancient channel, the traces of which are scattered, is 20 m away from the eastern end of the wall. Beyond the northern end of the channel is a gentle slope which merges into the stream at a distance of 40 m. Even today, this slope has patches of green grass, indicating that the ancient channel may have extended upto this point. But the outline of the channel here is not as distinct as in the central portion. This part of the channel may, in the ancient times, have been the course of the stream itself, and hence, its outline is not sharp. The same holds good for the slope where the water from the channel took a south-westerly turn as mentioned above.

The stream water, when full during the monsoon, was in all probability diverted into the channel for protecting the main habitation area (INM-1). The water thus diverted could also easily have been utilized for irrigating the fields close to the channel on its west. It is obvious that the channel contained water only during the monsoon and also perhaps in early winter months. The palaeo-botanical studies of the charred grains from excavations show that the region was not semi-arid as it is today. The climate was certainly wetter as the discovery of a variety of pulses and beans indicates. With more and regular rainfall, the stream must have contained water for a longer period than it does today and so also the water channel. The ground water level, therefore, would have been higher, supporting a variety of rabi crops.

In order to understand the exact nature of the embankment, we carefully studied the surrounding topography and surfacial geology by using soil augur samples (in Dhavalikar *et al.,* 1988). The wall was built on a basaltic flat divide separating the rill system of the inner bend of the meander loop of the Ghod (Fig. 2.1). The height of the flat divide is 12 m above the present river-bed and the slope of the flat is drained by a stream running in a west-east direction to meet the Ghod with a discordant junction. On the other hand, the drainage on the slopes of the flat is well entrenched into the late Pleistocene older alluvium and the stream meets the Ghod with concordant junctions. These observations show that the *nullah* system on the slopes of the divide is younger than the drainage lines on slopes. This argument gains support by the presence of sub-recent, dark brown and less calcareous overbank flood silts on slopes. The occurrence

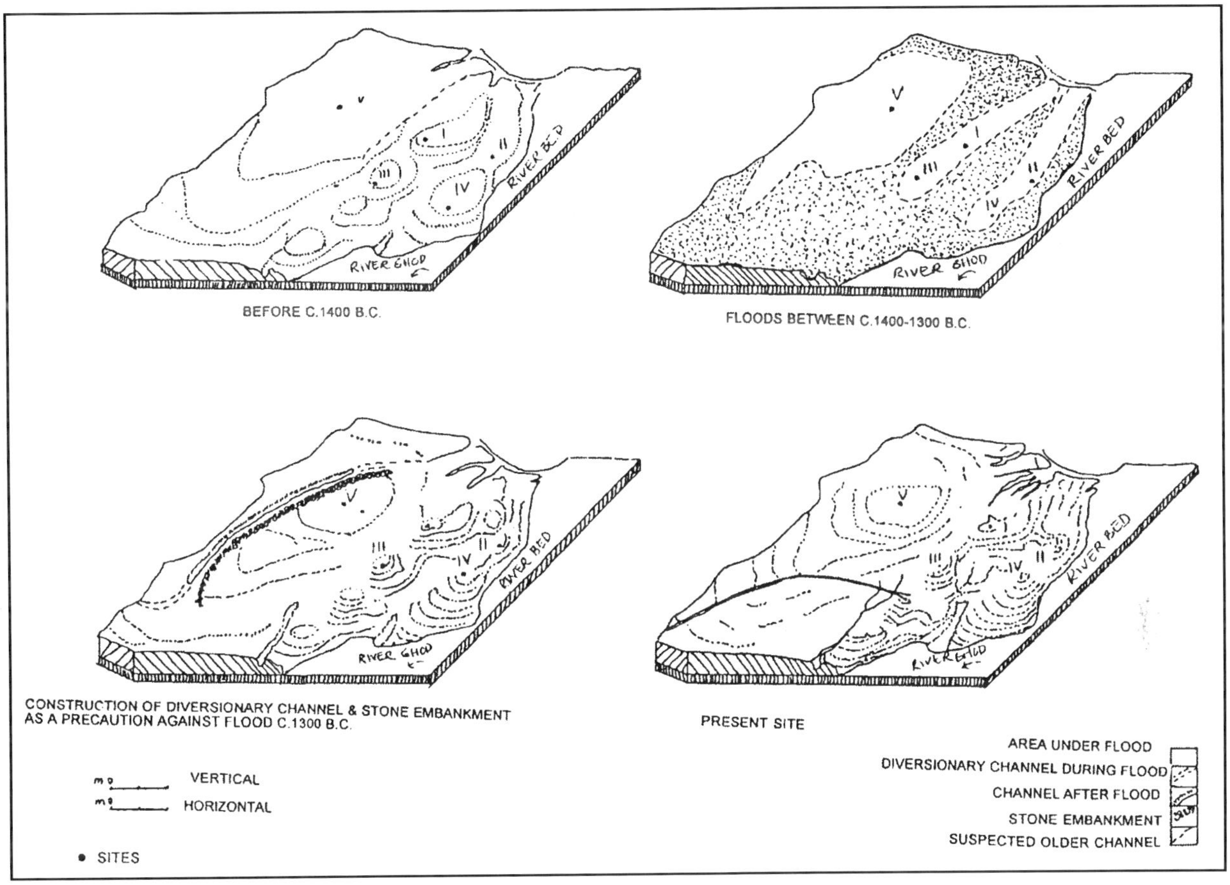

Fig. 2.1 Inamgaon, diagrams showing the river sources and embankment and irrigation channel.

of a few Early Jorwe potsherds in these formations indicate that these deposits have been formed during the Early Jorwe times (Period II). The low (6 m to 8 m) inset terrace on the present left bank is most probably the result of frequent overbank flooding during the Early Jorwe times. It is during this highflood stage that the tail water of the Ghod flood was definitely reaching the level of the wall under consideration.

Augur bore holes taken in the green belt showed the presence of dark brown sandy clay up to a depth of about 2.5 m (average), for a distance of about 120 m parallel to the wall. The occurrence of such thick clay on the divide flat which otherwise has a very shallow (20 cm to 30 cm) brown soil cover, definitely suggests that the clay was deposited along the green belt by the tail waters of the Ghod flood during the Early Jorwe times. As there is no possibility of the formation of a natural depression in the divide zone, it is certain that this clay-filled depression is the result of human activity. The dug-out channel on the divide flat must have served as a diversionary channel for flood waters, and the adjacent wall as a flood protection embankment.

IRRIGATION CANAL

The aerial photographs do not show up the embankment as it has now been completely destroyed by the farmers in whose fields it lay. The irrigation canal is also not very clear in the photographs, but its traces can be noticed. However, these traces are sufficient to support our hypothesis that the canal received water from the stream coming from north-east as it runs almost in a north-east south-west direction. The total length of the irrigation canal, as visible in the aerial photograph, is 420 m and its average width is 6 m. Yet another long channel running southeast-northwest was very distinctly seen in the aerial photograph. It is now marked by a green patch all along. It is likely that water from the main canal was diverted into this channel.

The above discussion sufficiently brings into focus the ingenuity of the first farmers of Maharashtra in utilizing their scarce water resources. The Chalcolithic irrigation system is the earliest and most convincing evidence of proto-historic irrigation in India. In this context, it may be noted that the Harappan irrigation canals identified by a French archaeologist in Rajasthan on the basis of satellite imagery are, according to some, palaeo-channels of rivers and not canals (Frankfort, 1992).

Another important feature of the Inamgaon irrigation system is that, the water was not only used for irrigation but was also stored in a tank. The recently unearthed brick-built tank of the Kushan Period (1st-2nd century AD) at Sringaverapura (district Allahabad, U.P.) was used only for storing water (Lal, 1992) and not for irrigation. The Inamgaon evidence is, therefore, the only unique example of a hydraulic system where the flood water of the river was diverted and stored, and the excess water was siphoned off for irrigating fields.

NOTES AND REFERENCES

Dhavalikar, M.K., 1988, *The First Farmers of the Deccan*, Pune, Ravish Publishers.

Dhavalikar, M.K., H.D. Sankalia and Z.D. Ansari, 1988, *Excavation at Inamgaon,* Vol. 1 (i & ii), Pune, Deccan College.

Frankfort, H.P., 1992, Evidence for Harappan Irrigation System in Haryana and Rajasthan, *Eastern Anthropologist* 45: 87-103.

Lal, B.B., 1992, Excavations at Sringaverapura, Vol. 1, *Memoirs of Archaeological Survey of India* 88, New Delhi, Archaeological Survey of India.

Dr. S.N. Rajaguru while commenting on the Chalcolithic irrigation system at Inamgaon writes:

"An embankment was built 300 m west of the main habitational area of a Chalcolithic settlement on the right bank of river Ghod at Inamgaon (18° 36′ N, 74° 32′ E), in district Pune in upland Maharashtra, where the present rainfall is around 500 mm per annum. The embankment made of local basaltic blocks was about 50 m long, 7 m wide in extent and 1 m deep. It ran parallel to a ditch equally long and deep. The ditch was located in the central portion of a meander loop of the Ghod. Flood waters of the river were channeled through the ditch into a large reservoir where water was stored and siphoned off into nearby black soil patches for cultivating wheat and rice. This is probably a unique site where early farming Jorwe Culture flourished between 1500 BC and 1200 BC, partly due to controlled water management in a drought-prone, semi-arid region of Maharashtra.

The irrigation system got defunct around 1000 BC probably due to weak summer monsoons which reduced flood frequency and intensity of the Ghod. This minor climatic change around 1000 BC is observed in another Chalcolithic site at Nevasa in Ahmednagar district Maharashtra. A buried soil, indicative of desertification of the site, was formed over habitational debris between 1000 BC and 300 BC. There is strong evidence for relative degree of aridity in parts of western Rajasthan and coastal Karnataka, around 1000 BC.

Chalcolithic embankment of Inamgaon thus provides good evidence of man's response to environmental change during the Mid-Holocene.

A few suggestions for field initiatives for revitalization of traditional water harvesting systems have been given below:

1. Outdoor Exhibitions: Exhibits could include models showing the damage and deterioration that has occured to traditional water harvesting systems, and the causes of such damages. Exhibits may also put focus on water rights and how they are managed.
2. Travelling and Visual Exhibitions: This could include a program on collecting opinions and suggestions systematically from communities of present condition, causes and future alternatives for rejuvenation of traditional water harvesting systems. Opinions should be collected from local communities on legal powers and procedures required for such rejuvenation.
3. Regional Workshops and Seminars: Subjects for discussion and manual contents should include evaluation of current legal (including rights) framework regulating traditional water harvesting systems state-wise, and alternative law, policy and rights framework from a water-shed perspective."

Editors

3

TRADITIONAL WATER SYSTEMS IN THE FORTS OF MAHARASHTRA

P.K. Ghanekar

ABSTRACT

This paper outlines water management systems in the forts of Western Maharashtra, each of which has a water storage system. However, very little information is available on this aspect in relation to forts. Various types of cisterns are seen on various forts like Sinhagad, Sivneri, Raygad, etc. and there is a general belief that the art of cave temples and type of excavating cisterns is similar. However, the latter are excavated at the junction of pervious and impervious rocks. There is an advantage in certain types of cisterns as the loss due to evaporation is minimum because of least exposure. The author emphasizes that there should be an effort to make use of water storage techniques in remote areas which will make enough water available to the people even during hot summers. This is a simple technique for harnessing the rainwater on the higher slopes of the mountains.

INTRODUCTION

Maharashtra is a land of forts. The last few centuries (AD 100 to AD 1790) witnessed great fort building activities under different dynasties such as the Satvahana, Rashtrakuta, Chalukya, Yadava, Bahmani, Mughal, southern Sultanates, Marathas, Siddis, Portuguese, English and the Dutch owing to which, the state has become a living museum of forts. Forts were a geo-political need of medieval Maharashtra.

Each of the fort possesses a kind of fortification and a water storage system. Very little information is available about the management of forts. The text *Adnyapatra*, written by about AD 1694, contains some information about storage of water under the sub-chapter "Gad Kot-Kille" which is given below:

> **तसेच गडावर आधी उदक पाहून किल्ला बांधावा. पाणी नाही आणि ते स्थळ तो आवश्यक बांधणे प्राप्त झालो, तरी आधी खडक फोडून तली, टाकी पर्जन्यकाळ पर्यन्त संपूर्ण गडास पाणी पुरे, अशी मजबुत बांधावी.**

It is necessary to make provisions for water before building a fort; if it becomes unavoidable to build a fort where water is not easily available, cisterns and ponds (or lakes) have to be excavated to make water available till the next rainy season.

गडावर झराही आहे, जसे तसे पाणीही पुरते. म्हणून तितक्यावरीच निश्चिती न मानावी. किं निमित्त की झुजांमध्ये भांडियाचे आवाजा खाली झरे स्वल्प होतात आणि पाणियाचा खर्च विशेष लागतो, तेंव्हा संकट पडते.

One should not rely on perennial springs because, during wars, the explosion of cannon balls fractures the rocks and water vanishes in the cracks. Besides, water consumption is maximum during wars.

याकरिता तसे जागी जखिरियाचे पाणी म्हणून दोन चार टाकी, तळी बांधावी. त्यातील पाणी खर्च होऊ न द्यावे. गडम्चे पाणी बहुत जतन राखावे.

One may develop 'reserved' water sources by making provisions for 2-4 tanks and cisterns. Water should be used with utmost care.

A close look at the position of water tanks and cisterns on forts would help to illustrate the above principles.

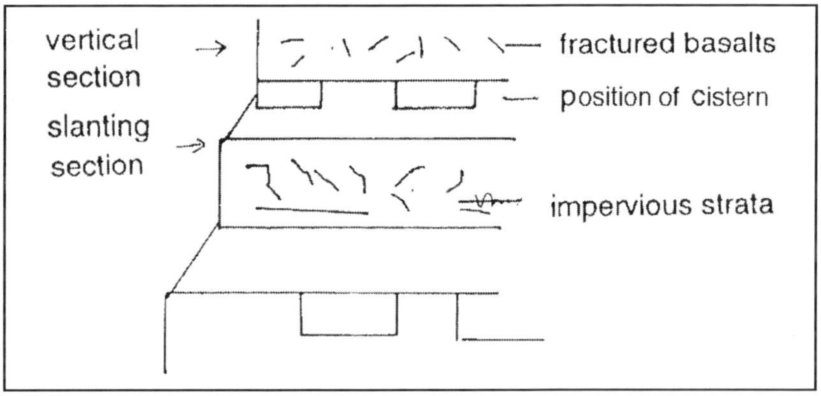

Fig. 3.1 Geological formations in the Sahyadri.

Most of the cisterns are located only in impervious strata just below the fractured basalt strata (Fig. 3.1). During rainy seasons, water percolates through the soil and the rocks, and moves down (due to gravitational pull and slopes) through hair-like cracks. Water cannot percolate when there is an impervious layer of rock. If a bowl-like cistern is excavated at this junction, water can be stored for a long time. Generally, water trickles into such cisterns throughout the year. Since the population on most of the forts was small, water in cisterns would last round the year and cater to the needs of the population.

This type of cistern is seen on very ancient forts like Sinhagad, Shivneri, Raygad (Raigad), etc. (Fig. 3.2a & b). Though no written evidence is available, it is generally believed that the art of constructing cave temples and excavating cisterns is very similar, the only difference being that cave temples are excavated in impervious rocks, while cisterns are created at the junction of pervious and impervious rocks.

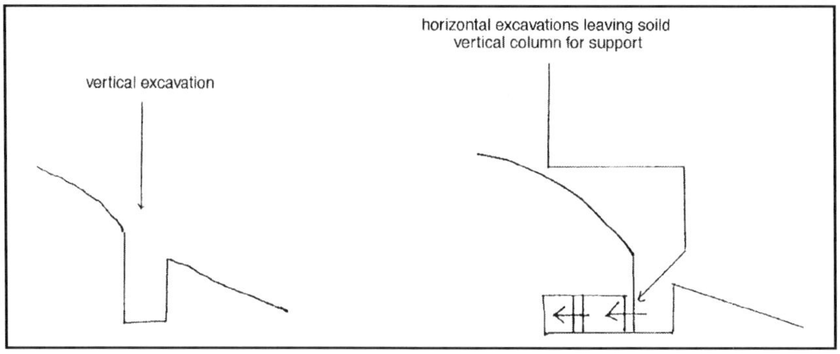

Fig. 3.2a Types of cisterns on forts.

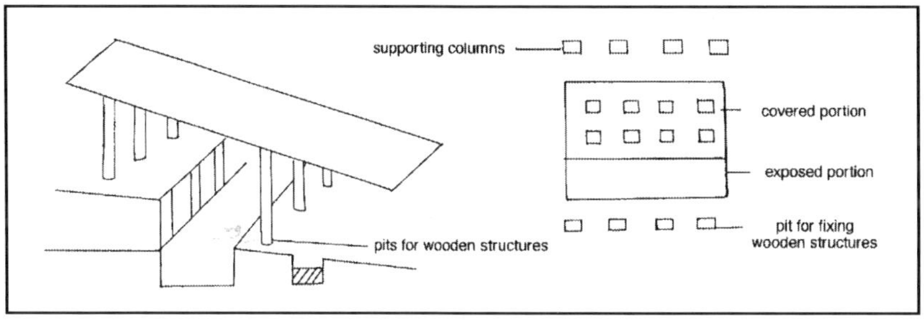

Fig. 3.2b Types of cisterns.

The main advantage of this type of cistern is that the water body is least exposed, thereby minimizing the loss of water through evaporation. Besides, the possibility of garbage accumulating in the cisterns is also avoided. At some places, a small pit is excavated for providing drinking water to animals.

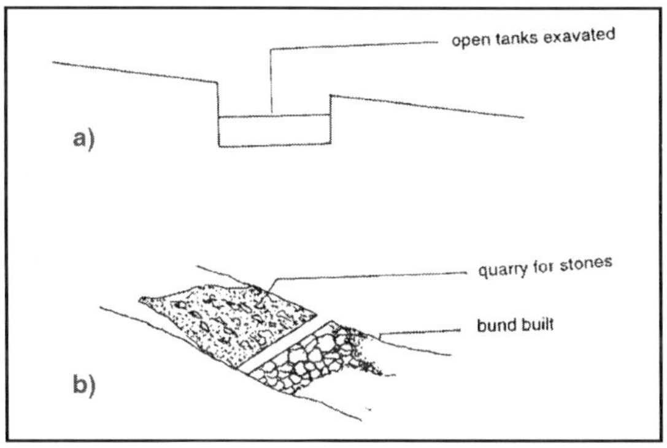

Fig. 3.3a & b Types of cisterns.

Cisterns of this kind are not found in the forts of later periods. Instead, we find only open tanks excavated on either side of a slope into which water was diverted (Fig. 3.3a). On some forts, particularly those built by Shivaji, very huge ponds were excavated in shallow ravines.

Major forts like Raygad, Pratapgad and Rajgad, etc. required huge amounts of dressed stones which were quarried from the nearby areas. Evenly grained, fractureless solid blocks were chiselled out from quarries located in a ravine or near the ravines. After sufficient amount of building blocks was quarried, a small bund was built, and thus a quarry was converted into a huge reservoir (Fig. 3.3b). The rate of evaporation of water, accumulation of garbage, growth of algae and other hydrophytes is comparatively more in such reservoirs. This stagnant water was probably used for purposes other than drinking.

The practice of inspecting water reservoirs, cistern cutting and excavation skills shows a declining trend during the late medieval times.

Most of the water systems on hill forts are working well even today. The ancient Dev Tank on Sinhagad fort is famous for its clean, cool and refreshing mineral water. But tanks like Gangasagar, Hatti talav, Hirkani talav, Baman talav, Kolimb talav, Kala haud, Bhavani talav, etc. on Raygad have deteriorated and hence they need to be restored.

If we can make use of these water storage techniques in remote areas where large dams cannot be built, enough water could be made available to the people living there even during summers. At least, an effort may be made at a few places initially, and if it serves the purpose, one can think of excavating such cisterns and water tanks with advanced excavating equipments, especially in the hilly mountainous areas.

वा. सि. बेंद्रे - *गड कोट दुर्ग आणि त्यांच्या वास्तू*

पान ९

किल्ला समृद्ध कसा ठेवावा? या विषय मनू काय सांगतो की "राजानेया दुर्गात नाना प्रकारची आयुधे, अनेक प्रकारचे धनधान्य, वाहने, बाम्हण, लोहार इ. शिल्पकलाभिज्ञ लोक, यंत्रे, गवत, आणि विपुल जलयांचा संग्रह करावा" (मनुस्मृति ७/७५-६)

पान २४

(वराहमिहीराच्या बृहत्संहिते मध्ये आलेला उल्लेख)

डोंगर असोत किंवा दऱ्या असीत, जमीन असो वा खडक असो, सर्वत्र कमी अधिक झरे वाहाणाऱ्या शिरा पृथ्वीत असू शकतात आणि त्या पाणण्याची साधने निसर्गातील उत्पत्ती स्थिती लयातच दृष्टिगोचर करून घेतायेतात.

पान २९

देशप्रांत प्रमुखांनी नंतरयुक्त जागी डोंगरांवरील नैसर्गिक तटबंदीचा फायदा घेऊन व पाण्या च्या पुरवठ्या प्रमाणे गंडावर वास केला व नंतर डोंगरांवर कृत्रिम तटबंदी बांधून त्यांचा आधार घेतला.

Two more aspects of water on forts:

1) Moats are of two types:
   a) Dry moats
   b) Water filled moats

Devgiri (Daulatabad) is an ideal fort where both types of moats can be seen. Here, there is a narrow ditch around the central towering citadel filled with water. The vertical walls of the moat acted as a barrier. Kandhar and Vijapur also possess such water-filled narrow moats which, in these cases, were used as a defensive tool or barrier.

2) Water tanks as emergency attacking method:

On the Raygad fort, the Mahardarwaja, i.e., the main entrance, situated in a ravine, is flanked by two towering bastions (Gomukhi Rachana). A few tanks are built on this fort at a height of 200 m, above the main gate, for defence purposes. By blowing the walls of these tanks, water is made to flow down and wipe out the attacking forces. Though this strategy was never actually practised at Raygad, its reference is noted in documents. There is a record of heavy rains in the year 1787 which destroyed one of these water tanks. The entire construction became a huge water reservoir, threatening the fortification walls and the bastion. Fortunately, there was no damage of any sort.

CONCLUSION

The historical references and the surviving tanks and water-harnessing cisterns are an excellent example of the use of simple technology for harnessing rainwater on the high slopes of the Sahyadri and other remote locations on mountain forts. The Maharashtra State Department of Archaeology should make a detailed documentation of such water sources because they can still provide drinking water to the nearby villages. Restoration of such systems will require relatively small amount of money, but will permanently solve the problem of drinking water in these remote areas. The techniques used on these forts could be replicated at similar areas in the Western Ghats. In any case, these systems need to be documented and preserved.

4

THE INSCRIPTIONAL EVIDENCE OF ANCIENT WATER MANAGEMENT SYSTEMS WITH SPECIAL REFERENCE TO WESTERN INDIA

Shobhana Gokhale

ABSTRACT

This paper gives a glimpse of ancient water management illustrating examples from epigraphical records and ancient literature. One of the earliest references to well-water is noted in the *Rigveda*. Kautilya's *Arthashastra* provides a wealth of information on irrigation tanks and wells. Inscriptions of different periods in Western India too record construction of dams and wells. The Junagadh inscription refers to a dam named Sudarsana built by Chandragupta Maurya. There are references of water tanks in the Buddhist caves located on the trade route in Western India. The inscriptional records underline the fact that water related activities were regarded as meritorious deeds in ancient India.

INTRODUCTION

In the Rigvedic pantheon, Varuna is regarded as the overlord of the waters and the universal monarch. Indra, another Rigvedic god, is considered as the liberator of waters. He defeats Vrtra, the demon of drought. The worship of nature gods is a significant hallmark of the Indian tradition. This tradition manifested itself in subsequent periods in different forms, since offering of water was considered as a meritorious deed. It appears that even in the Rigvedic period people did not depend only on natural sources of water. There are references to well-water in *Rigveda*, for instance, *Kulyā* and *Khanitrimā Āpah* (Max Müller, 1965: 3:45.3 & 7:49:2).

Even though irrigation was looked upon as a state activity during the Mauryan Period, Kautilya refers to privately-owned irrigation tanks and wells (Kangle, 1963: 3.9.32.34). Co-operative efforts for waterworks were encouraged (Kangle, 1963: 2.1.22.28). Kautilya mentions the words *setubandha* embankment; *prapā* storage of drinking water; and *āhāryodakasetu*. Such waterworks were to be undertaken by the king himself.

Besides this literary evidence, the earliest inscriptional reference comes from the rock-edicts and pillar-edicts of the Mauryan king Asoka. In the seventh pillar edict of Delhi

Topra (Hultzsch, 1969), it is recorded that,

> at intervals of eight Kosa (nine miles was considered a day's march of an army) wells were caused to be dug by me and flight of steps (Hultzsch, 1969) were caused to be built. Numerous drinking places were caused to be established by me for the enjoyment of cattle and men.

At Sopara, an ancient port in Bassein Taluka of the Thane district, Maharashtra, Pandit Bhagvanlal Indraji discovered a broken block of basalt bearing one-third of the eighth rock edict of Asoka. The existing fragment suggests that a complete set of his edicts must have been engraved near Sopara. In this set, the second rock-edict (Hultzsch, 1969) mentions that the wells were caused to be dug for the use of cattle and men. Cunningham (1962) has observed that distribution of water was considered as a charitable custom, and persons carrying water (*kavadi*) figured at Bharhut (Cunningham, 1962: Pl. 41).

At Junagadh in Gujarat, the inscription of Rudradaman (Kielhorn, 1981) which is written in Brahmi script (in the Sanskrit language) records the history of a dam called 'Sudarsana' which was constructed on the river Suvarnasikata and Palasini by the Mauryan emperor Chandragupta Maurya under the supervision of Vaisya Pusyagupta. During the reign of Asoka, conduits were made by the Persian engineer Tusaspha. The breach was 420 *Purusha* (feet) in length as well as in breadth and 75 *Purusha* deep. The dam was devastated due to a storm on *margasirsa krsnapaksha pratipada samvat* 72 = 19 November AD 150, and was re-constructed under the supervision of Pahlva Kulaip's son Suvisakha. After three hundred years, during the reign of the Gupta emperor Skandagupta, the dam was again destroyed by a storm. The inscription records the dimensions of the re-constructed dam (AD 455) which measured 100′ x 68′ in length and breadth and 42′ in height.

The inscription of Kharavela in Orissa (Jaiswal & Banerjee, 1929-30) records the construction of different types of tanks in his city. He brought the Tanasuliya canal which was constructed by Nanda king into his capital city of Sisupalgarh (200 BC).

The famous inscription of Naneghat (Buhler, 1964) of the Satavahana king Siri Satakarni and Naganika records the celebration of different sacrifices such as *Vajapeya, Rajasuya* and *Asvamedha*. The inscription is located in a cave on the ancient trade route which had linkages with the ancient ports of Kalyan and the Satavahana capital city of Pratisthana. On this trade route, which runs along the Junnar range, there are many water tanks to quench the thirst of traders. Junnar, where the above-mentioned *yajnas* were being performed, is 90 km north-west of Pune and Naneghat is 40 km west of Junnar. Being situated in the fertile basin and surrounded by five rivers – Mina, Kukdi, Ara, Puspavati and Ghod, Junnar occupies an ideal position. Today, on every river a dam has been constructed: Manikdoh on the Kukdi River, Vadaja on the Mina, Yedgaon on Puspavati and Dimbhe on the river Ghod. In the Satavahana Period, the sacrifices lasted for one year, for example Gavamayana sacrifice. The confluence point of five perennial rivers was considered an ideal place for the performance of such sacrifices.

In Maharashtra, the western coast is studded with nearly 1200 Buddhist caves. Kanheri, an important Buddhist site situated 10 km to the south-east of Borivali, the suburb of metropolitan Mumbai houses hundred and four caves, the majority having watertanks (*podhi*). These tanks recieved rainwater from the water channels which were purposefully excavated on the top of the caves. An inscription records the construction of a dam

Fig. 4.1 The reservoir by Punaka from Sopara.

(Gokhale, 1991) by Sethi Punaka of Sopara (Figs. 4.1-4.2), which is the earliest evidence of dam construction in Maharashtra. There is still a catchment area and there are remains of the ancient wall. It appears that the water tanks in the caves were sufficient for the occupants of the cells and that the dam was constructed across the stream and the collected water was utilized for watering the nearby fields.

Another Buddhist centre is Nasik which, because of its prominent geographic position, had linkages with the ports of Sopara and Kalyan and also continuous communication from North and South. Nasik was a Buddhist training centre and therefore it was visited frequently by Buddhist *bhikṣus* from all the four quarters. The inscriptions at Nasik register donations made by foreigners. One inscription (No. 15) records that one thousand *kārṣāpaṇas* (coins) were invested in the guild of potters (*kulārika*) and two thousand in the guild of makers of water machines (*odayantrikā*) (Senart, 1981), indicating the importance attributed to water management by thc Buddhists.

In the Vakataka Period, the king Devasena (Gokhale, 1967-68: 1-3) constructed a dam named Sudarshana in the Shaka era 380 (AD 458) near Vatsagulma, the capital of the Vakatakas (now Washim district in Maharashtra). In the same year, the famous Sudarshana dam in Gujarat was repaired by the Gupta king Skandagupta. The name of the dam Sudarshana was so popular that the dam constructed by the Vakataka queen Prabhavati Gupta near Ramtek was also given the same name (Jamkhedkar, 1992).

The Kandhar inscription (Sircar, 1963-64: 107) of the Rastrakuta king Krsna III (E.I. XXXV: 107) records the embankment named after Jagat Lunga where watering centres were established in summer (Gokhale, 1991: 60-67).

Fig. 4.2 Inscription on the reservoir of Punaka.

In the Yadava Period, and also in the later period, there are references to the construction of wells. There is one Sanskrit inscription of 1795 at Narayangaon (Purandare, 1928: 9-11) which specifically records the construction of a dam on the river Mina.

The earliest evidence of construction of well by a private individual is from Gujarat. It reads as follows:

Line 1-	Vapi 2 3 3 Sravana Bahule
Line 2-	6 Kumaradevaputrasya
Line 3-	Kumaradattasa

The inscription mentions that Kumardatta, the son of Kumaradeva, donated a well on Shravana vadi (dark fortnight) 6 in Saka era AD 233 = 311.

A review of these inscriptional records, which have registered aspects of the traditional water management, reveals that such activities were regarded as meritorious deeds, and therefore irrespective of caste and creed, great souls made donations to different kinds of water-centres for the welfare of public.

Finally, I would like to mention an interesting instance. A mother, who donated a tank at Kanheri (Gokhale, 1991), has specifically mentioned that the merit she has achieved by the donation would be shared by her children also. In ancient India, the meritorious work of establishing water-centres had additional qualifications. Water when mixed with Āvalā (āmalaka: *Emblic myrobalan*) (Shastri, 1969) would increase *punya*, the highest worldly merit of the donor.

Reading of the Inscription from Kanheri

Line-1- Soparakasa (indistinct)
Line-2- — patisa sethisa Pu
Line-3- n a k a s a lalaka deyadhama

NOTES AND REFERENCES

Buhler, G., 1964, *Archaeological Survey*, West Vol. 5: 64.

Cunningham, A., 1962, *The Stupa of Bharhut*, (Plate 41),Varanasi, Indological Book House.

Gokhale, S., 1967-68, *Epigraphia Indica*, Vol. 37: 1-3.
——, 1991, *Kanheri Inscriptions*, Pune, Deccan College.
Hultzsch, E., 1969, *Corpus Inscriptionum Indicarum*, Vol. 1: 135, Varanasi, Indological Book House.
Jaiswal, K.P. and R.D. Banerjee, 1929-30, *Epigraphia Indica*, Vol. 20: 71-80.
Jamkhedkar, A.P., 1992, *The Age of the Vakatakas*, in Discovery of Vakataka Temples at Ramtek (Shastri, A.M. (ed.), pp. 156-64, New Delhi, Harman Publishing House.
Kangle, R.P., 1963, *Kautilya's Arthashastra*, Vol. 1: 33 & 110, Bombay, University of Bombay.
Kielhorn, F., 1981, *Epigraphia Indica*, Vol. 8: 41.
Maxmuller, F., 1965, *Rigveda* (3:3:45 & 7:49:2), Varanasi, Chaukhambha Series (Reprint).
Purandare, K.V., 1928, *Quarterly Bharat Itihas Samshodhaka Mandal* (in Marathi), Part-4: 9-11.
Senart, E., 1981, *Epigraphia Indica*, Vol. 8: 88; reprinted (original year 1905-06).
Sircar, D.C., 1966, *Epigraphia Indica*, Vol. 35: 107; reprinted (original year 1963-64).
Shastri, A.M., 1969, *India as Seen in Brihat Samhita*, Delhi, Motilal Banarsidass.

5

WATER MANAGEMENT IN ANCIENT AND MEDIEVAL INDIA

M.S. Mate

ABSTRACT

This article discusses the experience of water management gained by our ancestors as per historical annals. Most of the information has been culled from the epigraphic sources which speak of the construction and maintenance of a large number of small tanks. Even though many of the evidences collected so far relate to peninsular India, attempt has been made to present the available evidence of various ancient water management systems even from other areas.

INTRODUCTION

The present exercise has been undertaken in order to evolve ways and means of utilizing available water without disturbing ecological balance, without the use of mechanical devices that consume energy generated by coal/oil/electricity, and without resorting to high-cost structures like huge dams. The emphasis would be on local initiative and innovation. In this endeavour, the efforts of our ancestors are likely to be a good guide; they may suggest ways of achieving our objective.

This discussion is prefaced by a glimpse into the social attitude of the people at large and of the thinkers in particular. It was this awareness that led them to undertake all sorts of efforts to conserve and use available water in the most profitable manner. Clear statements are to be found in the Smriti and the Puranic literature. One of the earliest of the Puranas, viz., the *Matsya Purana* (Apte, 1907: 154 & 511) makes the following statement:

एवं निरुदके देशे यः कूपं कारयेद् बुधः।
बिन्दौ बिन्दौ च तोयस्य वसेत् संवत्सरं दिवि।

A wise person who causes a well to be dug in a waterless (dry) land, (would) stay in heavens as many years as the drops of water therein.

The same trend continues in later literature and *Aparājitapṛcchā* (Mankad, 1950: 74, 37 & 38), a text of the 12th-13th century AD, expresses the concept in the clearest possible terms. It states:

> वापीकूपतडागानि नैकश उदगाश्रयः ।
> जलाश्रयं च संपाद्य कुर्यात् पुण्यमहोत्सवम् ॥
> यस्य गोपादमात्रं तु ह्युदकं धारयेन्मही ।
> वर्षषष्टिसहस्राणि शिवलोकं स गच्छति ॥

After having constructed *vāpī, kūpa, taḍāga* (stepwell, well, tank) one should organise a religious ceremony to mark the occasion. If a person creates a resort as small as the impress of a cow's hoof, he would enjoy *Sivaloka* for sixty thousand years.

The relationship of water to spiritual merit is not confined to religious and prescriptive texts. Those who excavated tanks, wells or built other types of waterworks have also stressed this aspect in their dedicatory inscriptions.

One has now to pose and answer an important question: how far these attempts are relevant today? To anticipate, I would say that they are extremely relevant. The answer is provided by the element basic to all our efforts, the availability of natural water, that is, rainwater. The level of water supplied by this source, today, is roughly the same as the level two thousand years ago. Kautilya's *Arthashastra* (Kangle, 1963: 2/24/5) dated to around the beginning of the Christian Era has enumerated the average annual rainfall in the sub-continent. The passage could be rendered thus:

Sixteen *dronas* is the amount of rain in forest areas, one-and-a-half times of that in wet lands, where sowing is in conformity with the nature of the region; thirteen-and-half *dronas* in the Ashamakas, twenty-three in the Avantis, unlimited in the Aparantas and the snowy regions and unpredictable as to time in lands where sowings are made with the help of camel.

According to the calculations of the editor, one *drona* is equal to two inches or five centimeters of rain. The comparison would be as under:

	Old	Modern
Forest areas/ Central Indian forests	80	60-100
Ashamaka/ Godavari basin	115	100-200
Avantis/ Western M.P.	68	40-60

Aparanta (Western Coast/Himalayan ranges) Unlimited
Deserts/Rajasthan - Unpredictable.

Of course, it has to be admitted that the measurements may not be as accurate as one would wish to have, but are enough to convey an idea of the general correspondence of the two. It follows that since the source and the quantity of water available was generally the same, the solutions would be similar.

Most of the information regarding irrigation works is to be culled from epigraphic sources. These have been brought together by Venkayya (1990); it has been enlarged and supplemented by Kuppuswamy (1992: 70-90). These inscriptions speak of the construction and maintenance of a large number of small tanks. They were built by throwing bunds of stone and earth across small valleys and catchment areas. The money and labour for the construction came either from a wealthy landlord, an official or a guild – but always locally. All the evidences so far collected and published relate to peninsular India, where extensive alluvial plains are not found.

Much attention was paid to the maintenance of tanks and other irrigation projects. This was achieved by royal patronage, generosity of individuals and by constant action by the village assemblies. It appears that the village assemblies had regular supervisory committee that would inspect the tank and advise or undertake repairs, etc. For this purpose, a regular staff was maintained. The assemblies were empowered to collect taxes, rents accruing from irrigation facilities and also to penalise those who failed to fulfil their obligations. Examples given by Venkayya (1990: 202-211) are quoted henceforth at some length as the details are of great interest in the present context. They also show that these practices were followed for centuries together.

During the reign of Pallava Dantippottarasar, a private individual made provision for the clearing (de-silting) of a tank known as Vayiramega-tataka at Uttaramallur. This endowment was accepted by the village assembly and it made arrangements for the removal of silt every month from the tank. Another record speaks of the gift of one thousand *kalanju* of gold by a local chief (one *kalanju* of gold equals to eighty-two grams). The interest was to be used to clear the silt from the tank for three months every year, from June to August.

One of the inscriptions from the same place specifies that a hundred *kalanjus* of gold received by the village assembly was to be properly invested and the income from this investment was to be utilized for maintaining a boat which would be used for clearing the Vayiramega-tataka of accumulated silt. It was further provided that this operation was to be carried out daily; everyday a specific area was to be cleared and the silt thus taken out was to be deposited on the bund.

Details of the routine arrangements are found in an inscription from Nangavaram, in Tiruchirappally district. It belongs to the reign of the Chola king Rajasekharavarman (10th century AD). A piece of land purchased by a private individual was given/donated to the village assembly which was entrusted with the task of cultivating it. The proceeds were to be utilized for the maintenance of the tank. If the village assembly failed to cultivate the land, the king could impose fine. Out of the proceeds, boat was to be maintained and a hundred-and-forty baskets of silt had to be taken out and deposited on the bund every day. Each basket consisted of about two hundred cubic feet of earth. For this purpose six labourers, a carpenter, a blacksmith and a fisherman were maintained as regular staff. Each of the labourer was given approximately five kilos of paddy as daily wage. The carpenter and the blacksmith who were to maintain the boat received about thirty kilos of paddy annually. The fishermen who supplied wood for the boat got about twenty kilos. The work of the labourers and craftsmen was supervised by a superintendent who got about eight hundred grams of paddy daily.

In the absence of a single donor, the entire village agreed to contribute to the building/ maintenance of a tank as evidenced by an inscription at Bahur near Pondichery (10th century AD). A committee for supervision of the tank was constituted and it was entrusted with both levying the contribution and de-silting the tank at regular intervals.

Penalties were prescribed to all concerned, individuals as well as assemblies, if they failed to pay or to complete the undertaking. From Uttaramallur comes an epigraph of the 9th century AD in which the penalty clauses are elaborated. Certain land-owners failed to pay their dues. The village assembly paid the amount for them and their land was taken over for the benefit of the tank for a period of three years. If at the end of that period the defaulters returned and paid up their dues, they were to be given back their land. Otherwise, the land was to be sold and the proceeds used for the maintenance of the tank.

If any person at Uttaramallur objected to this course, his own land was to be sold similarly and the sale proceeds credited to the tank, while the person was to be dealt with as a *grama-kantaka*.

Along with penalties for failure to perform assigned duties, certain allurements were also held out before the people. Spiritual merit was always there, but it was more or less nebulous, for more concrete were tax-exemptions. A person donated 200 *kalanjus* of gold, its interest was to be utilized for desilting the Vayiramega-tataka. In appreciation of this gift, the village assembly exempted that individual from certain taxes.

Records of a much later period, of the 18th century AD or still later, indicate that the age-old custom of responsibility and initiative in this regard revolved on local bodies and minor officials or landlords. Vast amounts of archival records are available for the Mughal Period as well as the Maratha rule, however, only a fragment of these are published. One such record comes from Bedla, an obscure village in Rajasthan. The village headman, known as Thikanedar, had kept meticulous records of all such transactions from 1856 onwards. The editor says in the introduction,

The tanks were maintained by the Thikanedar but the cost of maintenance was shared by the cultivators. Whatever amount the Thikanedar spent on repairs and maintenance was collected from the cultivators and if the cultivators of more than one village took advantage of it for irrigation purposes, then the cultivators of those villages shared expenses.

Local initiative in the field did not preclude royal or state intervention and activity. More especially when bigger problems like flooding of the rivers or providing irrigation to larger tracts of land were to be faced, royal initiative was always forthcoming. The most well-publicised instance is that of the river Cauvery. Karikaal, the semi-mythical Chola king is said to have constructed huge embankments on either banks of the river. During seasons of heavy rainfall, the river was prone to flood vast areas near the banks and erode cultivable lands. The construction of the embankments enabled the delta to receive adequate supply of water. Buchanan (1807), writing about the turn of the century, has noted the same problem:

The rivers which run along deltas, or along ground level, are liable to flow over their banks during the rainy season, it becomes necessary, in order to prevent the country being inundated, to raise walls or embankments to confine the stream.

Canals were dug from the river Yamuna during the Sultanate Period and were repaired and renovated by the Mughals (Randhawa, 1982: 79-80 & 278-279). The earliest example goes to the second century BC, when Kharavela dug a canal to supply water to his capital. The Sultanate canals were, however, mainly for irrigation.

Construction of dams for irrigation purposes has been recorded from the 4th century BC, when the Mauryas got the Sudarshan Lake constructed in Saurashtra. From then onwards, we have a number of records of dams constructed by various rulers. I would confine myself to discussing only two of them.

Both have been published in full along with their translation in English and as such are not reproduced herein. However, certain portions just cannot be avoided. Two verses quoted below from the Porumamilla inscription (Sukhthankar, 1982: 97-109) are a veritable guide or manual for builders of a dam.

धर्माढ्यो धनवान् सुखी स्थिरयशो द्रव्याभिलाषी नृपः
पाथःशास्त्रविदग्रजश्च दृहढमृत्संशोभिता चोर्वरा ।
माधुर्याम्बुवहा त्रियोजननदी तद्योगखण्डीगिरिः
सेतुस्तत्र विनिर्मितो घनशिलाभिर्नाल्पदीर्घः स्थिरः ॥

शृंगौ बाह्यफलस्थिरापरिवृतौ विस्तीर्णनिम्नोदरं
ऋज्वायामयुतं खनिश्च निकटक्षेत्रं फलाढ्यं समम् ।
अद्रिस्थानदृढं शुभा जलगतिस्तत्कर्ममर्त्यव्रज-
श्चेदृक् द्वादशसाधनैश्च सुलभः श्रेष्ठस्तटाको भुवि ॥

The two verses enumerate twelve ingredients which were considered essential for the completion of such an undertaking. It should be emphasized that the characteristics taken into account by the author of this inscription deal with every essential aspect of such an undertaking. The first and foremost is the prime mover, the State, here denoted as 'King'. The king should be endowed with righteousness, he should be rich, and should be desirous of happiness and lasting fame. In other words, he should be aware of the needs of the people (by satisfying which he would attain happiness and fame) and he should have the material means, money, needed to undertake the work. Then he should have, at his command, the services of experts in the science of hydrology (*Pathasastravid*). They should be assisted by a troop of craftsmen, masons, skilled in the construction of such a structure. The raw materials required, viz., strong and long stones should be available and the quarry should be as close as possible to the site of the intended structure. These were all preliminary requirements. Then comes the question of selecting the site for location of the dam. First and foremost, of course, is that the river should contain sweet water. The dam should be located at least three *yojanas* downstream from its source. A spot should be selected where there are strong hills on either side of the river so that the wall of the dam can be pinned against them. The ground here should be firm, neither sandy nor porous. It is further prescribed that the land around and in the vicinity of the intended lake (dam) should be fruit-bearing, that is, fertile, and should not be sandy or rocky. This is a very sound advice as a lake in a rocky or barren land would mean waste of money and effort. At such a site, a stone bund should be erected and sluices should be provided in the wall (so as to permit water to be carried to fields through channels).

This is a brief but complete guide to building of a dam, as remarked in the relevant section. The *Vastusastras* seem to be blissfully unaware of this branch of hydraulic engineering. Having thus narrated what should be called the 'positive' requirements, the epigraph also details the avoidable.

Structural and other practical considerations as well have been taken into account. The dam and the consequent lake should not be too near the boundary of the kingdom, a very wise precaution, as it would be constantly in the danger of an enemy attack and destruction. Long back Kautilya had defined 'neighbour' as the most natural enemy. *Kurma*, elevated mounds in the midst of the lake, were to be avoided. So was saline soil, scanty supply of water in the river and too extensive a stretch of land to be irrigated. Conversely, the land to be irrigated should be large enough to absorb the water stored in the lake, otherwise it would go waste.

Having enunciated the principles of sound dam construction, the epigraph goes on to describe the process of the construction of this particular dam that created the vast sheet called Anantraj Sagar. One thousand labourers were working at the site every day for a period of two years. A hundred carts were pressed into service. There was no limit to the amounts spent on the work. This effort in manpower and money resulted in the construction of a massive dam. The measurements are given in terms of *rekha dandas*. The length of the bund, including the hills was five thousand *rekha dandas*, the height was seven and width eight *rekha dandas*. The person who was in charge was one Devaraja, son of the minister Kumara Girimath and the patron of the dam was Bhaskar alias Bhavadura, son of Bukka I of the Vijayanagar Dynasty and the date of the inscription is AD 1369.

The Anantraj Sagar or its improved form (perhaps slightly enlarged or strengthened version) stands today some two miles to the east of the village of Porumamilla. The lake is seven miles in length and two-and-a-half in breadth.

> The bund consists of four natural hills connected by three earthen dams riveted by Cudappah slabs. The total length of the artificial bund is about 4,500 ft., total length including the hills is 14,000 ft. At the deepest section the bund is 12 ft. wide at the top and 150 ft. at the bottom and about 33 ft. deep.

Sukhthankar (1982), who has edited the inscription, suggests that one *rekhadanda* would be equal to one and quarter yards, that is about 45 inches. There seems to be some confusion in these calculations. If the height is 33 ft. which in earlier terms is recorded as seven *rekha dandas*, one *rekha danda* would be equal to 51 inches. Since the length mentioned in the inscription is 5,000 *rekha dandas*, it has to be equated to 14,000 ft., each *rekha danda* would then be equal to thirty inches; however, if it is to be calculated as 14,000 + 5,000, that is 19,000 ft., it would mean that a *rekha danda* is equal to 40 but not 45 inches.

The dam near Kankroli in Rajasthan, that created the beautiful Raj Samand, took fourteen years for its completion. The work was started in 1662 and was completed in AD 1676 (Chakravarti, 1957). Such a long time was required because three different but closely inter-related aspects had to be taken care of – the digging of the bed of the river Gomati (on which the dam was to be built) so as to deepen and enlarge it; building of the dam proper and the construction of spacious *ghats*; pavilions in front of and on top of the embankment. The epigraph associated with the work has given precise description of the whole operation and compares most favourably with the Porumamilla prescriptions.

It is narrated that when King Rajasimha expressed his desire to get a dam constructed, his priest and advisor told him that his desire would be fulfilled only if he satisfies three pre-requisites. These were, according to the inscription, *Sraddha*, full faith in the divine; friendship, at least absence of enmity towards the Lord of Delhi (अविरोधत्वं दिल्लीशेन), and thirdly, ample funds. The first probably refers not only to faith in the divine but also in his own determination to get the work done. The second was a very practical piece of advice as the Udaipur rulers were vassals of the Mughal emperors of Delhi. The third, financial ability, was equally practical and valid. The king fortunately had all three with him. The site selected speaks of considerable knowledge – it was a gap between two fairly large hills and close to land that would benefit from the irrigation from the lake. The lake was to extend over a very large area which had sixteen villages on it. The names of these are listed in the inscription. However, it is silent on their fate – how they were rehabilitated, whether the villagers were given alternate lands or monetary compensation or just driven out is not clear.

Urban water supply was a comparatively late phenomenon. Cities of ancient India were generally located along the banks of perennial rivers or tanks and lakes with their own springs. In order to get access to water, easy flight of steps known as *ghats* were constructed; the most well-known being at Nasik and Varanasi. Tanks and *kundas* were similarly provided with *ghats*.

Towns and villages away from the rivers depended on wells. The administration took steps in some cases, to build percolation tanks in which rainwater was stored. They were located at levels higher than the ones where wells existed. The more ancient of such tanks is to be found at Badami in Karnataka and the comparatively later one, known as Nagar-Tale, was at Devagiri.

With the advent of the Islamic Sultanates, the accent shifted. Instead of people going to the water, water was brought where men wanted. Thus came into existence complex systems of water supply. The most extensive systems were to be found at two of the early capitals of the five Sultanates of the Deccan, viz., Ahmednagar and Bijapur (*Gazetteers of the Bombay Presidency*). The earlier of the two appears to be from the former city. Slightly later in date was the waterworks at the military-cum-political centre, Daulatabad. The Mughals introduced similar systems at two places, Aurangabad (*Maharashtra Gazetteers*, 1977) and Burhanpur (Pangare, 1992: 43-44). The latest in the series was built in Pune under the Peshwas in the second-half of the 18th century.

The one from Ahmednagar is to be dated to the first part of the 16th century, Bijapur got it in the late 16th, Aurangabad and Burhanpur during the late 17th and Pune in the 18th century. Interestingly, the Marathi ballads of the period call this system 'Japani', i.e., Jahapanhi, indicating the source of the technology. It has to be noted that except at Daulatabad, all other systems are now buried under modern buildings and habitations. As such, one has to depend on the data recorded a hundred years ago by the *District Gazetteers of the Bombay Presidency*. This information is, to some extent, supplemented by occasional discoveries, mostly while digging the foundations of new buildings. To some extent this data is supplemented by our surveys conducted at Daulatabad.

Ahmednagar is situated on the eastern bank of the river Sina. The river is, in fact, a small stream and is mostly dry in the better part of the year. It, however, provides the low-lying area necessary for the system to be brought into existence. The system has fifteen different sources and barring one, all are on the eastern side of the river. In 1884,

Fig. 5.1 Different types of water lifting systems.

eight out of the fifteen were in working order and brought water to the city. Now hardly two are in operation (Mate, 1999).

These systems had some elements in common: (a) assured sources of potable water; (b) pipelines, masonry conduits to carry water from these sources to the outlets; (c) arrangements for preventing blocking of the lines; (d) private or public outlets and arrangements for lifting water wherever needed; and (e) drainage of used water. These could be described as follows:

a) Wells or artificial lakes (dams) were located at a height of 100 feet or more, and were situated in excellent catchment areas. In some cases, two or three bunds were constructed, one below the other, so that silt would settle in the upper lake and allow purer water to go to the lower one and eventually to the pipelines.
b) Pipelines were usually made of terracotta, with pipes 3 to 4 inches in diameter and nine to eleven inches in length. One end of the pipe was narrower so as to fit in the next one. At places, such pipes of 14 ft. diameter were found. These were enclosed in stone masonry walls. Brick-built conduits, some 6 ft. in height, to enable a person to walk through it, were built. Such conduits were noted at Bijapur and Pune.
c) The pipeline and conduits were dotted with air-ducts. These were in the form of hollow-bricked, tower-like structures, some eight or ten feet in height. They were open to the sky and, thus, allowed air-bubbles to escape. The base of these towers was pit-like, that is they were traps to catch the silt carried by the pipes. Another method was to build small masonry tanks which received water from the pipelines and after allowing the impurities to settle, clearer water was allowed to go further.
d) Water coming down the pipes was stored in small tanks either in the house or in public places, from where it could be used. Such public tanks were in existence in Pune till some ten years back and continued to receive water from the Katraj reservoir, the source. Water was lifted from these storage tanks by *rahats* or Persian Wheels (Fig. 5.1).
e) Waste water was drained out of the habitation areas through well built and graded drainage lines. These were generally open.

NOTES AND REFERENCES

Apte, H.N., 1907, *Matsya Purana*, Pune, Deccan College.

Buchanan, F., 1807, *Journey from Madras through Mysore, Canara* and *Malbar*, London.

Chakravarti, N.P., 1957, Rājaprashasti Inscription of Udaipur, *Epigraphia Indica*, XXIX, New Delhi.

Gazetteers of the Bombay Presidency,
XVII, Ahmednagar, 1884, Bombay.
XXIII, Bijapur, 1884, Bombay.
XVI, Nasik, 1883, Bombay.
XVII, Pt. 3, Poona, 1885, Bombay.

Kangle, R.P., 1963, *Kautilya Arthashastra*, Bombay, University of Bombay.

Kuppuswamy, G.R., 1992, Irrigation system in Karnatak-building aspect, *Quarterly Journal of the Mythic Society*, LXXXIII.

Maharashtra State Gazetteers, 1977, Aurangabad and Bombay.

Mankad, P.A., 1950, *Aparājitapṛcchā of Bhuvandeva*, Baroda.

Mate, M.S., 1999, *A History of Water Management and Hydraulic Technology*, New Delhi, B.R. Publishers.

Pangare, Ganesh, 1992, *Mughal System Still Supplies Water at Zero Cost, Down to Earth*, Vol. I, No. 10, New Delhi.

Randhawa, M.S., 1982, *A History of Agriculture*, New Delhi.

Sukhthankar, V.S., 1982, Porbmamilla Tank Inscription of Bhaskara Bhavadura, Saka 1291, *Epigraphia Indica*, XIV, pp. 97-109.

Venkayya, V., 1990, Irrigation in Southern India in Ancient Times, *Archaeological Survey of India: Annual Report*, pp. 202-211.

6

WATER SYSTEMS AT UDAYAGIRI: A SEARCH FOR ITS MEANING

Meera Dass

ABSTRACT

In this paper an attempt has been made to study the Water Management system at Udayagiri in District Vidisha of Madhya Pradesh in the light of recent field work. The study throws light on some of the aspects of water distribution system in the area which have been overlooked by earlier workers. The author has grouped the tanks, channels and drains in the area to four water systems and explained all the systems in details and also commented on the water rituals. The systems at Udayagiri were not for irrigation purposes but water was manipulated to emphasise the sacred nature of the site. The development of the site was a celebration of Chandragupta Vikramaditya's victory on Malwa. The holy rivers are released here in honour of this celebration.

INTRODUCTION

The large panel of Vishnu in his Varaha *avatara* (401/402 CE), carved on the eastern face of Udayagiri hills (Fig. 6.1), has been written about by almost all scholars interested in the art of ancient India such as Begnold* (1818), Cunningham (1876), Garde (1929), Patil (1948), Mitra (1963), Harle (1974), Agarwal (1977), Williams (1982), Khare (1985) and Huntington (1985). Udayagiri hills are located 3 km to the west of the ancient city of Besnagar (Vidisha and 5 km to the north-east of the present town of Vidisha in Madhya Pradesh). Focus of the archaeologists in the early 19th century was, however, on Buddhist remains and it is therefore not very surprising that archaeologists working in the Vidisha region such as Lake (1910) and Bhandarkar (1913-15) do not mention this important panel at all in their works. How pre-conceived was their approach can be seen from the fact that Udayagiri was declared as a Buddhist site by both Cunningham (1876) and Bhandarkar (1914) although detailed examination of the site and remains by the author failed to establish the claim. On the contrary, it appears that the early occupation could have been in the nature of sun worship, a hypothesis that can only be corroborated by further excavations. The approach was also fragmentary with focus on iconography and epigraphs.

Fig. 6.1 Varaha Panel at Udayagiri 1914 (Courtesy ASI Photo Archive).

Patil (1948) tried to make amends and describes the site in some detail along with the caves and sculptures in them. He, however, sees the site as an assemblage of monuments although he is able to increase the number of caves from ten, as defined by Cunningham (1876), to twenty.

Without undermining the contribution made by these scholars, an attempt is made here to find answers to questions ignored in previous studies due to the fragmentary approach. The paper brings into focus the 'non-monumental' remains along with extensive field research with emphasis on both interpretive observation and collection of fresh rather than empirical data. It aims to bring out the meaning and reasons for the presence of the monuments on the site, its spatial organization, the relationship between the various components of the site and its relationship to the large landscape as a whole. In short, architecture, iconography, epigraphs, archaeology, textual studies and numismatic finds were re-read along with close observation of the site, layout of the caves, visit to the museums, and participation in all events related to Udayagiri. One of the methods adopted was to identify the original location of objects by visiting the site with old photographs.

The holistic approach also brought the question of relative chronology into the study resulting into the discovery that the site was crafted under one single campaign lasting approximately twenty-eight years from 401/402 CE to 426 CE (Fleet, 1888).

Implicitly, it means that the entire site was developed on the basis of a grand design laid out during the reign of Chandragupta Vikramaditya II of the Gupta Dynasty.

This paper explores the extent of the King's involvement on the site along with retracting the water systems and their symbolic representation based on iconographic studies combined with site survey. Comparison with the ancient water works in the neighbourhood and their similarities and differences are analyzed. The meaning and use of these water bodies in relation to the monuments and sites they are a part of, is argued and the visual impact of the water alongside the sculptures and caves is examined.

WATER RESERVOIRS, LOCATION AND DISTRIBUTION CHANNELS

Udayagiri consists of two hills joined together with a low ridge or a saddle. The hills are aligned northeast-southwest, forming a crescent-shaped pocket in the west with ancient river Bes (Halali) hugging it in the north. It is on the east face of the hill that most of the caves are located, although some of the caves are also carved on the northern face of the 5 m wide and 30 m long passage that divides the saddle from the northern hill (Fig. 6.2). To the east of the passage, which is also the entrance to the cave complex, is the large Varaha panel (Cave 5) facing east and at the west end of the passage is the second large panel showing Vishnu (Cave 13), facing north, in his cosmic sleep on the

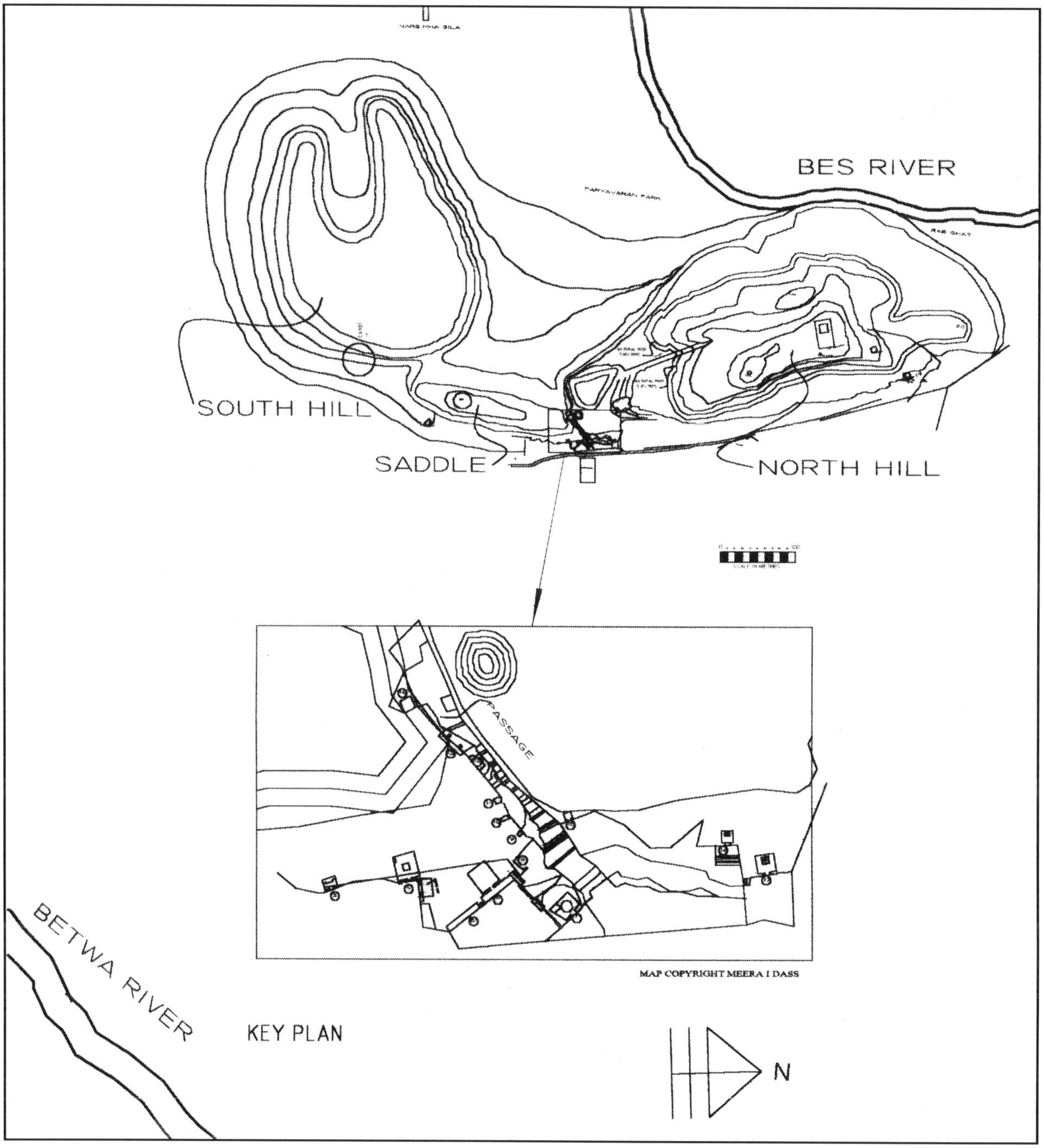

Fig. 6.2 Location of caves at Udayagiri hills 5th century site.

Sheshanaga. These two panels at the two ends of the passage set the tone of the underlying scheme of the development at Udayagiri. Varaha *avatara* of Vishnu marks the beginning of *Varaha Kalpa*, the present *Kalpa*. Myths associate *Anantasayana* Vishnu with the long night and the end of each *Kalpa*. The deep ravine-like passage running from east to west can be read as the beginning of time to the end of time. Not surprisingly, Narasimha *avatara* of Vishnu, which also represents a time that is neither day nor night, is located in between the two panels. Smaller caves with Vishnu in *sthanaka* pose are carved alongside the Narasimha image on the southern wall. The northern wall of the passage, on the other hand, is totally plain except for one notch with a very damaged image of a goddess.

The western end of the passage leads to a high embankment of a tank, two sides of which are formed by two sides of the northern hill divided by a valley. There are three other tanks and two major channels apart from minor drains forming four independent water systems at Udayagiri (Fig. 6.3). The largest tank (Tank 1) is located to the east of the saddle and is directly in front of the Varaha panel and Cave 5 and 6. Old photographs from the ASI photo archives show the tank to be of a much larger size and much closer to the Varaha panel (Fig. 6.4). Closer examination of the pattern of decay at the bottom of the sculpted panel showed that water might have touched the sculpture at one time. As we shall see later, the tank may have been of much larger proportion, like a *sagara*, and may have extended to Cave 2 in the south. This point, however, requires scientific investigation.

Tank 2 (Fig. 6.3) is on the north-west of the passage and is the second largest. There are five rock-shelters on the top level of the embankment. One of the rock-shelters appears to have been the source of perennial water to this tank. A 3.5 m high shell character is etched deep into the front of this rock-shelter. There are three places at Udayagiri where shell characters in this particular style are engraved. Shell inscription, so named by Pincep, the well-known epigraphist, because of its resemblance to the form of shells, has still not been satisfactorily deciphered. All the three inscriptions act as billboards as if announcing something.

An elephant path leads one to the top of the northern hill and follows the valley to the north of Tank 2. The embankment, it appears, also acted as an approach to the northern hilltop. Plinth of a Gupta Period temple was unearthed by Bhandarkar (1915) on the northern hilltop in the only excavation that has ever been taken up on the site. It is a high plinth of 4 m height and 21.5 m x 35 m size. This unusually large plinth (larger than Deogarh) is formed of stone masonry grids filled in with debris and cladded from outside by rectangular stone blocks of roughed outer surface. The temple was contemporary to the excavation of caves in the same hill and formed part of the overall scheme.

Tank 3 (Fig. 6.3) is located to the south-west of the temple plinth. This tank, which is 5 m below the temple level has an 8 m x 0.75 m x 0.90 m monolithic cistern aligned to its east and is probably part of the same water system. This cistern is to the south of the plinth and at the same level. Old photographs show a drain-like structure attached perpendicular to the south wall of the temple plinth. This structure, which may have formed part of the drainage system, was removed after 1914. There is, however, all possibility of the tank having been ritualistically associated to the temple. Excavation of

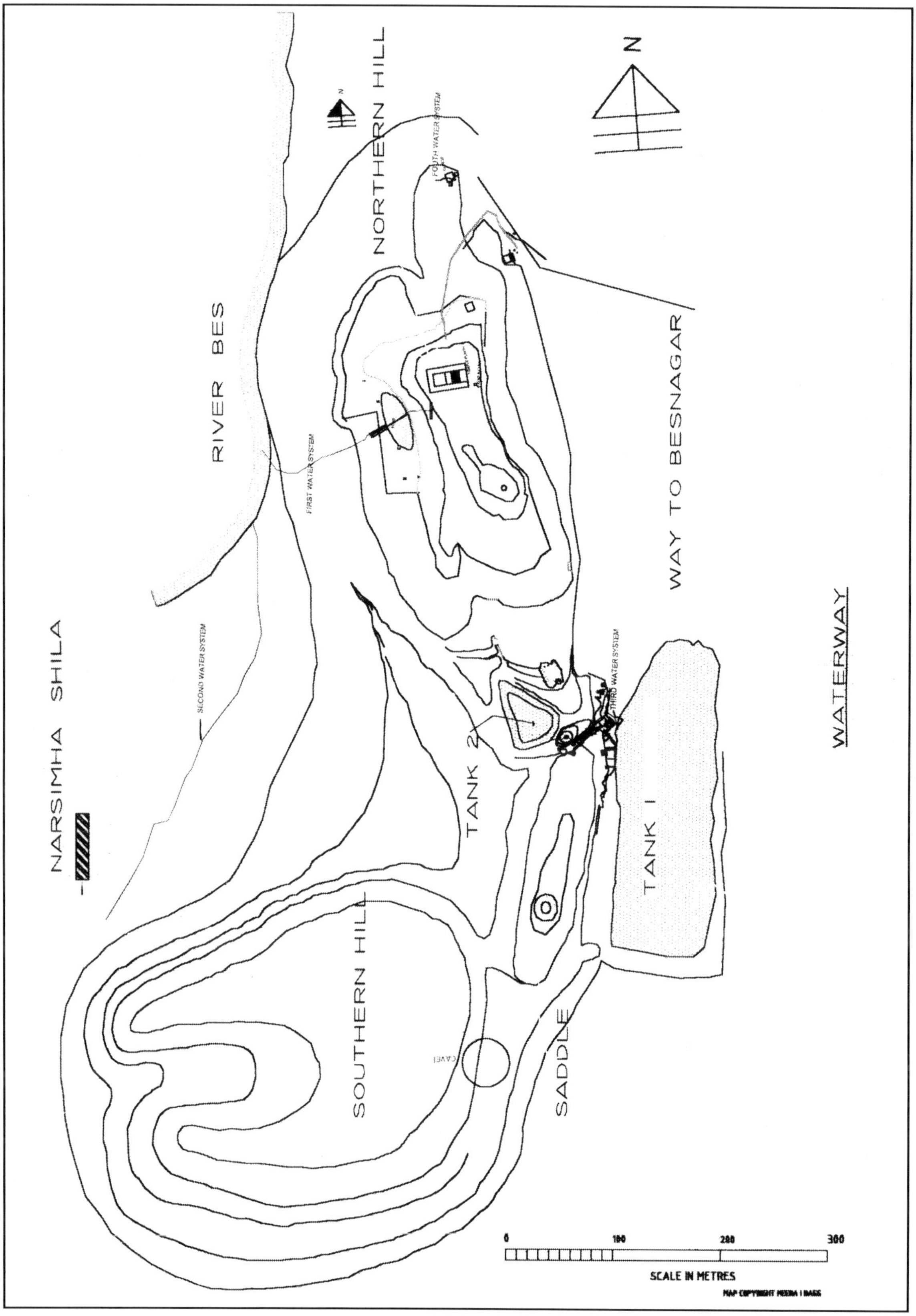

Fig. 6.3 Water systems at Udayagiri 5th century caves.

Fig. 6.4 View of Udayagiri caves showing a much larger tank in front 1914 (Courtesy ASI Photo Archive).

the tank may provide vital information regarding these rituals and the chronology of the temple.

In relation to the northern hill, this tank is situated to its north-west end and has a sheer drop of 50 m to the river Bes below. On the vertical surface of this cliff and very near to the tank are ten post holes in two rows. Just below them on top of a projected ledge, at the water level, are more postholes. The postholes could be the remains of some timber structure attached to the side of the hill. The proximity of the remains to the tank makes one wonder if the timber structure had anything to do with the lifting of water from river Bes below. The level of the water in the river has gone down as is indicated by the discovery of *ghats* by Lake (Lake, 1910) some 30 m from river Bes, during his excavations on Besnagar mound. The water level was found to be just 15 cm higher than the lowest step but the strata of *bujri* and shingle, lead him to conclude that the riverbed had sunk to 3 m-3.6 m below. Building of Halali reservoir, in recent years, has lowered the water levels further.

At this point Ras Ghat, a deep trench (3.0 m deep and 1.5 km long), which cuts across the crescent shape to the west of Udayagari hills, joins the river. The beginning of the trench is marked by a large image of Vishnu in his Narasimha *avataras*. This 6 m high image of Narasimha is engraved deep into a flat surface of inclined rock facing south. It is popularly known as Narasimha *shila* and probably marks the west end of the boundary of the sacred hill of Vishnu.

THE FOUR WATER SYSTEMS AT UDAYAGIRI

The tanks, channels and drains can be grouped into four water systems (Fig. 6.3). The first system consists of the cistern on the northern hilltop and the tank located 5 m below it. The water from the temple was connected to it and its use may have been ritualistic. The water lifted from the river below (probably) may have been used to fill the tank. Currently, the cistern and the tank appear to be the only sources of water on the hill. The second water system is towards Narasimha *shila*. Further investigations are being carried out to determine its use and extent. The third water system is much more discernible. This system connected Tank 2 to Tank 1 in such a way that it flowed in the channels provided along the passage. The meaning and the purpose of this water system is discussed below. The fourth system is a much smaller system serving only Cave 20 located at the northernmost point on the northern hill. This is a Jain cave and was built last in the series of caves carved on the hill. It appears the Jains were following the extensive water management tradition. Two small tanks were scooped out of the rock in such a way that the water flowed through the cave.

The four water systems could have been rain-fed but flowing water was critical for the water architecture and, therefore, lifting of water from the river below or presence of natural springs became important. As mentioned above, traces of the two are seen at Udayagiri and further investigations have been carried out by the author (Dass, 2001) to ascertain their presence on the site. To understand the purpose for which these extensive water systems were put into place, it is important to compare them with the larger irrigation waterworks in the Vidisha region.

ARCHAEOLOGY OF TANKS AND WATERWORKS IN VIDISHA REGION

Cunningham (1876) mentions remains of ancient tanks and waterworks in his report on Vidisha region. Cunningham noticed three embankments set up across the narrow valley between Sanchi and Satdhara during his study of Buddhist monastic sites in this region. Two of these embankments were re-examined by Marshall, who included them in his map of Sanchi. Shaw (2001), a research scholar working in the region, discovered 16 embankments in an area of 750 sq. km. area around Sanchi, during a field study aimed at evaluating the archaeological and cultural setting of Buddhist monasteries in Central India.

Shaw's work on the ancient irrigation works in the Sanchi area is significant as it not only discusses the distribution and form of the dams but also examines the socio-economic and religious infrastructure that underlay the construction and management of these dams. The dams are located in close vicinity to the 'early historic complexes' of Buddhist *stupas* or monasteries. Independently standing images are invariably found at the top of the embankment or near them. Where they are not present, they have been removed to a nearby shrine. Shaw estimates the dates of the tanks on the basis of the images and finds them to date from 1st century BC in most of the cases.

Some reservoirs have spillway while others have deep trench on one side. Shaw's study also demonstrated that the size and form of the embankment were in harmony with local catchments and run-off volumes while some of the larger reservoirs show a familiarity with the problems of flood control. This suggests that engineers who built them were already accustomed to irrigation reservoirs. That the reservoirs were designed for irrigation purposes raises questions regarding the nature of agriculture and cropping. Management of these reservoirs and the spread of Buddhism are some of the questions raised in Shaw's study.

Canals did not accompany the reservoirs. However, Bhandarkar (1914-15) discovered a canal near Heliodourus Pillar during his excavations. Heliodour's Pillar is a *Garuda dvaja* that was consecrated by Heliodorous, son of Dion and an ambassador of Antialkidas the Greek governor at Taxila, to Vasudeva-Sankarshana and is located to the north of river Bes just outside the ancient site of Besnagar. Bhandarkar unearthed two 1.65 m high parallel brick walls 2.1 m apart running in the north-south direction for 60 m that joined another set of walls running in east-west direction at a depth of 3 m 'just below the solid railing level'. Bhandarkar concluded it was the remains of a Mauryan Period irrigation canal (*nahr*) firstly, because they were not connected with any structural remains and secondly, they were filled with alluvial earth which may have accumulated due to floods. Some lime mortar was scraped from the bricks that 'adhered firmly to one another' and on analysis was found to be of a very high quality with 'full recognition of the purpose served by sand and clayey matter in making the material, as well as the lime'. A circular signet-ring, consisting of a '*nandipada*' and a *svastika* design with letters 'Golakasa' in 1st century BC characters written in the centre, was discovered from the canal.

Recently, excavations conducted some half a kilometer to the east of Betwa, for the sewage disposal system, have revealed remains of what could be an ancient water system. The author (Dass, 2002) found two masonry walls of undressed stones forming a channel approximately 3 m wide and about 4 m deep. At half the distance there appeared to have been some disturbance due to floods. Black cotton soil seems to have caved in at this level and disturbed the masonry. Further investigations are required to determine its extent, use and chronology. However, on the basis of the depth at which it is located and the pottery collected from the depth of 4 m it appears to be of antiquity.

PURPOSE OF THE WATER SYSTEMS

As is apparent from the large waterworks around the Buddhist sites in Vidisha region, they were not directly connected to any structural remains and were meant for irrigation purposes. Although not directly connected to any structural remains, the proximity to ancient remains is clearly demonstrated by their location. It is, however, the presence of *Naga* figures around these tanks that suggests some sort of a Buddhist control over the water. *Nagas* were ancient snake deities but during the Buddhist period they were relegated to being guardians of relics as *dvarapalas*. Buddhists may have adopted this symbol on account of its popularity and widespread following. It also indicates the appropriation of the ancient *Naga*-cult sites for Buddhist use.

The presence of the canal near the Heliodourus Pillar, or in other words, near the Vasudeva-Sankarshana temple, suggests religious interdependency between the temple and the canal or water system. The Hindu parallel to *Naga* deities comes in the form of

Sankarshana (Balarama) whose early images from Vidisha region come with a *Naga* hood. According to brahmanical textual tradition, the *Garuda* and *Nagas* were related deities.

Engineering of water harvesting and its manipulation is intermingled with the spread of the religion. At Udayagiri, however, it is quite clear that the water was not harvested for irrigation purposes. Also the iconography on the site shows that the water on the site was not for mere consumption but had much greater role to play in the entire scheme of things.

WATER RITUAL AT UDAYAGIRI

At Udayagiri suggestions of water rituals come from drains and channels made around the three *matrika* caves to the north of Shiva Caves 4 and 6. Closer examination of these caves suggests that anointing of the *matrikas* or may be even submerging of the *matrikas* in water may have formed part of the worship.

This, however, may have been only a minor part of the rituals associated with water. Domination of repetitiously represented Ganga and Yamuna on the temple doors suggests a much larger water scheme (Fig. 6.5). The multiple *shakhas* (branches of a jamb) of foliage on the doorjamb and river goddesses Ganga and Yamuna at the threshold transposed the worshipper from the outside world of the mundane to the land of the gods within the cave. The map is symbolically organized with the two rivers defining the sacred landscape, purifying the initiated before entering the inner chamber. Parts of water cosmology symbols that the craftsmen of Udayagiri employed were lotuses and *purna-ghata* (a pot of abundance). Lotuses blossom in this world of the sacred space and sacred time whereas abundance is visualized in the form of *purna-ghata* overflowing with vegetative growth. Water is also present in the form of cosmic ocean on which Vishnu floats, sleeping on the coils of *Sheshanaga*. On the lintel of Cave 19, gods and demons are shown churning the ocean, depicted in the form of wavy lines, from the depths of which the earth is brought out. This feat is enacted in the sacred enclosure defined by the two river goddesses.

Fig. 6.5 Ganga on her Vahana Crocodile from Besnagar (Photo by the author).

This is the conceptual map of Udayagiri as depicted in its iconography. Cartographically, the two rivers Bes and

Betwa, garland the hills like the *vanamala* of Vishnu, and define the sacred land. It is clear from the imagery on the stone that water is integral to this cosmological scheme. Traces of water canals, channels, tanks and cisterns are some of the remains of the water network that knitted the landscape into one conceptual, mythical whole. Harvesting and manipulating water, therefore, was the preliminary and fundamental element in the exercise.

The myth of the descent of Ganga is enacted here at Udayagiri, albeit in a miniature form. Sage Agastya of the Rig Veda who is reputed to have humbled the Vindhya, stayed in a hermitage to the south of Vindhyas on Mt. Kunjara. He is known to have given Vishnu's bow to Rama who visited him while in exile from Ayodhya and once drank the ocean dry. Bhagirath who could not get any water to perform the rites of his ancestors did penance to bring down the celestial river Ganga to earth. However, the immensely powerful river could be brought down from the heaven only with the help of Shiva who received the full might of her force in his matted hair. Meandering through the dark hair, she is known to have then gently descended to the earth, purifying the souls of the ancestors who could then ascend to heaven. From the matted locks of Shiva she is known to have descended in seven streams known as *Sapta-Sindhva.*

The seven strands of hair on the *mukhalinga* in Cave 4 could be representative of the *Sapta-Sindhva.* Water after the ritualistic ablution of the *linga,* was drained out of the cave through the hole in the outer wall. The *matrikas* in the half-cave nearby went through a similar ritual. The drains and the watermarks highlight the course of the drained water. The caves were closed with door shutters, while the *matrikas* were partially cut off from the outside with a 90 cm high railing. The holy water was received below in a tank that stretched across to Cave 7 to the north and Cave 2 to the south.

The water from here overflowed into the tank on the east of the caves through a channel cut along with the rock-cut caves in the passage. The channel was cut along with the steps thereby dividing the steps into two levels. Garde of Archaeological Dept. of Gwalior State levelled this level difference in 1929. On reaching the eastern edge the water dropped into the tank that at one time touched the feet of Varaha. The marks of the water thus touching the feet of the god can still be discerned. The tank stands disconnected from the caves by a modern road. Old pictures show the water much closer to the caves. The photo (Fig. 6.4) also shows the tank to be of a much larger size. Location of Cave 2 towards the south makes one wonder if the tank was much larger and reached up to that cave. The reason for the location of Cave 2 could be attributed to the size of the tank.

If one studies the flow of water with the sacred scheme, the meaning becomes clearer. The water from the north tank (Tank 2) appears to have flown along the northern wall of the passage. Only one notch with a goddess with raised right hand is carved. The image is badly damaged and from the pose of the maiden it appears to be goddess Ganga. If the morphology of the passage, the tank and the images is interpreted, then we realize that water may have been perceived not just as ordinary water but as Ganga herself. The direction of Ganga was from the end of the *Kalpa* towards the present *Kalpa,* falling into the tank (Tank 1) below, perceived here as *sagara.*

The waters of the *sagara* appear to have touched the feet of the mighty Varaha. The wavy lines of the rippling *sagara* depicted on the Varaha panel reflected in the waters of the tank and the cosmic act of Vishnu in his Varaha *avatara* enlarged it to twice its original form and size in the reflection. The shine on the body of the god gives the whole scene and the depiction a timeless quality, as if he is still wet from his act of rescue.

Such imagery and water architecture had never been attempted before. The visual impact of this in stone and water was so strong that centuries later it continued to inspire artists of Mahabalipuram, where the descent of Ganga was carved to match the size and scale of this original version. 'Kiritarjuna' panel at Mahabalipuram was carved on a large surface of rock and a tank was constructed above to hold water that was released to enhance the effect of the carving. The water was collected in a pond all around the rock to make the rock appear like a cosmic mound emerging out of primordial waters.

CONCLUSION

Elaborate water systems were installed at Udayagiri. A comparison with the large dams in the region demonstrates that the water systems at Udayagiri were not for irrigation purposes. Such extensive works were not required for the supply of drinking water either. Therefore, the reason for making such efforts for lifting water and letting it flow along laid out routes had to be other than irrigation or drinking. The entire water architecture at Udayagiri is critically dependent on flowing water.

Study shows that the water was manipulated to emphasize the sacred nature of the site. The emphasis was brought about by visually employing water to enhance the effect of the images carved on the face of the rock. Images that were large and powerful visually were reflected in the water to enlarge and enhance the effect. The cascading and shimmering water created drama and added to the meaning of the concept behind its visualization.

Metaphorically, the flowing waters on the site were compared to the goddesses Ganga and Yamuna carved on the lintels and panels. Sacred, like the sacred rivers of Ganga and Yamuna, these waters were for reverence and like the king who is allegorically represented as Varaha, the sacred rivers, which are also symbolic of the sacred land from where he had come, are symbolically represented here as actual waters.

We are reminded here that the development on the site was a celebration of Chandragupta Vikramaditya's victory over Malwa. The holy rivers are released here in honour of this celebration as the gods and *rishis* alike come and bless him. It is an important site of the king who came here personally along with his minister Virasena.

NOTES AND REFERENCES

* Lieutenant John Henry Begnold sketched the Varaha pancel in 1818 and this is the earliest reference to the carving. The sketch is now in the library of the Royal Asiatic Society in London.

Agarwal, V.S., 1977, *Gupta Art: A History of Indian Art in Gupta Period,* Varanasi.
Bhandarkar, D.R., 1913-14, Excavations Besnagar, *ASI Annual Report:* 187-225.
——, 1914-15, Excavations Besnagar, *ASI Annual Report:* 66-88.
——, 1915, Excavations, *Progress Report of Archaeological Survey of India, Western Circle:* 59-72.
Cunningham, A., 1876, *Archaeological Survey of India,* 3, Varanasi.

Dass, M., 2001, *Udayagiri: A Sacred Hill, its Art, Architecture and Landscape,* Ph.D. dissertation, De Montfort University, U.K.

——, 2002 (in press), Heliodorus Pillar from Besnagar: Its Capital and Worship, *Journal of the Asiatic Society,* Bombay.

Fleet, J.F., 1888, *Inscriptions* of *the Early Gupta Kings and their Successors,* Corpus Inscriptionum Indicarum, Vol. 3, No. 3, 6, and 61, Calcutta.

Garde, V.D., 1923-40, *Annual Administrative Report of the Archaeology Department Gwalior State,* Gwalior.

Harle, J.C., 1974, *Gupta Sculpture,* Oxford.

Huntington, S., 1985, *The Art of Ancient India,* New York.

Khare, M.D., 1985, *Vidisha,* Bhopal.

Lake, H.H., 1910, Besnagar (Art XVIII), *Journal of the Bombay Branch of the Royal Asiatic Society,* Bombay: 135-143.

Mitra, D., 1963, Varaha Cave of Udayagiri, *Journal of the Asiatic Society of Bengal* 5: 25-28.

Patil, D.R., 1948, *The Monuments of the Udayagiri Hills,* Gwalior.

Shaw, J., 2001, *The Sacred Geography of Sanchi Hill: The Archaeological Setting of Buddhist Monasteries in Central India,* Ph.D. dissertation, Cambridge University.

Williams, J., 1982, *The Art of Gupta Empire and Province,* Princeton.

7

PRE-MUGHAL WATER SUPPLY SYSTEMS IN THE DECCAN (AD 1300 – 1650)

M.S. Mate

ABSTRACT

This article highlights that there is very little evidence of pre-Mughal water systems in the Deccan in the time period of AD 1300 to AD 1650. It seems that the rulers of the Deccan paid little attention to the irrigation systems as against those in Karnataka or Tamilnadu where tank irrigation enjoyed the highest priority with the kings and other administrative bodies. In the North, however, dams were built and canals were dug from the time of Firoz Shah Tughluq. Examples of step-well from various areas indicated a change in the distribution of water systems which were constructed by the rulers to bring water to their palaces and gardens. The smaller tanks built at a number of spots in the town catered to the needs of the general public. It is to be noted that several examples of water system lie buried under modern habitation and one has to take recourse to the written documents. The author's excavations in Aurangabad region have revealed extensive arrangements for water supply beginning with 5th century at Daulatabad. It is also pointed out that there was no arrangement for controlling flow of water in our ancient systems. It is suggested that small-scale systems should be constructed with locally available materials and constant maintenance must be provided for its upkeep.

INTRODUCTION

One of the surprising aspects of the period under consideration (AD 1300-1650) is that there is very little evidence, either written or monumental, that would indicate the existence of any measures or systems associated with irrigation. Unlike in neighbouring Karnataka or Tamilnadu or further south, the rulers of the Deccan seem to have paid little attention to irrigation works. In the southern states, tank irrigation was popular and its construction, maintenance and utilization enjoyed the highest priority with the kings as well as the local administrative bodies. Numerous epigraphs testify to this interest. Venkayya (1990) has ably summed up the data available up to 1902. Recently, Kuppuswamy (1992) has brought together a vast amount of data from Karnataka. This written evidence testifies to the existence of large dams, bunds on smaller streams, small tanks, with a provision for the maintenance of these bunds and tanks, as well as for de-silting them. Such works aimed at a fair and just distribution of the water thus available. In the north also, dams were built and canals were dug from the time of Firoz Shah (Randhawa, 1982). Epigraphs of the Deccan Sultans, and histories of their rule like those of Firishta or Tabataba are silent on these aspects while they do mention the construction of palaces, gardens, etc.

Supply of water for daily consumption depended on rivers, wells and tanks popularly known as *kunds*, which were in turn dependent on the rains. Most of the towns of the pre-Mughal, in fact pre-Sultanate Period, were located on or very near to rivers/streams or natural lakes and in order to make an easy access to water, flights of steps known as *ghats* were constructed by wealthy persons. A fine example of the pre-Sultanate Period (14th century AD), is available at Nevasa in Ahmednagar. On the eastern bank of the river Pravara are found *ghats* of the Yadava Period. Similarly, flights of steps were constructed on wells of larger sizes. These can be technically called 'step-wells'; but in art-historical parlance the term is used to designate a variety of wells found mostly in Gujarat and Rajasthan. These were architectural monuments with a considerable amount of sculpture and ornate galleries. These step-wells were meant not only to make access to water easy but were also luxurious and cool resorts. Wells with steps, belonging to the Yadava Period, are present in the inner perimeter or Mahakot area of the Daulatabad fort. One is known as the Saraswati Well because of the image of the deity Saraswati set on its wall. It also has an arrangement for fixing a *rahat* on it. Another well in the south-eastern sector has two flights of stairs.

Kundas fed by natural springs are found at a number of places in Maharashtra. The process of the construction of the *kundas* and their sacred character is interesting. Water-holes near localities were enlarged, given rectangular or square shapes and flights of steps were provided on all the four sides. In more elaborate versions, miniature temples were built around them or niches were provided in the surrounding walls. One of the better examples of such a *kunda* is to be found at Loni-Bhapkar, a small village some 10 km from Morgaon on the Pune-Baramati road. It is 60 ft. square and 20 ft. deep and on its bank is a small Vishnu temple belonging to the Yadava Period. This association of the *kunda* and the temple is not accidental, one is the result of the other. In most cases, the stone excavated to enlarge the *kunda* forms the raw material from which the temple is constructed. The association of the temple with the *kunda* bestows on the latter some sanctity entailing responsibility of maintaining and keeping it clean.

With the advent of the Sultanates in the Deccan, a profound change took place. Water was brought to the habitations instead of the habitations being situated near water. This gave rise to extensive systems of urban water supply. The most extensive systems were constructed at two of the early capitals of the five Sultanates, viz., Ahmednagar and Bijapur. The earlier system, at Ahmednagar is dated to the 16th century, while Bijapur got it in the latter half of the same century; slightly later in date were the waterworks at the military-cum-political centre, Daulatabad. The systems were constructed by the rulers or their noblemen and water was brought to their palaces and gardens. In addition, small tanks were built at a number of spots in the township and these catered to the needs of the general public. It may be noted that except at Daulatabad, all other systems are now buried under modern habitation which overlie those of the Medieval Period, and as a consequence, one has to depend on the data recorded a hundred years ago by the *District Gazetteers of the Bombay Presidency*. This information is, to some extent, supplemented by occasional discoveries, which are accidental, mostly while digging for foundations for new buildings. To some extent, this data is supplemented by reports of the Archaeological Survey of India carried out in the early decades of the 20th century. The picture of Ahmednagar and Bijapur, which unfolds before us, is indeed very interesting.

Ahmednagar was situated on the eastern bank of the river Sins. The river is in fact a small stream and is mostly dry in the later part of the winter and the entire summer season. It has been receiving water from fifteen different sources and barring one all are on the eastern side of the river in keeping with the slope of the ground. In 1884, eight of the fifteen conduits were in working condition and brought water to the city, but today not even one-third of the conduits are functioning. The one coming from the west originated at Nimbgaon, and collecting additional water at Nepti, reached the western areas crossing the river through terracotta pipes which are no longer to be found.

Clockwise, the conduits came from Pimpalgaon, Vadgaon, Imampur, Shendi, Varulvadi, Kapurwadi, Hasan, Bhingar, Shahpur and Bhandar. In between Kapurwadi and Hasan were two minor works named Anandi and Nagabai. The Vadgaon-Pimpalgaon channel owes its construction to Salabat Khan, a nobleman in the court of Ahmed Nizam Shah (1490-1508). It was repaired in 1630 at a cost of a hundred thousand rupees. The channel from Pimpalgaon to Vadgaon is now totally ruined. At Vadgaon, there was a covered well and from that well water was brought to the city, a distance of about 6 km. The main outlet was in the palace of Chengiz Khan, and from thence to the king's palace, the Jami Mosque and then to several dipping wells or cisterns. In later years several other tanks were built and connected to this channel. It was estimated that it carried one lakh of gallons of water everyday (B.G. Ahmednagar, 1884: 671).

The Kapurwadi channel originating from a well about 2 km to the east of that village (8 km from Ahmednagar), was also built in the same period (1490-1508) by Siddi Samsher Khan. It was repaired under Aurangzeb, about a century and a half later. The aqueduct supplied water to a deep well in Burhannagar and to some fifteen tanks in the eastern parts of the town. The Bhingar channel made in the reign of the Burhan Nizam Shah (1508-1553) by two of his noblemen, Salabat Khan Gurji and Nymata Khan Dakani (Samnan term in North Persia), was brought from a covered well not far from the source of the Bhingar stream and below the source of the Kapurwadi and Nagabai channels. It passes through the town of Bhingar and skirting the eastern part of the cantonment, waters the Farah Baue to the south-east of the town. The Shahpur channel has its source at the foot of the hill on which stands the tomb of Salabat Khan. The ravine is small and of little depth and when the conduit was built it was closed by two masonry dams. Near its head, the conduit passes under the high road and opens into a large dipping well. On the opposite side where it enters the conduit, it takes a fresh departure and joins the Bhingar channel. The Anandi channel has its source about 3 km north of the city and provides water to the northern parts. Two tanks, one near the Delhi Gate and another inside the city, received water from this channel, both called Anandi after their builder Anandrao. The Nagabai channel has its source one and half km below the Kapurwadi channel and its original source is an open well. It was built during the reign of Ahmed Nizam Shah (1490-1508). The water of this channel was brought by an 'anicut' as far as the village of Nagardevala and from there it was taken to fill the fort ditch by sets of double eastern pipes, laid side by side and covered with stone masonry. The work of constructing conduits for providing water to this city was begun almost simultaneously with the establishment of the capital here and continued for well over a century under three successive rulers.

Bijapur had water near the surface and wells were sunk everywhere so that the population at large had enough supply of water. It was only when the Sultans started conceiving plans of large palace-complexes and gardens that the need for additional and much greater supply of water was felt. As such the earliest water supply works at Bijapur were undertaken around AD 1550, i.e., half a century later than the works at Ahmednagar. The first major work was the Torvi channel which was a complex arrangement. A masonry dam was erected at a spot about a mile to the west of Torvi village which is three miles (4.80 km) to the west of Bijapur. Water from the dam was brought up to Torvi via a duct-cum-stream, then it passed below the village of Torvi through underground pipes up to Afzalpur where another large reservoir was built. Another dam, some half a mile south-west of Torvi, supplemented this water. Afzalpur also received water via an aqueduct raised on arches. An aqueduct, passing sometimes 60 ft below the ground level, carried the water from this lake to the city of Bijapur. Air shafts were built at regular intervals and wells were provided for in which the water was poured and then allowed to proceed in smaller conduits, thus reducing the force of water and the strain on the pipelines. In course of time, as the needs of the kings and the populace grew it was thought necessary to have additional sources of water supply. During the reign of Ibrahim Adil Shah, that is, the latter half of the 16th century AD, a dam-lake was constructed to the south of the city which was one mile (1.60 km) in length and covered an area of five hundred acres. It was situated at a much higher level than the city and thus water could be raised to greater heights within the palaces. Water from this lake (Begum Talav) was brought through pipes of fifteen inches diameter encased in a masonry wall of 6-8 ft. about 15 to 50 ft. underground. Along the course, large masonry square towers were built 800 ft. apart. To relieve the pressure of water, each one was raised 20 to 30 ft. above the level of the ground. These also intercepted the silt and prevented choking of the pipes. Water enters the tower at a comparatively low level while the take-off pipe leaves it at a much higher level. The towers were periodically cleaned. Some of the larger towers in the city were distributing centres, from which a number of pipes lead water to other centres like small distributing tanks. For example, the tank on the north of the Meccan Masjid has some seventy pipes emanating from it.

Another interesting feature, worthy of attention, is the sub-terranean tunnel which brought water from the Surang Bawdi near Torvi to the Ibrahim Rauza. Its course can be traced with the help of the air shafts located at regular intervals. For the greater part it is cut in murum, and at some places, it is 60 ft. below the surface of the earth. Only one side was built of brick, the other being left open so as to allow water seepage – thus it is termed as a percolation channel. Water from these various conduits is stored in large wells and tanks for the use of the people. The largest of these is the Taj Bawdi which is 223 sq. ft. with twelve moats; near the Shahpur gate is the Chand Bawdi, in the south-eastern side was the Bari Bawdi and in the north-eastern side is the Masa Bawdi (B.G. Bijapur, 1884: 578-81).

The explorations and excavations conducted by the author in collaboration with the Marathwada University, Aurangabad, have revealed extensive arrangements for water supply beginning with the 15th century and fully maturing during the late 17th at Daulatabad (Fig. 7.1). However, it has to be admitted that precise dating of each work and system could not be done, as they followed each other in quick succession, often merging or complementing each other.

The traditional sources consisted of wells with steps and a few ponds adjoining Hindu and Jaina temples that served the population of the pre-Islamic Period. Fresh water springs on the hill of Eogiri sufficed for the garrison and the small number of people that could be accommodated on the top of the hill. These traditional sources were hardly enough for the expanding population and hence a pond was created to the immediate north of the hill. It was known as Nagar-tal. Today, the area of the pond is all silted up but, in the olden days, water (rainwater) flowing down the slopes of the adjoining hills could be stored here in large quantity. The situation of the reservoir is interesting. Not only is it a good catchment area but it is located on a level much higher than the township which is to its south. This ensured that wells in the lower city would get sufficient water through seepage or percolation.

The next and most significant step was the blocking off of the huge valley to the north-east of the township. The maximum length of the valley is 1.263 km and the

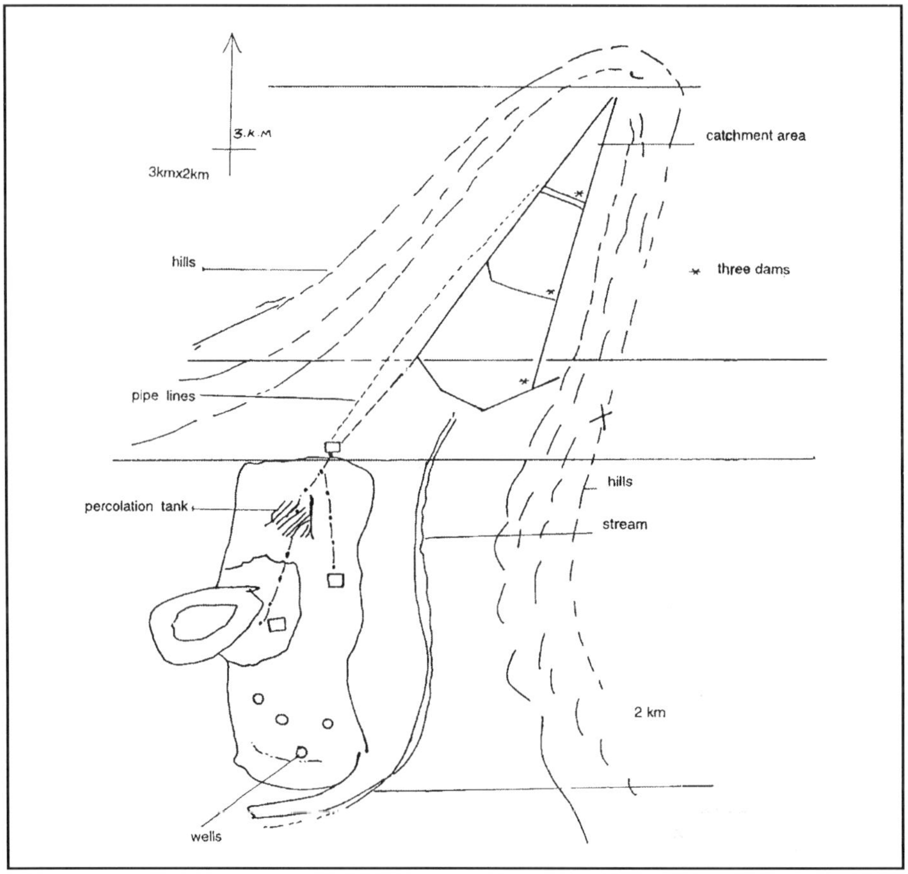

Fig. 7.1 Urban water supply system at Daulatabad, 15th-16th cent. AD.

maximum width, represented by the stone dam of the lowermost reservoir, is 165 m. The depth of the valley from the plateau on either side goes on increasing as it goes southwards. At the source, it is 9 m while at the other end it is 45 m. The uppermost reservoir is today filled up with fine silt. The dam at this point was an extremely strong and well-built wall of stone and lime-morter masonry, reinforced by a row of arches on its southern face. From its top a terracotta conduit put in a brick mortar encasing went down to the town. The bund of the next or middle reservoir was earthen. The third and the final had a stone masonry dam. From this dam, one open and one underground channel carried water to the town. During the rainy season, water from either side gathered into the reservoir. The open channels were built of brick, 25 cm broad and 35 cm deep with the bottom corners slightly rounded. The surface is covered with smooth lime-plaster. The channels stick to the sides of the hills and have gentle slope. These channels, both open and underground, empty themselves in the settling-cum-distribution tanks near the ramparts and the Ellora gate. All the water carried by the channels came in the settling tanks. Silt carried by the water was allowed to settle in these tanks, purer water reached the southern end which opened in enclosed terracotta pipes laid underground. The levels of the various tanks and the inlets and outlets in these tanks were so arranged that water pouring down through the channel never directly entered the underground pipelines, a measure necessary to protect them from silting. The progress of the pipelines is marked by air shafts at regular intervals. The airshaft consists of a brick-built hollow tower open to the sky. Water from the terracotta pipes emptied into a miniature tank at the bottom of the tower, and levels of the inlets and outlets were so arranged as to allow lighter and cleaner water to go out. The size of the shaft was such as to allow a man to descend into it to clean it.

Daulatabad also affords a glimpse into allied problem. Numerous conduits and pipelines brought a large amount of water to the habitation area. This must have raised the concomitant problem of disposal of used water. This aspect has not been touched in any earlier records or literature very probably because concrete evidence was lacking. Daulatabad, however, revealed such an arrangement. In the outer township (Ambarkot) were found drains which were properly laid out and built. The portions recovered from the excavations showed that the depth was 30 cm and width 25 cm, the channel being built of brick and mortar and plastered smooth with lime-plaster. The limited nature of the excavations prevented the excavators from finding out whether the system was in existence all over the town or only in certain areas.

Another line, consisting of stone pipes and much larger terracotta pipes set in a strong stone wall, was laid in the western side of the ramparts of the outermost enclosure that is the Ambarkot. The pipes have a diameter of 45 cm and two lines are set near or above each other. The entire hill on the northern side was skirted by a brick wall and rainwater running down the slopes was diverted and collected in small tanks from which it went into the pipelines. Some scholars believed that the lines were fed from a tank, some 5 km further to the north. However, extensive surveys have failed to locate the conduits that might have joined the extant pipes with the pond. Hence, it is only logical to conclude that the pipes carried rainwater only. As at Bijapur, they fed the ditch which circled the town.

An important lacuna, not only in the system at Daulatabad but also in the systems found in other centres such as Ahmednagar or Bijapur, is that there was no arrangement for controlling the flow of water. There were no valves or cocks that would shut off the flow. This was a defect common to all ancient systems, even the highly evolved Roman pipes had no such arrangement, water pouring out of them twenty four hours of the day.

A necessary adjunct to these structural arrangements was the utilization of water-lifting devices, especially since the Deccan Sultans had a predilection for patterned gardens with channels of running water in them and fountains, water-lifting became necessary. This was achieved by the use of the Persian Wheel or *sakiya* as it was then known. It was constructed of strong timber parts and was rotated by a pair of bullocks. The peculiar mechanism used in medieval India is illustrated in a number of miniature paintings of the period.

Much of the information so far narrated, except that regarding Daulatabad, is drawn from published sources and it gives a historical perspective. The main or the only principle used in these systems was that water keeps its level. The systems have used materials locally available and easy to be deployed like stone and terracotta, the only energy used is that of animals.

Regarding the current status of this system, except one channel at Bijapur, the rest of the systems are now defunct, the reasons being two-fold. Disuse leading to lack of maintenance and the intervention of modern constructions, these systems could be brought to life again if more durable materials are used, specially for the conduits. Terracotta lines are easily disturbed by the roots of the trees that grow in their vicinity. Either more durable materials like PVC pipes will have to be used or the terracotta pipelines will have to be encased in strong masonry walls. Secondly, periodic de-silting of the tanks that serve as the source of water, as well as cleaning the pipelines would be necessary. The one lesson for the future is that small-scale systems could be constructed with locally available materials and skill but constant maintenance would be required for its upkeep. And the task cannot be shouldered by all those who are to benefit from it as was done in ancient South India.

NOTES AND REFERENCES

Gazetteer of the Bombay Presidency, 1884, Vol. XVII, Ahmednagar district.

——, 1884, Vol. XXIII, Bijapur district.

Kuppuswamy, G.R., 1992, Irrigation System in Karnataka-Building Aspects, *Quarterly Journal of the Mythic Society*, LXXXIII/1: 70-90, Bangalore.

Randhwa, M.S., 1982, *A History of Agriculture in India*, (3 Vols.), New Delhi.

Venkayya, V., 1990, Irrigation in Southern India in Ancient Times, *Archaeological Survey of India: Annual Report*, pp. 202-211.

8

THE HYDRAULIC SYSTEM OF SOME EARLY HISTORIC SITES OF KALAHANDI DISTRICT, ORISSA

Baba Mishra and Pradeep Mohanty

ABSTRACT

Man's relationship with water has been vital, complex and varied from the earliest times. It is a well known fact that almost all the ancient civilizations in the world grew on the banks of rivers – Egyptian civilization in the Nile Valley; Mesopotamian in the Tigris-Euphrates Valley; Indian civilization in the Indus Valley; Chinese in the Yellow River Valley; and Andean civilization in river valleys of coastal Peru, etc. The relations between water supply and human settlement through the ages have not by any means been simple; on the contrary, they have been essentially reciprocal subject to perpetual re-adjustment. If on the one hand settlement may be restricted by shortage, on the other human requirements may lead to an increase in the supply of water made available. Nature imposes certain limitations, but within these there is scope for a wide range of adjustment (Clark, 1944; Smith, 1975; Mate, 1998).

INTRODUCTION

In India, during Proto- and Early Historic times, urban centres tended to grow on important and large water-courses, rivers, as they were considered sacred and good for trade and commerce. The earliest urban centre of the sub-continent, that of the Indus, illustrates this phenomenon, and this trend continued in the Early Historic Period as well. The present paper deals with the unique water management system of some of the early urban centres of Kalahandi district of Orissa (Fig. 8.1).

HYDRAULIC SYSTEM

Hydraulic system in the Early Historic Period (c. 6th century BC to AD 500) in the Tel River Valley was remarkable for its ingenuity and indigenousness. Sites like Asurgarh and Kharligarh unravel some clues to study their unique water management system.

Asurgarh (literally meaning 'the fort of the demons') is an ancient port-town, located near Rupra Railway Station, about 2 km north-west of the Narla village. The fort, which

Fig. 8.1 Kalahandi district of Orissa.

is square on plan with each side measuring about a kilometer in length, had four wide gates in four cardinal directions and at each gate was installed one guardian deity. The exterior fortification wall was built on a foundation of rubble. The interior height of the wall is 16 m and the width is about 20 m. The river Salund flows by the western side of the fort providing a natural boundary and meets the river Tel at a distance. The fort is circumscribed by a moat, 50 m X 25 m in depth and breadth respectively, which is fed by a huge ancient tank still existing and covers an area of 200 acres. It is said that water was brought through two sluice gates to fill up the moats. It was designed in such a way that when the fort was surrounded by enemies, a secret sluice might be opened so that the whole area both inside and outside of the fort would be flooded with water and consequently the enemy would be washed away. The central part of the fort would remain as an island if such a flood was created because this part of the fort was on an elevated horizon. Presumably, the palace was constructed at the centre of the fort (Figs. 8.2-8.4). It seems that a regular water supply provision into the residential area of

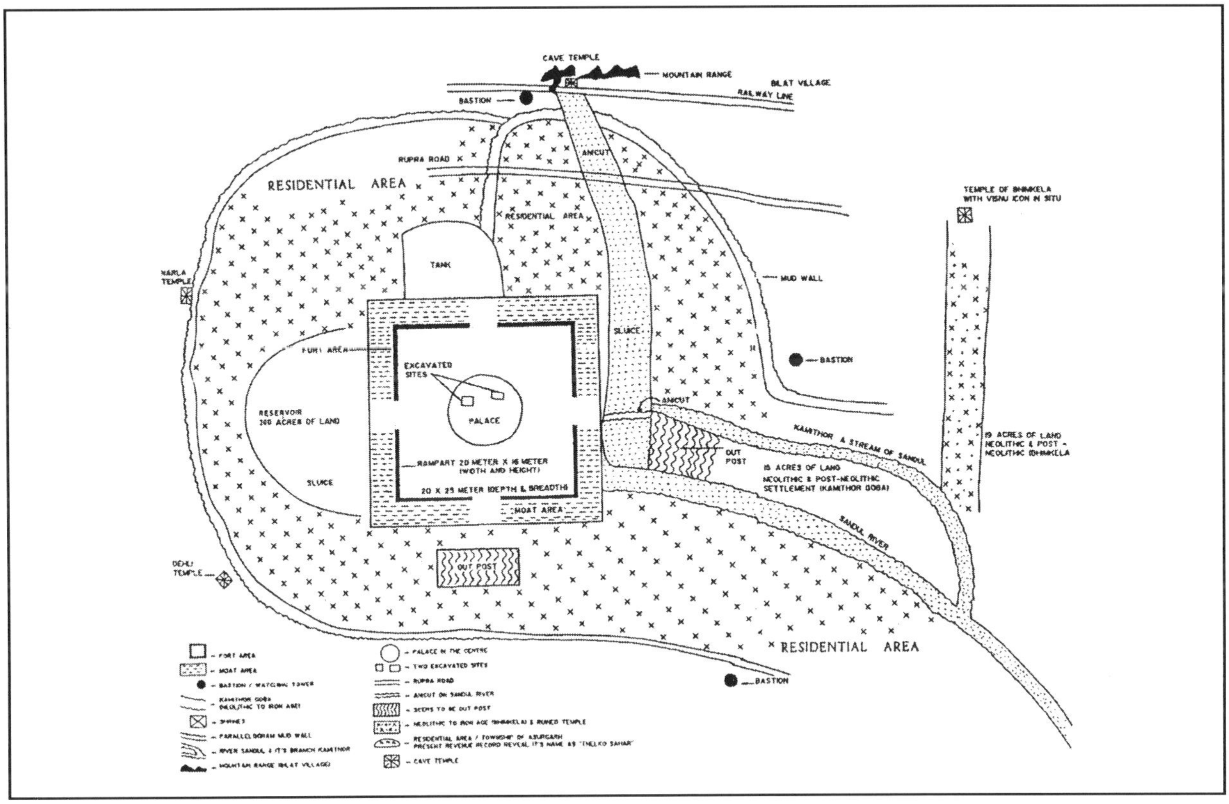

Fig. 8.2 Asurgarh urban complex, (3rd century BC to 5th century AD), Total fort area-60 Acres.

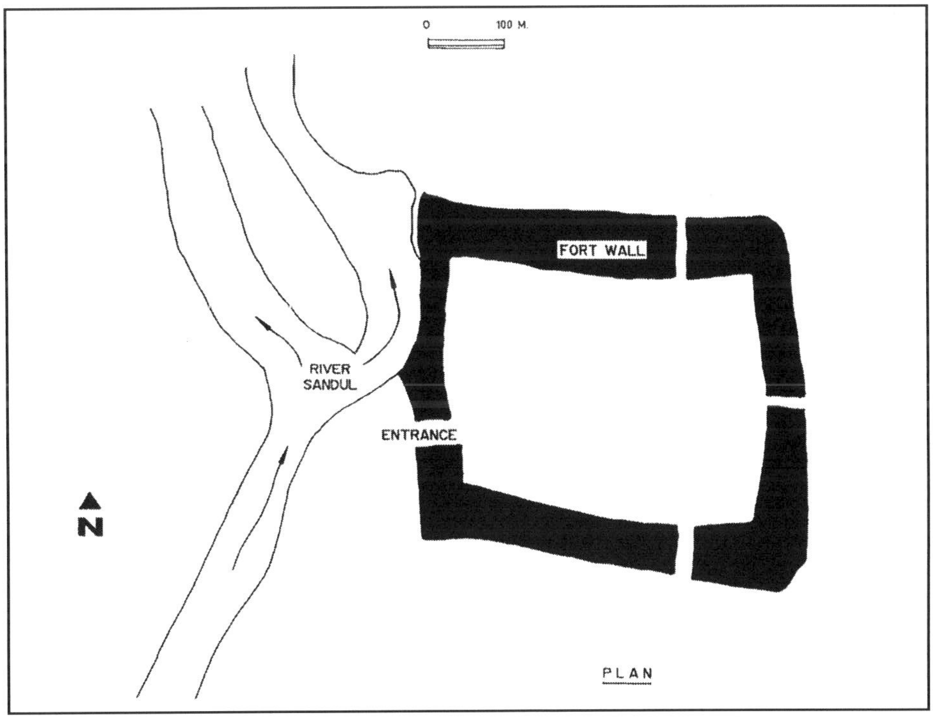

Fig. 8.3 Asurgarh fort, Asurgarh Kalahandi, Orissa.

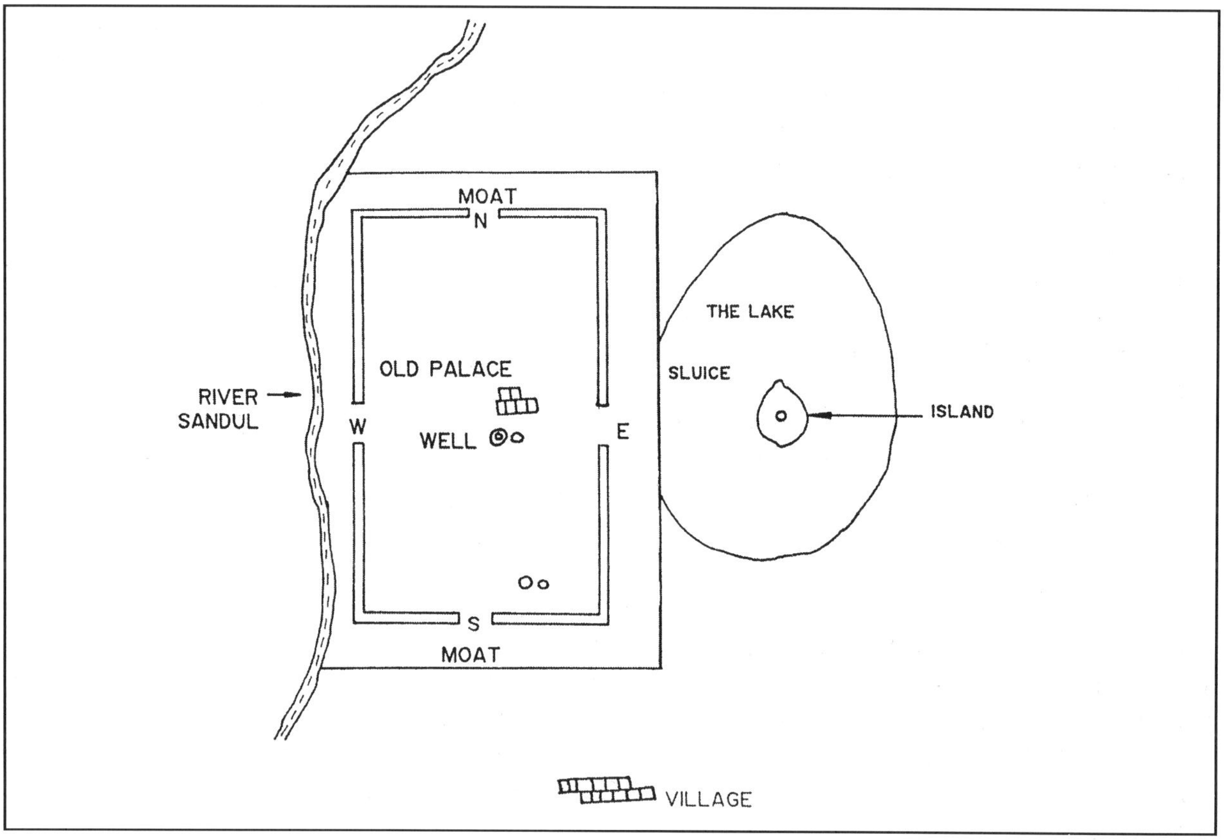

Fig. 8.4 Asurgarh, Kalandi Orissa.

the fort was designed from the embankment of the Salund River through the sluice gate. It is also said that the flow of the river Salund was diverted by erecting an embankment towards the north-west corner of the fort in order to facilitate irrigation and filling up of the moat of the fort (Mohapatra, 1986: 291; Deo, 1995: 129).

The utility of water through hydraulic system in Asurgarh region for agricultural purposes is not far to seek. Even in modern times, the water of the tank is lifted for irrigational purpose.

The settlement pattern of Kharligarh, a fortified Early Historic site, was another hallmark in the hydraulic system of the region. The site lies on the confluence of the rivers Buda and Rahul, which ultimately meet the Tel off Kharligarh. The fort area is about 150 acres and is surrounded on three sides by the river Rahul in U-shape. The other side, not encircled by the riparian system, was however, protected by a mammoth wall of burnt bricks. Close to the western rampart, a moat was excavated connecting both the rivers. At a place where the western wall touches the bank of the river Rahul, there are huge mounds of stone and large-sized bricks giving indication of some big construction activity in the past. Here the embankment was constructed to divert the water of the Rahul to the moat as well as the residential area of the fort.

The hydraulic system of Amathgarh, an Early Historic fort-town, is most amazing. Amathgarh is located on the crossing of a highway connecting ancient Kosala and Kantara. The ruins of this fortified settlement are strewn on the foothills of Bajragarh hill on the left bank of the Tel River. The fort area is located on an elevated horizon about 20 m from the present bank of the river. The velocity of the water at this particular spot is so high that, within a span of thirty years, two bridges have already been washed away, and the third one is under construction. What sort of technical skill was employed during the Early Historic Period to lift the water from the river Tel remains enigmatic due to the construction of many modern structures on the site.

In the rural areas, indigenous technology was employed in the sphere of hydraulic system until the amalgamation of princely states. The 1947-48 revenue records and the copper-plate charters of Nagavamsi kings reveal two revenue nomenclatures like *kata* and *munda* which served as a dividing line in the revenue settlements. *Munda* stood for small embankments, constructed at the top of the village and *kata*, a big reservoir, was usually located at the end of the village. Within the space between *kata* and *munda*, was located the habitational area, surrounded by several hectares of agricultural land. At the time of water scarcity due to abnormal monsoon, the water of *kata* and *munda* was utilized for agricultural purposes. During monsoons, *kata* and *munda* were filled up by diverting the rainwater and seasonal *nullah*.

Apart from having utilitarian values, these ponds and reservoirs or *pushkaras*, etc. served religious purpose too, like purification, ritualistic bath and the water of these was used for consecration of kings (Kosambi, 1981: 68). The construction of such artificial ponds for religious purposes finds mention in many ancient texts. Very often, a pond was dedicated to the mother goddess or fertility deity (Kosambi, 1981: 68-69). Trial excavation within the Asurgarh fort has brought to light the layout of a brick temple located at the southern corner of the fort where a small tank was also excavated, and a large number of nude terracotta female figurines were found thus lending the belief to fertility rite (Behera, 1982: 7). This find corroborates the belief of *pushkara* serving the purpose of fertility cult.

NOTES AND REFERENCES

Behera, S.C. (ed.), 1982, *Interim Excavation Report*, Department of History, Sambalpur University.

Deo, P.K., 1995, Forgotten Forts of Colonnade (Part-1) Asurgarh and Hoard of Punch-marked Coins, *Orissa Historical Research Journal* 14 (3-4): 32-48.

Clark, G., 1944, Water in Antiquity, *Antiquity* 17/69: 1-15.

Kosambi, D.D., 1981, *An Introduction to the Study of Indian History*, Bombay, Popular Prakashan.

Mate, M.S., 1998, *A History of Water Management and Hydraulic Technology in India* (1500 BC to AD 1800), Delhi, B.R. Publishing.

Mohapatra, R.P., 1986, *Military History of Orissa*, New Delhi, Cosmo.

Smith, N., 1975, *Man and Water: A History of Hydrotechnology*, London, Charles Scribeners Sons.

9

WATER MANAGEMENT CONCEPT IN CLASSICAL INDIAN LITERATURE

Vijay Paranjpye

ABSTRACT

This paper discusses at length the traditional and ancient knowledge of water management in the Orient which had been ignored by occidental thinkers till recently. Drawing examples from classical literature of ancient peoples, the author highlights the great awareness among these different populace regarding water-related aspects. Water, one of the *Pancha Mahabhutas*, was highly revered by the Rigvedic people; water was an object of religious charity for Prophet Mohammed. Maintenance of water and water rights are elaborated in the *Koran*.

Concrete evidences of water harnessing in river basins are to be seen only in later treatises written during 500 BC to AD 400, a period in which great attention was paid to the development and use of water resources. The works of Patanjali and Panini refer to water channels. Water resource development comprising construction of reservoirs, dams, etc. was a state affair during the Mauryan Period, the references of which may be found in Kautilya's *Arthashastra* which also discusses the duties of the king towards water management and refers to land irrigation activities through co-operative efforts.

Indigenous traditions of dam construction evolved around the same time in East and South Asia. In Indian context, literary and epigraphic evidences rendering information on canals, dams and irrigation systems can be gathered from the time period 500 BC to AD 500. Classical examples of treatises dealing with water are Kashyapa's water wisdom, Varahamihira's ground water science, *Sukranitisara* of Sukracharya, etc. The author emphasizes that dam and reservoir constructions developed in India as a science, the science of hydrology. It is also stressed that sustainable and socially just development of water resources is possible only when certain fundamental principles are followed. Ancient treatises and epigraphs give us such a set of principles.

THE PROBLEM

The second half of the 20th century saw an exponential growth of dams in the developing countries. Most of these structures are large (15 m or more in height), water impounding structures which have displaced millions of people, submerged hundreds of thousands of hectares of forests, and practically destroyed the cultural lifestyle of hundreds of indigenous communities in an irresponsible and thoughtless manner. Consequently, major people's movements have emerged in Asian and Latin American countries with such great strength and conviction that many mega-dam projects have either been cancelled or are facing stalemate positions in courts or on field. These social and environmental movements are the results of a process where the elite and articulate communities in developing countries have pushed for development projects which involve the transfer of water resources from the rural, forest-dwelling or mountain-dwelling communities, to the urban industrial elite. This unjust appropriation and transfer of a fundamental resource has been at the heart of social conflict throughout the 20th century.

The most critical factor which will impose severe limitation on all large-scale projects in the future is the involuntary, and coercive displacement of large human populations, because the government authorities concerned or the funding agencies have failed to demonstrate either the will or the ability to conduct and implement satisfactory rehabilitation programmes. In most cases, the physical hardships and the economic and psychological trauma has been so great that the 'oustees' are willing to enter into a prolonged conflict of attrition to save their lands, access to water and forests, cultural traditions, languages, moral and religious beliefs. Costs of such social and environmental damages are almost never included in the economic analysis or the feasibility studies conducted by different agencies. The professionals and technocrats have acquired the engineering skills to impound water behind walls, but they have practically no competence in 'social engineering', which requires patience, humility and compassion for pursuing a just process of long term rehabilitation. The major constraints in achieving the goals of sustainable and just development of water resources are as follows:

(i) An ignorance about and neglect of the traditional principles of River-Basin-Development.
(ii) A disregard towards the 'socially determined priorities' in water use.
(iii) A transgression of the ecological philosophy and principles of surface and ground water management.
(iv) A lack of careful analysis of the traditional systems of 'water-rights', and a reluctance to consider the merits of some traditions which may be relevant in future as principles.
(v) The over-emphasis on large and mega-dam projects by the Third World governments and funding agencies like the World Bank. This emphasis is not justified because the established departments of public works, irrigation and hydro-power have failed to give sufficient importance to the smaller scale, dispersed water-shed development alternatives.

INTRODUCTION TO TRADITIONAL KNOWLEDGE

There is a large body of traditional and ancient knowledge related to water, which has been orally transmitted over generations. In the case of India, for example, it was done through an intricate system of recitation and chanting. Contrary to the Western belief, these ideas underwent considerable change, and periodically, the whole body of knowledge was documented in the form of a treatise with references, examples, authentications and acknowledgements ascribed to earlier thinkers. Western science and thought have unfortunately often remained oblivious to such knowledge in the Orient. Worst still, unable to translate and interpret such literature in the modern scientific idiom, such knowledge and documents were either ignored or relegated to the category of 'mythology'!

In recent years, however, this unfair treatment of traditional knowledge appears to have been abandoned and Western thinkers have started looking for solutions to many of the contemporary problems in what is now being recognized as traditional wisdom. In what follows, recourse has been taken to various serious treatises for developing a framework of a water-related philosophy. The underlying principles are stated in simple terms at the end of the paper.

The basic thesis of this paper is that the sustainable and socially just development of water resources is possible only if certain fundamental principles are adhered to. Further, the degree of deviation from these principles would be directly proportionate to the social and ecological non-sustainability of the development projects.

WATER WISDOM IN DIFFERENT ANCIENT CULTURES

The ability of water to change its form with changes in temperature has led to its large-scale dispersion and incessant movement. In the form of rain and snow-melt, it feeds the springs and streams which may trickle or cascade down the hill slopes. It may tumble gently or come crashing down through rapids and falls. But whether it rains as drizzles or downpours, storms or cyclones on land or through typhoons and tempests in the sea, the water has to keep moving. On land it cuts streams, brooks and gulleys, merges into powerful rivers cutting valleys and deep gorges, settles into ponds and lakes. But eventually, water has to flow massively and quietly through flood plains culminating in deltas and estuaries, interfacing and merging into the oceans. There is a general consensus on the view that the physical and morphological changes on the earth's surface and the evolution of life forms were actually the responses and manifestations of the great hydrological cycles spurred on by fire and heat and moved on by the currents of air and the gravitational pull of the earth.

THE VEDIC PHILOSOPHY

It were these elements or the *pancha maha bhoota* which captured the imagination of the great philosophers of the Vedic Period (the Vedas consist of four treatises, of which the first, namely, the Rigveda is a collection of hymns composed between 2000 BC and 500 BC, evolved over time). The concept of life itself was understood and encapsulated through the hymns in the Rigveda. Each hymn was linked to the next in a logical sequence of ideas, verifications and proofs to form the holistic philosophy of the *Vedanta*.

Although man has preferred to settle in areas where water was dependable and plentiful, he was often forced by circumstances to migrate to areas where it was deficient in amount, inferior in quality or erratic in behaviour. When water supplies failed, or became silt-laden or polluted, or when floods had swept away the sites of habitation, the communities abandoned the locations and moved to safer and more reliable areas. But history is also replete with examples where the causes of migration lay as much in the acts of failures of men themselves as in the caprices of nature. Consequently, man's endeavours to achieve a more satisfying relationship with water, running or otherwise, have moulded his character and the outlook towards the world around him. The ancient tanks and wells, aqueducts and reservoirs, some surviving and serviceable, are reminders of the capacity for constructive thinking and co-operative ventures which played a part in human advancement. Some cultures and larger civilizations codified these ideas in scriptures or treatises or anthologies of experiences. Sometimes what remained was only the epigraphs and tablets or hieroglyphics in ancient monuments. Some ideas were integrated into the ethics and laws through edicts, and some entered the substantive positions of thought and philosophy.

THE MUSLIM CONCEPT OF WATER RIGHTS

Another lineage is the Holy *Koran*. Prophet Mohammad saw water as an object of religious charity. He declared that free access to water was the right of every Muslim, and that no Muslim should want for it. This noble principle has indeed become the basis for the whole body of Muslim jurisprudence and social traditions, as well as regulations governing the ownership, use and protection of water supplies in the Muslim countries have faced a relative scarcity of water throughout the historical ages, and therefore it is natural that they practised very strict codes of water use and water sharing. Property rights in water long antedated property rights in land, especially in these arid and desert lands. Rights were associated primarily with the use of water, first for drinking and then for agriculture. In the case of water courses, all persons living in its vicinity shared the water rights, but were also held responsible for its maintenance and cleanliness. The entire community was responsible for the care of water courses which were either natural or man-made. Cleaning was to start at the head or origin of the canal, descending to each waterside family in that order. All users shared the cost in proportion to their irrigation rights. The traditions of such records of rights and duties were best developed in the early history of the Babylonians, Sumerians, Assyrians and Mesopotamians. In most cases, however, water was inseparably linked to the concept of property in these regions. The origin of springs were greatly revered and therefore protected from misuse and vandalism. The brief historical review of dam building in the ancient lands of North Africa and West Asia (1900 BC to 500 BC) mainly reveals an evolution of the techniques of river harnessing. Since there are no written treatises or documents describing the thought behind such structures or the social relationships involved, one can only surmise about the thinking which may have taken place during the conception and creation of such structures.

The architectural achievements were admirable and great, but one cannot construct anything that could be called a philosophy of water-harnessing or the general principles of dam building. In the case of the Mohenjo-daro and Harappan civilizations, one does find the existence of a tank with channels, and its utility for the city and the adjoining agricultural areas. And even if these ancient people had developed a philosophy of water use, we do not have any access to it, since written records of it are not available.

So, for constructing what may be called a philosophy of the harnessing of water in river basin, we have to wait till the period 500 BC to about AD 400, when elaborate treatises were written in languages which are understood today.

THE HINDU AND BUDDHIST THOUGHT

The Buddhist and Hindu thought and literature during the period 500 BC to AD 400 paid great attention to the development and use of water resources. This oriental ideology reveals itself through the writings of several philosophers and *rishis* (saints) or enlightened individuals who continuously added their perceptions to an inherited body of knowledge. As such there was not a single scripture, but several anthologies which were memorized and passed down through generations. Occasionally, a philosopher would convert the received knowledge into a definitive treatise.

As described earlier, in the Rigveda, the elemental aspects were given great importance, but the practical aspects were not ignored. The *ghatachakra* and *asmachakra* were references to what is commonly known as the Persian Wheel, which minimized human labour and increased efficiency through mechanical irrigation. The wheel strapped with water pails was the method for lifting water into artificial channels meant for irrigation. *Khanitrima* are dug-outs and channels, and *kupa* were described as wells unfailing and full of water.

In the times of Panini (5th century BC), rivers were tapped for irrigation and he mentions Sindhu (Indus), Sarayu and Chandrabhaga as sources of irrigation. Patanjali also describes the river Devika and its banks as specially suited for growing paddy crops. He also describes a periodic supply of water through channels for use during droughts, which were not uncommon in many towns and villages.

Water resource development became an important feature of the Nanda-Mauryan periods, with state participation as the main plank in the establishment of irrigation enterprises. Under the Mauryan rule, irrigation was a matter of great solicitude. The most astute advisor of kings in that period was Kautilya, who wrote the famous treatise *Arthashastra* (a term used in modern Indian languages to denote 'political economy' or 'the science of economics'), which gives elaborate descriptions of the duties of a king towards the development of agriculture. He states that the king should construct reservoirs for providing perennial water supply and adds that for those private individuals who construct them of their own accord, the king shall provide sites, roads, timber, etc. without any charge until the private owners realize profits worth twice the initial expenditure incurred. This principle of 'state subsidy', so commonly encountered in modern democracies or 'welfare states', was so well codified over the years that two well-known treatises, viz., the *Arthashastra* and the *Sukranitisar* absolutely concur on it, even though historically they are separated by several centuries.

The *Arthashastra* refers to the concept of *kheyas* (irrigation canals), and *bandhyas* (bunds) constructed through co-operative efforts. These were expected to create lands like the *kosala*, or lands which were eulogized as *adwamatkrah*, i.e., lands which can rely entirely on irrigation rather than on rainfall. Such co-operative ventures were the order of the day and since the systems were a product of the prevailing agro-climatic conditions and needs, the work was performed by the farmers with involvement and conviction. That these canals were well maintained and that the water supply was regulated through monitored sluices is evident from the fact that the kings appointed 'superintendents of agriculture' or *Agronomoi* (district officials who supervised irrigation and land measurement) as described by Megasthenes, the Greek traveller and historian (appointed ambassador to the court of Chandragupta Maurya), who visited India during that period and wrote his travelogue *Indika* – a history of India.

Kautilya (or stylized as Chanakya for his Machiaevellian spirit) commanded the Superintendent of Agriculture to grow winter and summer crops according to the supply of water available for irrigation. One can read that the water rate was added to the land revenue raised by the state from a particular tract. The classified types of irrigated lands were subjected to differential revenue rates which included the water-cess.

THE EXPERIENCES IN INDIA AND SRI LANKA

The efforts in India and Sri Lanka towards river control were considerably different. The rulers of Sri Lanka and the kings of Peninsular India followed the practice of creating thousands of ponds and tanks in villages, all of them interconnected to form a cascade along the river course. The height of these structures rarely exceeded 5 m, as the pondage they were expected to create was meant to be adequate only for the adjoining village or town.

Dams were constructed during this period, and the one that needs special mention is the one constructed by Pushyamitra, during the time of King Chandragupta of the Mauryan Dynasty. This feat of Mauryan engineering skill lasted for nearly eight hundred years with periodic renovations and additions, as is evident from the rock inscription of Rudradaman located at Junagadh (literally translated as 'old fort') in the state of Gujarat in Western India. During the time of Emperor Ashoka (273 BC to 232 BC), the Yavana governor Tushaspa added conduits to this dam. The inscriptions indicate that the lake Sudarsana was destroyed during a storm by the waters of rivers like Suvarnasikata, Paatasini and other streams emerging from Mount Urjayat. The subsequent history is traced in the Junagadh inscription of Skandagupta dated AD 455-456. Thus, during the period 500 BC to AD 500, one finds several references, epigraphic records and literary evidences which furnish information on dams, conduits, canals and irrigation systems including the administrative and tax/revenue collecting procedures, and irrigation interest as the *paniyaka* which refer to cisterns commonly dug near the Buddhist caves (leni), where monks established their monasteries. Such 'leni' at Ajanta and Ellora (verul), dating back to the Saka-Satavahana period, survive to this day with *stupas* and figurines, colourful paintings and frescoes which form major tourist attractions. Another inscription from the city of Amravati and Mathura mentions the superintendent of *paniyagharika* (water houses) and *pushkarani* (water tanks) and *udapana* (pond). The reservoirs and tanks were clearly distinguished and a *naga* statue was installed as a symbolic protector near the reservoirs, a practice still commonly encountered at the tanks and reservoirs as far south as the island states of Sri Lanka and Bali in Indonesia. "The *nagas* were considered as guardians of water, and the invocation of this divinity might have been for the purpose of adequate water."

While India was rich in mineral resources, she appeared to be weak at the agricultural front. The Sanskrit and Buddhist literature is full of references to famines, and the state taking recourse to equitable distribution of food stuffs. This situation changed when the rulers were conscious of the importance of a sound agricultural economy. *Sukranitisar*, a treatise attributed to the sage Sukracharya during this period, advocates remissions of land revenue if the peasant invested in land improvement and reclamation. Further, no tax (*bhaga*) was to be levied on persons who constructed tanks, artificial water courses and the like, as well as those who brought fresh land under cultivation, until they earned twice their outlay. The earlier mentioned lake Sudarsana was rebuilt in this period by Ciratdatta. It was 420 cubits in length, 420 cubits in breadth and had a height equal to seven men (*sapta purusha*) or about 40 ft. The Pratapgarh inscriptions also mention the water wheel (*arahata* or *araghata*), and the Nasik Record mentions the *odayantrikās* or water pumps/hydraulic engines in the 2nd century AD. Another scholar, Bana, also mentions *tuliya yantra* which may be interpreted as a *water pump*. Mentions of these contraptions are found in inscriptions not only in India, but in Nepal, Cambodia, Indonesia, Sri Lanka and Java (the Tugu Bekashi rock inscription).

In the South Indian peninsula, there were village tanks dug out in practically every conceivable place within the Krishna and Cauvery River basins. Persons constructing tanks and maintaining them at their own expenses were granted the ownership of 1/10th of the area of land irrigated by the tank. The important point was that the people were not dependent solely on the state, since religious merit and material gain were directly associated with the construction of tanks and canals. Consequently, tanks were built by kings, temple authorities as well as by people who did not hesitate to come forward to undertake these ventures. Clearly, there was no despotic element in the development of tanks, conduits and canals in this region, since there appeared no reason to draft in forced labour or slave labour for this purpose. These were, of course, the larger reservoirs like the 'Ratta samudra' for which certain specified taxes and incomes were kept aside and paid labour was used. Most agricultural villages had two tanks, which were under the care of the village assemblies, for getting silt removed before the rains set in.

KASHYAPA'S WATER WISDOM

Although the mythical Bhagirath is popularly known for his efforts to divert the water of the river Ganga from the north to the southern direction, it was really Sage Kashyapa's treatise on agriculture, that gave a comprehensive foundation to the philosophy and principles of building dams and reservoirs. This great classic also provided the engineers and the king alike with a code of conduct for dam construction and river-basin management.

The passages on the selection of sites for reservoirs on the basis of the land gradients, soil structures and the situation of human habitations are so comprehensive that they can provide an object lesson to planners, promoters and builders of dams in the 20th century. Kashyapa gives a detailed account of the shapes and sizes of reservoirs, buttresses, embankments, causeways and channels and sluices suitable for various locations. 'The king', he says, 'should take care that when the reservoir is full, it should not be a source of danger to the village, city ramparts, gardens fortresses, etc. either due to overflow or breach.' For this, he suggested monthly inspections and had numerous canals dug for sluicing away the overflow.

Feeding of bipeds, quadrupeds, birds and reptiles, he says, is always laudable as it adds to the general happiness and prevents epidemics. He also insisted on protecting the perennial springs feeding the reservoir. He suggested that mountain rivulets, forest brooks and natural lakes must also be protected so as to guarantee the sustainability of the reservoir. Kashyapa goes on to list out different species of plants like rattan (*Calmus rotany*), the banyan (*Ficus indica*) and other ficus species, khadira (*Acacia catechu*), birjara (*birch*), bamboo, neem, kadamba (*Nauclea kadamba*), etc. as ones suitable for plantation in the vicinity and periphery of reservoirs. Today, we know that these plant species have characteristics like soil holding capacity and germicidal properties. Since Kashyapa was keenly conscious of the merits of de-siltation, he must have advocated these plantations more for avoiding siltation than as measures of beautification. The need for the protection of brooks, mountain rivulets, etc. is an indication of his realization that protection of the origins of rivers aids the health of river basins, or, what is generally described as 'catchment area treatment' in modern dam building parlance.

On lands where water reservoirs cannot be dug, he suggests four types of canals depending on geoponic conditions. He prefers higher levels in the upper catchment for digging reservoirs so that, passing from forest to forest, they may benefit the king's subjects. The breadth of the canals that he recommends varies between 4 to 10 'hastas', i.e., 6 ft. to 15 ft. These canals, he says, should terminate in a lake. He lays down the procedures for determining the best time for digging, examining the soil, the direction of the roots, the mixtures of sand, rock and lime for preparing the mortar, etc. and most important of all, he says, the king should worship Varuna, the lord of waters, the earth goddess and the forest goddess and only then order the construction of a well, a village pond or a reservoir. Kashyapa saw the obvious need to approach the natural cycles and elements with great precaution and humility so that their 'natural goodness' was not destroyed due to human indiscretion. The worship and prayers were also meant to restrain human greed and to recognize the rightful place of the forest and other life forms. It was, indeed, a highly sobering piece of advice given to the king and engineers alike. Kashyapa describes various kinds of reservoirs: *srimukha, vijaya, pranta, dundubhi, chudamani, bhadra, jaya, nanda, sankara,* and gives details about the characteristics of each type.

The most striking of his ideas, which is of great relevance today, is the concept of 'optimal size' of a reservoir. In his estimation, the optimal size should measure 4000 cubits in length, a medium reservoir should measure 2000 cubits and a small one about 1000 cubits. It must, however, be appreciated that the scales or size of the reservoirs indicated were not to be treated as absolute standards, but were intended to stress the point that for each location, the size should depend on the societal needs, competence in co-operation, the nature of forests and mountain streams in the upper reaches of the river basin, the location of the human habitations, etc. and not only on the basis of technological capabilities of the engineer or the technical maxima. There are literally thousands of *bandhas* in Southern India which are a testimony to the mastery acquired by the ancient people in the techniques of harnessing water. They were built to satisfy the year round needs of the local population and not for gratifying the vanity of kings and noblemen.

The graceful and ancient temples in South India or the majestic courtyard of a thousand columns at Chichen-itza, or the ruins of the Mayan civilization in Mexico and Guatemala are all a testimony to the artistic skills of the craftsmen as well as the bold and majestic vision of the architects and rulers who commissioned them. It was not as if they were incapable of building huge structures, and yet when it came to the harnessing of water in river basins, they applied a scale which did not transgress the ecological limits of the river basins in question. The Mayans used the concept of steps and terraces for reducing the water run-off and irrigating slopes of the high mountains, while the South Indians constructed thousands of village tanks and ponds, reservoirs and canals and dispersed them all over the countryside like little beads and ornaments to accentuate the beauty of river basins for the benefit of beasts and men alike. An exact contrast to these practices are the gigantic mega dams which tame and imprison the rivers in concrete and iron shackles exclusively for the benefit of man.

While discussing the ancient water wisdom, we cannot skip two more scholarly sages, viz., Varahamihira and Chakrapani. The writings of these two masters of water management indicate that they had accurately established the relationship between water-laden clouds, the surface run-off on the land, and the sub-terranean aquifers. So, while Kashyapa and Kautilya as surface hydrologists, were busy in the task of advising rulers on the development of river basin run-offs, Varahamihira and Chakrapani were deeply immersed in the science of geo-hydrology. Their treatises quoted the names and contributions of earlier writers like the works of Saraswata, Gargya, Samwasya and Kemadri, more as a mark of respect and reverence for the old seers than as an acknowledgement of intellectual property rights. What could be more true to the spirit of intellectual honesty and scientific temper?

Chakrapani, another great water expert is known for his work *Vishwa Vallabha*. His analysis of several plant species and their natural locational relationships with the underground water table was so elaborate and detailed, that today it can only inspire wonder and amazement at the ecological scholarship of this great seer. Chakrapani, from the city of Mathura, wrote a treatise on the use of water which lies below the surface of different kinds of land. He developed techniques for detecting water in arid soils, mountainous country and below marshy lands, which are worthy of serious consideration. Chakrapani mentions floral and faunal indicators of species for finding underground veins of flowing water not far below the surface, and also for locating aquifers up to a depth of 200 man lengths (*purusha*), or about 1200 ft. below the land surface. A great achievement indeed!

VARĀHAMIHIRA'S GROUND WATER SCIENCE

Varahamihira, another important geo-hydrologist of the ancient times, not only specialized in the understanding of the relationships between floral and faunal species and sub-surface water, but also in the environmental factors which govern the nature and types of landscapes and the ecological linkages and inter-dependencies between floral and faunal species and communities. Varahamihira's work *Brihat Samhita* is a tightly written thesis consisting of *slokas* or verses. It is to his credit that he did not advocate water divining, but insisted on the use of observation and verification for exploring underground springs. The 54th chapter, 'Dakargalam', consisting of 125 stanzas or *slokas*, literally means 'key to, or winning the existence of water'. It is written in a spirit of scientific empiricism. It is, therefore, unfortunate that Western writers, who traced the development of hydro-science, remain silent about the contribution made to this science in ancient India. Writers who worked on this subject in the first half of the 20th century, e.g., Meinzer, Baker and Horton, Chau and many others, do not discuss Varahamihira or Chakrapnai or any of the scores of scholars who wrote extensively on this subject. Take for example the clear identification of the clouds and rain as the origin of all springs and sub-soil water through the mechanism of filtration. The western history of hydroscience recognizes Vitrvius (15 BC) for establishing the fact that all ground water is derived from rain, but is unaware of Varahamihira's work where 'pregnancy of clouds', the 'quantity of rainfall' and the 'signs of rainbows' are sections immediately preceding the section on 'ground water exploration'. Hopefully, this chapter will arouse interest among occidental scholars about the advances made in hydroscience in ancient India.

Varahamihira recognized three basic types of environments: (a) *Anupa*, characterized by rivers, ponds, marshes and mountains, where *hansa, saras* (cranes), *chakravaka* and such other water fowl are seen easily, and where *sasa* (rabbits), *varaha* (wild boar), *mahisa* (buffalo), *ruru, rohit* (flamingoes) and such other animals show a preference for their habitat. Such lands have dark coloured fields, gardens and orchards with trees like *sati kadali* and *iksu*; (b) The *Jangala* is clean like the sky, elevated, with less water, and consists of trees like *sami, karira, bilwa, arka, pilu*, etc. The deer (*harina*), *ena, prsata, gokarna, khara*, roam freely among sweet, fruit-bearing trees; c) The third type is *Sadharana* which is the interface between the first two and carries most of the characteristics of *Anupa* and *Jangala*.

Varahamihira studies over a hundred plant species for their association with animals, with each other and with the location of water. He was particularly interested in the association of plants and termite mounds, and described the sources of ground water located at a depth varying from 229 meters to 160 meters underground in arid and semi-arid regions. Of special interest to him were Phreatophytes. The roots of such plants extended to great depths and reached the water table. Consequently, they could grow well independent of the periodicity of rain, e.g., salt brush (*Atriplex canscens*), cashew (*Acacia gregii*), cottonwool (*Populas* sp.), willow, wild rye and greasewood.

In stanza 47, he describes the occurrence of ground water at a depth of 7' 6" in association with *virana* and *durva* grasses, while the thorny *sami* occurring naturally is associated with ground water at a depth of 170 m. He recognized the power of the tap root to penetrate soil and rock, however hard they may be, to reach the water table. He identified mutualism and commensalism among *neem, ficus, palmyra*, etc. He also pointed out that it is similar both in case of excess and deficit of water. With these observations, he combined his knowledge of animals – termite mounds, frogs, snails, tortoise, mongoose, lizards, scorpions and land leeches which go into long summer sleep.

Varahamihira recognized four locations for water reservoirs, viz., (a) atmospheric moisture (clouds) and (b) land-surface, water in lakes, ponds and rivers (c) moisture soil zone and (d) ground water, and that all these were inter-related. The temperature of sub-soil water is cool, but he also identified the occurrence of springs from the depths of the earth which could be warm, hot or boiling. For the surface reservoir, he recommended expanses of water from east to west since they are subject to less evaporation losses and the waters are not spoilt by the action of waves raised by the westerly winds. Varahamihira also suggests the plantation of shady trees on the banks of reservoirs to prevent soil erosion, evaporation losses, pollution and sedimentation. For the wells, tanks and reservoirs which were to be used for drinking purposes, he recommends a mixture of *anjanam, musta* tubers, *usira* powder of *rajakoshalaka, amlaka* and *kataka* nuts. With this treatment, water which may be brackish, turbid, pungent or of bad taste and odour would become clear, tasteful, good smelling and would be endowed with good qualities. All these plants are recognized for their medicinal values and found practically throughout the Indian peninsula. Six different coagulants are known, of which *alum* is recognized as the easiest to use for getting rid of suspended particles. In addition, various mineral, vegetable substances and seeds of *Strychnos polatorium* were to be used. The process involved techniques like boiling and filtration.

To summarise quickly, Varahamihira looked at water resource development in relation to (i) plant responses, (ii) animal responses and (iii) geophysical responses, etc. which could lead him to high relative humidity levels, and eventually the ground water reservoirs. He used nine different kinds of indicators for studying geo-hydrology.

One more critical experience from the ancient world is related to the existence of *deva-vanas* (sacred groves) located at the origin of every major river in the Indian sub-continent. The Ganga, Yamuna and Brahmaputra emanating from the Himalaya; the Narmada, emanating from the Satpura mountain ranges in Central India; and the Krishna-Godavari in Southern India have all got two peculiarities that deserve to be mentioned. At the origin of each river, there is a Shiva temple, a tank usually with the head of a cow carved in stone (*gomukh*) from which emanates the river, in some cases literally, and in others, idiomatically. And secondly, around each river origin there is a sacred grove of a small or large dimension. All this is a fact, and what follows is mainly Hindu folklore. And even though the story is a part of the Hindu mythology, without any material evidence, the symbolism reveals interesting ecological perceptions and interpretations of lands. From the times of Mohenjo-daro, the bull (nandi) and the cow have been the ancient state symbols. A part of the secular interpretation is that the bullocks and cows were the animals which enabled the social transition from the hunting-gathering stage to the stage of settled agriculture in many parts of the world, and most certainly in India. It is, therefore, no surprise that the pastoral communities as well as the settled agriculturists in India revered the possession of these useful creatures, which provided milk, fertilizers and at times, fuel in the form of dung cakes. The mythological symbolism notwithstanding, the linkages between the origins of rivers, the existence of sacred groves and for enabling the infiltration of water run-off certainly cannot escape our attention. And last but not the least of the ancient concepts, we have the tradition of *parikrama*. All pilgrimage centres in India are chiefly along the rivers culminating at the origins of the great rivers in India, Nepal and Tibet. The simple idea was that the best way to teach man the truths about nature and life was to make him walk up and down the river course.

The foregoing section makes it clear that dam and reservoir construction was not merely a response to needs but that it was developed as a science. Literary works referred to this systematized practice as *pāthas-śāstra* or the science of hydrology. Engineers specialized in the construction of irrigation works were known as *jalasutrada*. The location and selection of the site were given great importance. Besides Sanskrit and Pali languages, literature on irrigation and tank construction is abundant in Tamil language. In Tamilnadu, one finds Megaliths on rocky high grounds or hillocks, and the most notable feature is that they are almost always found in association with large irrigation tanks. Agricultural and urban communities, highly specialized in the manufacture of iron implements, were the Megalith builders. The authorship of the artificial tanks in Southern India can be ascribed to the Megalithic folk. Historically, it was the Singhalese king Karikaal who actually engineered the idea of raising embankments, cutting canals and digging tanks. All the subsequent dynasties followed suit and employed engineers, consulted relevant treatises and applied different techniques because they were anxious to accomplish their tasks without blemish. Karikaal was a South Indian king belonging to the Chola Dynasty. He ruled over Tanjavur, Tirucchirapalli and some parts of Putukotta during the 2nd century AD. His work is described in the *Shilappadhikaram*. He constructed tanks/ponds, dams and canals for supplying water for agriculture.

Thus, while the Mauryan rulers in Northern India were practising irrigation based on treatises written by Kautilya, Kashyapa, Chakrapani and Varahamihira, the southern kingdoms had simultaneously and independently developed the science resulting in the treatise by Vishwakarma entitled *Vastushastram* or the science of building and construction. The water diviners were called *kupadansakas* and carried out their profession, and also worked as inspectors of wells. An inscription of the Vijayanagar king Virapratapa Bukkaraya II (AD 1338) speaks about the accomplishments of the hydraulic engineer Singaya Batta who was the master of ten sciences (*Dasavidya Chakravarti*). The king also maintained *varigraha karana* or the department of water works.

JUDEO-CHRISTIAN IDEAS

Judeo-Christian ideas can be derived from the Old Testament, wherein the relationship of man with nature was as a conquest, with nature looked upon as being in the service of man. Take for example the *Psalm* (104:10-14) which reads as follows:

> He sendeth the springs into the valleys which run among the hills. They give drink to every beast in the field; the wild asses quench their thirst. By them shall the fowls of the heaven have their habitation, which sing among the branches. He watereth the hills from chambers .... He causeth the grass to grow for the cattle, and herbs for the service of man ... (The Old Testament)

The message here is clear. Water, birds, fowls, cattle, grass, branches of trees and herbs are all in the service of man.

This anthropocentric view-point has pervaded and later moulded the entire relationship between man and nature in the Judeo-Christian world view. A verbatim modern version of this Biblical *Psalm* is rendered by professor Otto Hittmaier in his keynote address to the International Commission on Larger Dams (ICOLD), at the Vienna Congress in 1991. He says "Man's first duty is to his species. We should obey the Biblical command to go forth and subdue the Earth." This basic approach to water harnessing, coming from a president of the ICOLD, and which is ostensibly rooted in positive science, is a typical example of the way in which religious positions are used for justifying human action. Realism, pragmatism, etc. are also used along with religious rationalization of human action. This is found in another famous proverb used tellingly by the Swedish expert in water harnessing, Ms Malin Falkenmark, who is known to have said: "You have to break an egg if you want to make an omelette." In modern development philosophy, this dictum is used not only to break an egg, but also to smash it, and better still, to blow up the whole kitchen, just to make an omelette.

TRADITION ON THE NILE AND IN MESOPOTAMIA

The egyptian Pharaohs of the Old Kingdom (c. 3200 to 2130 BC) had a passion for grand structures, which they believed would immortalise them. On the other hand, their subjects were ardent agriculturists who had settled along the narrow fertile valley and the lower deltaic reaches of the great Nile River. The annual flooding of the Nile had brought enormous quantities of silt and spread it evenly on the inundation plains, making them fertile and productive right through the millennia – a classic case of sustainable agriculture quite similar to the civilization that had emerged in the other flood plains of the Indus, the Ganga, the Euphrates and the Yangtze in Central and South Asia.

On the Nile, however, the Pharaohs saw a tremendous opportunity in the loamy soil which could be made into excellent bricks, and the rock structures which could provide the slabs for constructing tombs for the kings and queens. It is, therefore, no surprise that it is in this valley that we find the oldest large dam structure at Wadi EI Gavavi. History has recorded that this masonry structure, which was 15 meters in height, was constructed about 4900 years ago at Kosheish on the Nile to provide drinking water to the great North African city of Memphis.

It is interesting to note that any dam structure equal to or greater than 15 meters in height is considered to be a large dam as per the classification provided by the ICOLD. Unfortunately, the ICOLD has not emphasized the point that the concept of 'large' dams is highly relative in nature, and that even a 15-meter high dam like the one in the reaches of a river as great as the Nile should actually be considered 'small' for the situation. It is precisely to these circumstances that it served its purpose and survived for at least some length of time, in spite of being 'large'.

Of course, it is possible that some of the water from the structure at Kosheish was used for irrigating the vegetable gardens and orchards which supplied food to the city dwellers. What was remarkable about this was not the antiquity alone, but the fact that the dam was just high enough to stop the waters at the end of the annual flood, after the main silt load had passed over the spillways to spread over the mouth of the delta. One can safely assume that the height of this dam was kept down to 15 meters mainly because of the imperatives laid down by the silt-carrying nature of the river. This conjecture is based on the fact that during the same period, the Egyptians had been quite capable of building enormous structures like the pyramids and temples of monumental scale with the use of rock slabs. They had also mastered the concept of the arch and the vault which were reserved for construction and for the chambers and chapels inside the great tombs. It is quite obvious that such monumental architecture must have been based on despotic system of using slave labour. But it is also to the credit of such a civilization that the principle of long-term sustainability was at the root of the structural forms of the apparently useless pyramids and the extremely useful dam which supplied drinking water to the city of Memphis. They could have built the dam higher. But they did not because on the one hand they knew that a high dam would soon get silted up, and on the other, they did not need more water than that held by a 15-meter high dam. While they flouted extreme profligacy in constructing the pyramids on the near-inanimate desert sands, they also showed an equally heightened sense of prudence while constructing a dam across the great Nile which to them was alive and dynamic.

Not very far from Egypt, but in an equally ancient country, is the valley of the Oronted in Syria, where we can still witness the oldest dam in use. It is a rockfill structure of about 6 meters, built by the Assyrians about 3300 years ago. What could be a greater tribute to the concept of sustainability and permanence than this structure of supreme antiquity?

The Romans, on the other hand, were no great dam builders, in spite of being skilled civil engineers. They were more concerned about transporting and distributing through aqueducts the water which was collected comprehensively in hilly watersheds. In southern Spain, however, there are two Roman dams still in use: Prosperina and Cornalbo. The Prosperina is an earthen dam with a masonry-faced core wall of concrete. Engineers regard it as the forerunner of the modern earth dam. The Cornalbo also has a masonry wall consisting of cells filled with stones or clay. Structurally, it has a slope facing the reservoir.

It was only in AD 550 that the arch gravity-dam was built at Dar on the present Turkish-Syrian border by Byzantine engineers. The true pioneer among the arch dams was of course the Kebar in Iran in the 14th century. This 26 metre high dam spanned a narrow limestone gorge. The central portion was curved against the water flow and was supported by two abutments. Yet the Persians, Babylonians and Assyrians had been building reliable dams from 700 BC to 250 BC. In the south of Arabia an earthen dam had been built, which was 14 meters high and 600 meters in length. Marib, as it was called, was flanked by spillways, and had a system of irrigation canals which provided water to farmers for more than a thousand years.

Dam building in the ancient times was definitely not an unmitigated success. In the Nile Valley again there is evidence of masonry-faced earth dam (2700 BC) which failed shortly after completion, when, in the absence of a spillway, it was overtopped by a flood. Dadd-EI Kafara, built 30 km south of Cairo, the failure of this dam must have caused a flood of a great magnitude and intensity because of the addition of the impounded water shock-released to the downstream plains. The moral of the story is obvious: if one disregards and transgresses the ways of nature and the ecological imperatives, then such actions can only end in disaster.

THE BEAVER GENIUS

As we start travelling back into geological history, we come across the receding glaciers towards the end of the Ice Ages. At the snout of these receding masses of ice, rock and debris there gushed out the streams of melted snow which eventually turned into larger rivers. And along these rivers lived the beaver, an animal belonging to the sciuromorphic family of rodents evolved in North Asia, Europe and North America quite a long time ago during the Oligocene Age. Giant beavers lived during the Ice Age and their fossil remains have been found. They became aquatic in the later part of their evolutionary process.

Today, the beaver, along with other cousins – the weasels and badgers – are commonly found in Canada, Northern Europe, Northern Asia and occasionally in the highlands of Tibet, Ladakh in South Central Asia. These incredible creatures are known to construct dams across streams, thereby creating lakes and ponds which provide the beavers the security and food which they need for their survival.

The beaver dams can be as high as 5 meters and can run to more than 100 meters in length. The ponds provide protection to the amphibian beavers from predators on land. A full-grown beaver can weigh up to 30 kg and can have a length of one meter. These adorable rodents eat the bark of twigs and trees which they can easily gnaw down with their large incisor teeth. Their houses consist of tree poles and branches plastered together with moss and mud. The entrance to these beaver houses (dams) are often under water and, therefore, very safe from attacks. What is even more amazing than the dams themselves is the fact that they occasionally build canals up to 600 meters long, through which they float sections of food trees which float down until they get trapped in the beaver dam. The invention and construction of dams can thus be traced back to a period long before man walked on this earth, and certainly long before man thought of the characteristically insolent regime of intellectual property rights. The Indian communities in North America made good use of beaver dams, as food and water was plentiful, not to speak of the ready-made firewood and furs.

It is also conceivable that dam structures were conceived and erected by the cave man quite independently of the beaver. Those early humans who lived in tropical Africa, Australia and the monsoon regions must have realized that the streams dry up in summer and that even the springs turn to a trickle if it does not rain for long. And then, it must have been a matter of experimental observation after which he thought of throwing rocks across streams in order to create ponds on either side of the rock bund. He also could not have missed noticing that the fish, which he so loved to eat, had a preference for shallow pools created by the aerating action of the waterfalls.

These pools became additional 'water holes'. These rudimentary structures across streams were the precursors of the so-called Gabion dams made from boulders lashed together with steel wires or reeds and rattan. But, since such instances are not a part of recorded history, they can be called conjectures, however plausible and convincing they may appear to be. Whatever the truth, the fact remains that even ancient man did strive for securing sustainability and permanence as regards food and water.

EMPEROR YU OF CHINA

Quite independent of their evolution in the West Asia, dams were being conceived and constructed all over the Orient and at the tip of South Asia, in what is known today as Sri Lanka and in some parts of Southern India. In China, for example, a stone crib was built across the Guckow River in 240 BC. This structure was 30 m high, 30 m long and would easily have qualified to be designated as a large dam. But the historical importance of this early dam notwithstanding, it was really the efforts to control the floods of the Yellow River (Huang He) and the Yanhtza, that formed the governing plank of China's struggle for keeping the civilization going. Chinese emperors have tried to control the floods of the Huang He for thousands of years, without success. The Yellow River carries tremendous loads of silt which it scours from the Loess Plateau, which has a 750 meter thick layer of fine silty soil. The Huang He erodes this soil and, in the process, becomes the most heavily silted river in the world, carrying to the sea about 2 billion tonnes of soil each year. Since a dam would serve no purpose as it would get silted rapidly, the Chinese constructed dykes and levees which have stood precariously between the river and the population. Yet, the river changed its course 26 times during the last 3500 years, killing thousands, and sometimes even millions of people.

The Chinese dynasties throughout their history have risen and fallen solely on account of their failure to control floods. The experience in China has been totally humbling and the great rivers Yangtze and Huang He flow untamed. So overpowering is the force of the great Yellow River that the Chinese can only take solace by looking at a giant statue of the mythical emperor Yu, which stands on a cliff near Zhengzhau, 700 km south-west of Beijing in Northen China. Yu symbolises prosperity with one beneficent hand outstretched, and with the other, he carries the tool with which the Chinese people erected dykes and dug irrigation canals for eight thousand years – from the time they are said to have arrived on the flood plains. The dykes keep getting raised with sheer human labour, and simultaneously the river-bed also keeps rising as the silt is deposited within the restricted areas between the dykes and the embankments. When such embankments break, the resulting floods are even more disastrous than the natural floods.

In South and South-East Asia too, there was a considerable amount of dam building activity going on through the ages. The Buddhist kings of Angkor in Cambodia used large numbers of slave labourers to build canals and dams. The structures known as Barays were trying to control the Mekong River. The smaller rivers were dammed and the larger ones diverted through canals. The engineering skills in dam construction were greatly surpassed when they built the temple city of Angkor Wat in the eleventh and twelfth centuries.

THE EUROPEAN EXPERIENCE

After following this brief history of dam construction in the ancient period, a reader may wonder why this activity did not take place in the so-called 'advanced' regions of Europe. The ecological reason is that Europe has had ample and well-distributed rainfall throughout the year which obviated the need for constructing dams. And with a touch of irony, one may say that there appears to be no evidence of a 'civilization' in Europe in those early millennia which paralleled the ancient civilization in other parts of the world and which required regular irrigation facilities or urban water supply. From the beginning of the 17th century, North Europeans focussed on drainage of their large expanses of swamps, fens and marshes which they wished to tame and harness for civilized living. However, in the Middle Ages, small barrages are known to have been built to maintain water levels in the navigation canals.

It is evident that most of what the English, Dutch and the French learnt about dam construction had already been established as a long tradition in West Asia and North Africa, or in the scriptures and practices in India and Sri Lanka.

CONCLUSION

A careful analysis of epigraphs, treaties and some of the scriptures and mythological or historical references provide us with a set of ancient principles which must govern any sustainable and equitable development of water resources, not only in the developing countries, but also in the so-called developed world. They are:

1. The 'Sanctity of the Origins' of water sources, and therefore the protection of upper-catchments, then the middle regimes, the flood-plains and finally the estuarine and deltaic mouth of the river in that order.
2. The principle of 'Least-Interference', in the natural flows of water. This is derived from the respect and primacy of the natural order and the 'protection of the hydrological cycle'. Long term obstruction of water flows leads to ecological and hydrological hazards.
3. 'Suvarna Madhya' or the Golden Mean, for deciding and optimizing the scales of development structures. This optimal solution is to be derived within the social, technical and economic limits and competence, and also within the administrative and financial capacities.
4. The inseparability and inter-dependence between land, water and forests as elements of a holistic eco-system. This refers to 'Sacred Groves' (*Deo rais/Deo bans*) which are invariably found at the origins of all rivers in South and South-east Asia. These form an integral part of the cascade system of a series of village tanks interlinked with diversion and distribution systems.
5. The significance of the principle of protection of and compassion for all plants and animals who have an equal right to drinking water.
6. The principle of respecting the direct correlation between surface water and ground water reservoirs. This would achieve the judicious and conjunctive use of the water resources.
7. Holistic integration of all principles and functions via:

a) Sages and Philosophers	-	Conceptualization
b) Kings and Chieftains	-	Commissioning
c) Peasants/User	-	Execution, Participation, Distribution and Equitable Sharing of Benefits

This would achieve transparency, simplicity and simultaneous accountability between participants.

The basic thesis and conclusion of this paper is that 'the greater the degree of convergence between the features of the water resource development project and the seven principles indicated above, the greater is the degree of sustainability. Conversely the greater the degree of divergence between the project features and the seven principles, the greater would be the degree of unsustainability and socio- and economic disaster.'

SECTION II

TRADITIONAL WATER MANAGEMENT SYSTEMS IN CONTEMPORARY TIMES

10

DATA ON EXISTING TRADITIONAL WATER SYSTEMS IN HIMACHAL PRADESH

R.G. Arya

ABSTRACT

This paper summarises the existing status of coverage of rural habitations by drinking water. By March 1994 all the census villages were provided with drinking water facilities as one dependable source of potable water was available within a radius of 1.6 km. Details of survey on the status of drinking water supply in rural habitations are given here.

HISTORICAL BACKGROUND

Himachal Pradesh came into being on 15 April 1948 as a centrally administered territory by integration of 30 erstwhile princely states. At that time the state had four districts, viz., Chamba, Mahasu, Mandi and Sirmour. Its area then was 25,839 sq. km. In 1948, safe drinking water facilities were available only in 300 villages.

EXISTING STATUS OF COVERAGE OF RURAL HABITATIONS BY DRINKING WATER

Coverage unit has been changed from village to habitation since 1st April 1993. All the census villages were provided with drinking water facilities by March 1994 on the criterion that at least one dependable source of potable drinking water was available within a radius of 1.6 km. A survey on the status of drinking water supply in rural habitations was carried out by the Irrigation and Public Health Department in 1991 under the guidelines of Rajiv Gandhi National Drinking Water Mission and later on it was re-validated by an independent agency, i.e., Regional Engineering College, Hamirpur. As per the figures finally included in the report issued by the Mission, there are 6,402 (14.62 per cent) NC (Not Covered), 12,878 (29.41 per cent) PC (Partially Covered), 24,502 (55.96 per cent) FC (Fully Covered) aggregating to 43,781 rural habitations in the state. The district-wise break up is tabulated in the following page (See Tables 1, 1.2, 1.3):

TABLE 1

Sr. No.	Name of Dist.	NC	PC	FC	Total
1.	Bilaspur	31	1025	1269	2325
2.	Chamba	1181	605	5976	7762
3.	Hamirpur	1	902	1036	1939
4.	Kangra	262	2759	2698	5719
5.	Kinnaur	105	20	199	324
6.	Kullu	819	122	2329	3270
7.	Lahaul Spiti	20	1	325	346
8.	Mandi	837	1632	4889	7358
9.	Shimla	2081	3482	1275	6838
10.	Sirmour	1558	351	1631	3540
11.	Solan	543	425	2298	3286
12.	Una	19	320	755	1094
	Total:	**7157**	**11644**	**24980**	**43781**

TABLE 1.2

During 1994-95, 1995-96, drinking water facilities were provided as under:

Year	NC	PC	Total
94-96	538	262	800
95-96	778	147	925
96-97	1156	194	1172
Total:	**2472**	**603**	**3075**

TABLE 1.3

The district-wise source details in habitations

Sr. No.	Name of District	Ground Water	Surface Water	Rain Water	Traditional Water	Other Sources	Total
1.	Bilaspur	827	786	0	461	0	2074
2.	Chamba	1717	2433	3	2598	836	7587
3.	Hamirpur	1057	485	0	231	1	1774
4.	Kangra	1602	1317	11	1369	466	4765
5.	Kinnaur	76	217	0	24	2	319
6.	Kullu	0	3392	0	0	0	3392
7.	Lahul Spiti	1	290	0	57	0	348
8.	Mandi	833	3924	0	1483	840	7080
9.	Shimla	233	3917	5	2518	9	6682
10.	Sirmour	644	2249	0	535	9	3457
11.	Solan	344	1090	0	1215	316	2965
12.	Una	832	123	1	21	116	1093
Total:		**8126**	**20223**	**20**	**10512**	**2595**	**41536**

Source : Survey data of status of drinking water in rural habitations 1991-93.

In the survey, sources were classified as under:

(i). Ground Water : Open well, tube well (deep/shallow), infiltration gallery, well.
(ii). Surface Water : Pond, river, stream, lake, canal, spring.
(iii). Traditional Water : Local methods practised for collecting surface/rainwater/ground water for drinking purpose. These include ponds, *baoris*, open wells, springs, ditches and *khaties*.
d. Others : Non-conventional methods of collecting drinking water as practised by tribals and local residents.

TECHNOLOGY MISSION ON DRINKING WATER AND RELATED WATER MANAGEMENT

A mission was approved in district Kangra under Technology Mission (now renamed as Rajiv Gandhi National Drinking Water Mission) for which a sanction for Rs. 615.72 lakhs was accorded for providing drinking water facilities to 238 villages. All the villages, except one which was submerged in Pong dam reservoir, were covered at the expenditure of Rs. 703.01 lakhs.

URBAN WATER SUPPLY AND SEWERAGE

The urban water supply systems in most of the towns are quite old and have outlived their purpose. The sources of the schemes need augmentation while the distribution system in almost all the schemes needs replacement and rehabilitation. Though it had been assigned a second priority in the past, now the priority has been assigned to state/district headquarters besides the towns of tourist interest. Till March 1997, an expenditure of Rs. 92.81 crores has been incurred for augmentation of sources of schemes of 10 towns, and work on replacing and rehabilitation of 3 towns is still in progress. During the 9th Five Year Plan period, this sector needs larger outlays.

ACCELERATED URBAN WATER SUPPLY PROGRAMME (AUWSP)

For the towns having a population up to 20,000, the ministry of Urban Development has sponsored a new programme. The OPH department has accordingly planned schemes since 1995-96 which are to be sanctioned and funded by GOI. Four schemes have been sanctioned under this programme out of which one scheme has been completed and the execution of the rest is in progress.

CAPITAL FUNDS

Funds are also available for water supply and sewerage schemes for the capital town of Shimla. Sewerage schemes have a direct impact on the pollution of water as also on the environment. Eighty per cent of the water from sewerage schemes generally returns as sewage whose adequate treatment is a necessity. As most of the towns in the state attract tourists and serve as health-resorts, environmental improvement assumes much significance.

STATE OF IRRIGATION POTENTIAL

The geographical area of the state is 55.67 lakh hectares out of which the net cultivated area is 5.83 lakh hectares. It has been assessed by the *tehsil*-wise master plans that assured irrigation can be provided by major and medium schemes to 0.5 lakh hectares and by minor schemes to 2.85 lakh hectares, thus aggregating to 3.35 lakh hectares.

The material and financial achievements of CCA from 1951 to March 1996 are as follows:

(i) By the schemes provided by the Agriculture
and Rural Development departments & private *kuhls* is 92, 796 hects.

(ii) By the schemes designed by the State
Irrigation and Public Health Department in March 1996 is 90, 862 hects.

Thus, the total sums up to 1, 83, 658 hects.

As per the statistics maintained by the Directorate of Land Records (Revenue Department) of the net sown area, about 16 per cent area is being served by the *kuhls*. According to 1991 census of minor irrigation, the irrigated area is about 17 per cent although much area has been added in CCA over the past decades. There are, thus, variations in the statistics on the aspect of utilization of irrigation potential created. To sort out the variations, the IPH department has approached the Director of Census of Minor Irrigation to undertake scheme-wise field survey on the utilization aspects.

MEDIUM IRRIGATION PROJECTS

The details of expenditure incurred and physical achievements of completed/ongoing schemes are given is Table 2.

TABLE 2

Sr. No.	Name of Project	Expenditure (in lakhs)	Physical Achievement (in hects.)	Remarks
1.	Giri Irrigation	823	5263	Completed
2.	Bhabour Sahib Ph-I	115	923	—do—
3.	Balh Valley	1065	2410	—do—
4.	Bhabour Sahib-II	1142	2490	Ongoing revised Target of Commissioning 12/97
	Total:	**3145**	**11086**	

Besides, CWC has checked the project report of FIS Sidhata in Kangra district for Rs. 33.62 crores to provide assured irrigation to the CCA of 3150 hectres.

MAJOR IRRIGATION PROJECT

The report of the first major irrigation project of Shahnaahar in Kangra district has been approved by CWC for Rs. 143.32 crores to provide assured irrigation to the CCA of 15,287 ha. The share of Himachal Pradesh is Rs. 54.83 crores and of Punjab Rs. 88.49 crores. The project is yet to be started by the department.

HILL AREA LAND AND WATER DEVELOPMENT PROJECT (1982-92)

During the last decade the USAID assisted Hill Area Land and Water Development Project (HALWPD) took important measures to develop and support the design and construction of small irrigation schemes, with particular emphasis on development at Chak (outlet) level. It developed co-operation between the state agencies on one hand, and between the government departments and the farmers on the other hand in order to provide integrated development.

In its implementation, state IPH and Agriculture and Rural Development departments were mainly involved. In all 878 irrigation schemes consisting of irrigation tanks, flow and lift irrigation and tube-wells were constructed or rehabilitated in 10 districts (Table 3).

TABLE 3

Number of Schemes Completed

Sr. No.	Department	FIS	LIS	T/W	Hydrauns	Total
1.	Agriculture	240	21	21	5	287
2.	Irrigation & Public Health	219	138	81	—	438
	(i) New					
	(ii) Rehabilitation	153	—	—	—	153

ISPAN consultants reviewed the experience of farmers' organizations about irrigated agriculture which was created under the above project from 1984 to 1992. The study would benefit the department or government in furthering the involvement of farmers in irrigated agriculture.

IRRIGATED SCHEMES WITH NABARD ASSISTANCE

Keeping in view the financial crunch, to expedite completion of ongoing irrigation schemes, financial assistance in the form of loan was taken from NABARD for 61 minor and one medium irrigation schemes. Forty-nine schemes were completed by March 1997 and the remaining are to be completed during 1997-98.

The programme was further extended during 1997-98 by inclusion of 52 more schemes under minor irrigation. Under Rural Infrastructure Development Fund (RIDF), 19 schemes have also been approved.

Details of Minor Irrigation Schemes completed by IPHD up to March 1996 are (See Table 4):

TABLE 4

Minor Irrigation Schemes Completed

Sr. No.	District	L.I.S	F.I.S	T/Wells	Total
1.	Bilaspur	39	26	—	65
2.	Chamba	14	130	—	144
3.	Hamirpur	42	9	—	51
4.	Kangra	84	42	66	192
5.	Kinnaur	—	39	—	39
6.	Kullu	13	37	—	50
7.	Lahaul Spiti	5	40	—	45
8.	Mandi	38	163	12	213
9.	Shimla	18	158	—	176
10.	Sirmour	41	76	13	130
11.	Solan	53	40	38	131
12.	Una	38	3	185	226
	Total	**385**	**763**	**314**	**1462**

TRADITIONAL WATER SYSTEMS

A peep into the traditional water systems of Himachal Pradesh is of historical as well as practical interest. While the study would provide an insight into the development of existing systems, it would also provide an approach to utilize their vast inbuilt potential through modernization to meet the drinking water needs and to provide irrigation facilities. The status of the systems in these categories is as follows:

DRINKING WATER SUPPLY SCHEMES

As per the details given in the Table 1.3, which is based on the survey carried out in the state during 1991-93, there are 10,512 traditional sources. By and large, the traditional water sources have been retained by both urban and rural people, and are used in the event of failure of the existing systems as a supplementary source of water. These sources are not defined but are quite relevant as most of the schemes, both in rural and urban areas, are intermittent. It is also true that there are imbalances in the distribution due to networks, which in the case of urban scheme are pretty old and have outlived, while in the case of rural schemes, include many scarcities. These systems have now assumed a secondary role and are in a state of neglect so far as hygiene and repairs are concerned. As usual, there is no or little patronage from the government departments/agencies, and also there is general apathy of the communities towards these sources. In the new (or existing) schemes, contribution of these traditional or spot sources in terms of supply is ignored. These sources are extra or redundant and are sometimes abandoned depending upon their utility which in turn depends on the efficacy of their supply. Ever increasing need of water makes them still relevant. There is, however, a big snag in it being integrated into the main systems. The emphasis of the modern water supply schemes is on the adequacy of the available water in a single source which can afford proper analysis and control on the qualitative aspects by providing the necessary treatment. In the case of the multiple sources, the control on the treatment would be lost and the municipality or the government/agency cannot guarantee on the safety. Main objections of the authorities may be valid to a large extent but the fact remains that people still make use of the traditional sources. Sometimes water from the springs and *baories*, even though impure, is considered better for drinking purposes compared to the water obtained from the municipal water taps which, in the process of its transmission and distribution, gets polluted, particularly in the intermittent supplies when the pollutants are sucked in by the distributory lines from leaking joints due to the vacuum created by the stoppage of supplies. It is true that the government agencies/municipalities cannot take on the responsibility of allowing the use of untreated water from the spot/traditional sources because of their large number. Some amount of rethinking would, however, be necessary considering the present state of use of water from these sources. A better approach could be to leave this burden on the communities after imparting the necessary know-how to them through educational institutions, research centres and government agencies who develop quick but effective methods of treatment of water. Technologies are available but they need to be further broad based.

Besides the general aspects, the traditional sources can be broadly classified as under although factually they are location-specific:

(i) Low Hills: The spot/traditional sources in the valleys are open-wells, infiltration galleries/wells in the rivers beds, tube-wells, both deep and shallow, and hand-pumps. Among the surface sources, springs and *baories* enjoy priority followed by flowing streams, *kuhls*, rivulets and rivers. The ponds and lakes are not given much importance because water gets polluted in them due to stagnation.

(ii) Mid Hills: There is greater emphasis on infiltration galleries/wells in river beds, shallow or deep tube-wells and hand pumps. Least priority is given to water from ponds/lakes and reservoirs.

(iii) High Hills: Emphasis is on springs, snow-fed streams, rivulets, rivers and also on infiltration galleries/wells in the river beds.

(iv) Alpine Zone: The mainstay is spring/perennial snow-fed streams/rivers which are used with suitable precautions to avoid freezing of the sources.

As per the survey details (Table 1.3), there are 2,595 non-conventional sources. Large number of sources are in Mandi (840) and Chamba (836) districts followed by Kangra (466) and Solan (316), where the tribal and nomad population is higher. These people have adopted non-conventional means like ditches for obtaining drinking water.

STEP-WELL

To fetch underground water, there are wells provided with steps. These step-wells are about 45 meters deep on an average. As per the survey carried out by the department in October 1992, the number of such step-wells are:

Sr. No.	Name of District	Number of step-wells
1.	Hamirpur	1485
2.	Kangra	1107
3.	Mandi	52
4.	Una	456
	Total	**3100 nos.**

These steps-wells are not in much use. It was proposed to convert these steps-wells into sanitary wells by providing RCC (Re-inforced Cement Concrete) slab pavement, hand pump mark III and a cattle trough at the cost of Rs. 47,000/- per well aggregating to Rs. 16.79 crores. The proposal was sent to the advisor TM, RGDWM in March 1993 and its sanction is under consideration.

IRRIGATION SCHEMES AND LAND CLASSIFICATION

The first settlement of land was done in Kangra district in 1850s, and the land was classified into various categories depending on quality and other attributes. The land records of most of the districts of Himachal Pradesh were brought out after a survey and land settlement work was carried out from the beginning of this century. In old areas of the state, the first such settlement of the princely states of Mandi and Suket was carried out in 1911-16. The second settlement of combined Mandi district was carried out in 1958-70, which is still operative. The other districts were also covered during this period.

A unique practice was followed earlier in the administration of the irrigation whereby the extents of private rights were defined on recognized resource in the districts of the state. This was known as 'Riwaz-i-Abpashi' or 'custom in irrigation' which is an important record of rights included in the claims of individuals and communities of a village during the process of land settlement. It was prepared for each village. Not all 'Riwaz-i-Abpashi' contained the same extent of information. The 'Riwaz-i-Abpashi' as a record of rights on a water source, be it an irrigation system or a natural stream or any other source of a village or an individual, is unique to Himachal Pradesh. These rights were systematically recorded in most of the districts of the Himachal Pradesh at the time of preparation of land settlement in the first quarter of this century except for district Kangra where first such exercise was carried out much earlier. In some districts, a second land settlement was also carried out updating the records.

It generally records any or all of the following:

- History of *Kuhl*, also names of beneficiary villages or individuals;
- Description of the method of diversion, reconstruction of the diversion structure in case it is washed away, and operation and maintenance of the *kuhl*; it also mentions penalties to be levied for non-participation in maintenance chores;
- Water distribution on rotation modalities;
- Attestation by beneficiaries of correctness of the record. This is done to verify the correctness of the contents of the record of rights and is signed by all prominent persons of the command area of the system.

Some of the classical examples where 'Riwaz-i-Abpashi' was applicable are Kripal Chand Kuhl, Dai-di-Kuhl, Diwan Chand Kuhl, Fateh Chand Kuhl and Kusmal Kuhl, all located in Kangra district.

NEW DEVELOPMENT ON WATER RIGHTS

The irrigation activity has undergone change after the enactment of Minor Canal Act, 1976. Now, the land records prepared for all holdings under Land Revenue Act serve as record of irrigation rights also and provide,

> a statement of customs, reflecting rights and liabilities in the state. This statement of customs is presumed to provide a record of customary rights of the water for irrigation or for the working of mills.

The above water rights would undergo further change after the amended Himachal Pradesh Irrigation Act comes into force for which a bill is under consideration.

NEW PROJECTS UNDER BILATERAL ASSISTANCE

There is a proposal to start the under noted projects for the year 1997-98:

TABLE 5

No.	Name	Agency	Objectives	Project Cost	Remarks
1.	Irrigation line of credit	Federal Republic of Germany	Creation of CCA & Chak developments in 10,000 hectares; rehabilitation in 3000 hectares	Rs. 140 crores	Study by consultant complete draft agreement awaited
2.	Drinking water supply to rural habitations in H.P.	—do—	To provide duly water in the rural habitants.	Rs. 203 crores	—do—
3.	Sewerage project for Shimla town	OPEC assistance	To improve the sewerage system.	Rs. 66 crores	—do—

Besides, the Himachal Pradesh Ground water Project amounting to Rs. 150 crores for providing 500 tube-wells that would provide irrigation facilities to 15,000 hectares is on the shelves of Department of Economic Affairs awaiting a suitable donor.

The following new concepts are proposed to be introduced by the IPH Department:

(i) Water Users Associations
Based on the studies of Action Research Project for involving the water users in the operation and maintenance of water supply schemes.

(ii) Participatory Irrigation Management (PIM)
A trial has already begun through Krishak Vikas Sangh (KVS) under USAID assisted HAWLPD. The concept could be extended not only to new irrigation projects but also the old schemes. The responsibilities of O & M shall be shared by the beneficiaries besides participation in other vital spheres to boost the agriculture produce.

Editors' Note

Many of the schemes outlined above have already been implemented and the progress reports with regard to these are awaited.

11

RE-CHARGING OF SPRINGS: A REVIVAL OF TRADITION

A.P. Joshi and Rumita Gupta

ABSTRACT

This article discusses the scarcity of water being faced by the villages of Himalayan zone, particularly Uttar Pradesh hills, which is the abode of many mighty rivers like the Ganga and the Yamuna. The water schemes of the Government, having a few limitations, have failed to fulfil the drinking water requirements of these villages. The revival and re-charging of traditional sources of water like the natural springs and nullahs, which are drying up due to de-forestation, earth movements, etc. is proposed as a solution to this problem. Rainwater may be preserved and used for re-charging these springs. This traditional technique is not only simple but also has several advantages over the governmental schemes.

INTRODUCTION

India has large water reserves – large enough to sustain its expected climax population of 1,700-1,800 million in the next century, provided we use and manage the water resources wisely and intelligently. The source of all these waters are the rivers flowing down the mountains, particularly the snow-fed rivers of the Himalayas. The mighty Himalayas, the 'water bank' of the Indian sub-continent, are endowed with several rivers like the Ganga, the Yamuna and their tributaries. Unfortunately, the Himalayas have always suffered the 'myopia' of our water technocracy, and in spite of being a part of and having contributed greatly to the mainstream of India's development, the people of this region have always been devoid of de-centralized planning, and of appropriate and modern technologies to harness this vast natural resource. The mighty rivers, the Ganga and the Yamuna, flow through the Himalayan lands without being of much use to the residents of the land. Garhwal/Uttarakhand has no suitable water policy. In fact, there is no easily available drinking water for its residents.

About 8,800 villages of Uttarakhand are suffering from the scarcity of drinking water. The mighty Ganga supplies about 46,870 crore cu. m. of water (about 25.2 per cent of the total water supply of India) to the plains every year while a mere 10-12 per cent of Garhwal lands manage to receive water from the same river.

About 42 per cent of the Indian population, residing in the states of Haryana, Uttar Pradesh, Bihar, West Bengal, Rajasthan, Madhya Pradesh, Himachal Pradesh and Delhi thrive on the waters of Ganga. Drinking water, irrigation, energy supply, industries and all other water-related needs of these states are fulfilled by these rivers of Uttarakhand. In fact, about 21,200 crore cu. m. of Ganga water goes to feed or charge the tube-wells in the plains.

Despite the fact that mountains are a constant source of water, the mountain dwellers do not have even sufficient drinking water. In case of Uttar Pradesh hills, hardly 12.7 per cent land is irrigated. Out of 17,000 villages scattered in 9 districts, 7 districts (13,000 villages) have been categorized as drought prone. Is it not ridiculous that the Uttar Pradesh hills which cater to country's water needs through great rivers – the Ganga and the Yamuna – is itself devoid of water? Most of the villages are located near natural springs which are now drying up due to de-forestation and earth movements.

APPROACH OF THE GOVERNMENT

The drinking water requirements of these villages are being met through the supply of water in pipelines. Certain limitations of this system like conflict among villages, poor repair and maintenance, disconnection of water pipes by the villagers, drying of springs which may result in the collapse of the whole system, etc. have led to the failure of water schemes in Uttar Pradesh hills. The Govt. has failed to provide a full-fledged scheme of drinking water for the residents of Himalaya.

PROPOSED APPROACH

The only option in such circumstances is to revive the traditional approach. Prior to the introduction of modern techniques of water supply, the villagers depended on natural springs and nullahs. These two sources served the immediate water necessity of the villages. Geologically, these outlets of water have been through internal seepage of water from upper catchment. At many places, the earth crust has created such fissures through movement. The rainwater/snow through particular catchment seeps down and springs down at the outlet. Where this seepage is higher, it is called spring, and where it is slow and low, it is called nullah. The villagers created tanks in nullahs for timely collection of water. In order to provide water to the villagers without much labour and material investing strategy, a multi-dimensional approach with traditional in-built system will have to be revived. This is quite possible through re-charging the nullah and the spring.

THE STRATEGY

The three major reasons for the loss of rainwater are:

(i) De-forestation in the catchment area has resulted in loss of rainwater which is usually conserved for re-charging springs.

(ii) As earth movement is a continuous process, the springs change their routes.

(iii) Disturbance of natural springs while laying pipelines for water supply has also caused change in water routes.

The last two processes are now out of human control. No doubt, afforestation can re-charge the springs, but it involves a series of intricacies, and is a time consuming process by itself. The spring can be immediately re-charged through creation of rain harvesting ponds at the catchment of spring.

POND

Himalayan geology and topography permits the application of this approach. The catchment areas of these springs are well defined, and can be identified by simple techniques. In fact, the rocks of Himalaya are sedimentary and bestowed with fine clay which can control the water seepage. The catchment area of a spring can be re-charged by way of constructing a pond with sub-ponds scattered around. This would immediately charge the springs. Two rains in a year will be sufficient to keep the spring charged throughout the year.

ORIGIN OF SPRINGS AND CONTROL OF FLOW

Ground fissures/ground cracks are tectonic lineaments developed due to tectonic disturbances in the geological and historical times. These fractures/lineaments can be oriented in any direction. Whenever these transversal lineaments are intersected by dipping planes on ground surface, rain filtered water emerges at that point and forms the natural water source named as spring. Some of the springs are perennial while some provide water only during rainy seasons. The discharge of the spring depends mainly on acquifer characteristics. To re-charge these desiccating springs, acquifer has to be re-charged. Acquifer geometry plays an important role in defining storage capacity.

Satellite imageries (LISS-II/III data) are the best measures to identify the acquifer zones. The other option is horizontal or near-horizontal drilling. If the characteristics of acquifer zone are properly understood, then the springs can be re-charged by storing rainwater or by controlling the surface run-off.

RAINWATER HARVESTING TO RE-CHARGE THE SPRING

For rainwater preservation, *khals*, a periglacial feature, have been initially identified. These structures are found where two ridges meet and have a natural depression. In such depressions, clay band is present below the soil cover which works as an impermeable layer. Porosity is quite less due to fine grained sediments. The seepage of water from these layers is very less. Such structures have been identified in Kot and Pauri blocks; in Kot block, they include Dhaungli Khal, Pawari Khal, and Kafilgadhera Khal. The water preserved can be utilized for drinking purpose after proper treatment.

CONCLUSION

The concept of re-charging springs through rainwater is not new but simply a revival of the traditional knowledge. The approach entails identification of the catchment area of spring, creation of ponds and development of a regulatory mechanism. The pond must be supplemented with sub-ponds around the catchment to sustain water supply. At later stages grass and quickly growing tree cover can help in strengthening and storage of water in the ponds. This device does not require any external support as it is a traditionally-proven methodology. This approach will have the following merits:

i) Simple technique,
ii) Defined rights, community ownership,
iii) Less maintenance,
iv) Clean water, and
v) Efficient water conservation.

To conclude, with the government failing in its efforts to supply drinking water to these villages, the revival of traditional techniques of water management emerges as a hopeful solution.

12

ON THE NEED TO CONSERVE THE TRADITIONAL URBAN WATER SUPPLY SYSTEM IN PUNE

Shubhada Kamlapurkar

ABSTRACT

The *sine qua non* of a city, in one way or the other, is water supply whether for sanitation, sustenance or industrial use. However, in India, water not only has an utilitarian value, but its aesthetic value has been, in many places, combined with its symbolic nature, representing power and prestige in the society. This fusion of the metaphysical with the physical is best represented in Pune and is reflected in the layout of the traditional water supply systems and its urban form which evolved under the Peshwas. In Pune, the socio-economic and socio-political pattern was not only displayed through architecture, but the whole urban spatial structure can be discerned through the layout of services, especially the traditional urban water supply system and the remaining physical infrastructure that affected it. But the profuse building activity, which is always irrevocably linked with prosperity on the economic front in the urban centres, drastically affects and alters the urban spatial structure. Today, development is posing a threat to the built and natural heritages. One needs to understand that conservation and planning are inseparable, and that the essence of conservation lies in providing a healthier and safer environment more responsive to cultural interest, having a greater respect for the past and flexible enough to accept conducive changes and development in the future.

INTRODUCTION

The indigenous qualities of urban community spaces, the outcome of traditional urban water supply (system), an efficient and ingenious creation, its capacity to stand the ravages of time and yet survive and stay beneficial over a period of 250 years, makes one look back and unravel its mysteries. Since such elements also contribute to the historic character of the city and give it a distinctive identity, they need to be conserved.

Under the rule of the Peshwas, Pune evolved as a civic entity, culturally developed and administratively efficient. It was the capital city of Maratha empire, a symbol of authority and power and the seat of dominant religious ideology. It was basically a

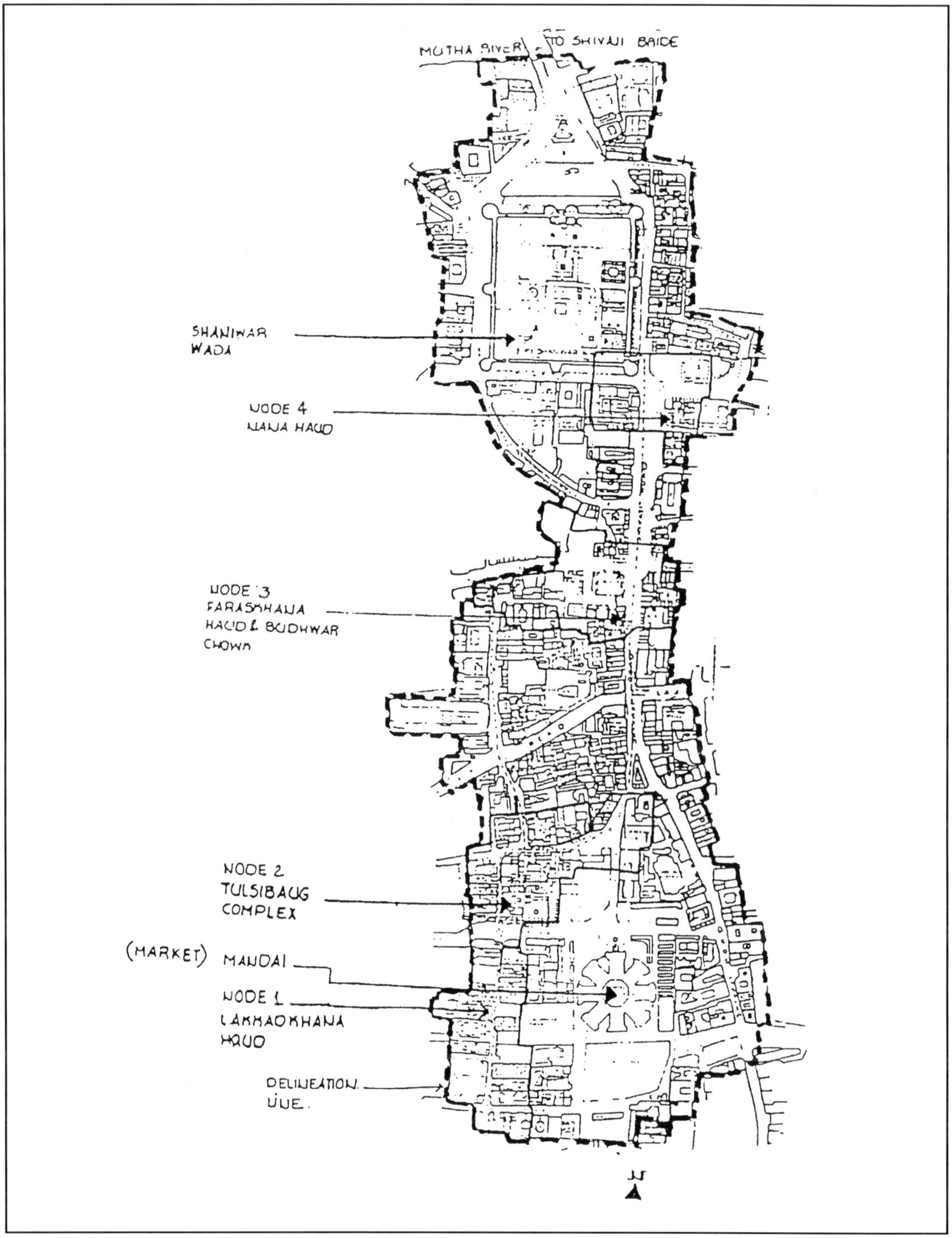

Fig. 12.1 Study area-Note: WADA-Nobleman's mansion; Haud-Water Cistern/Tank.

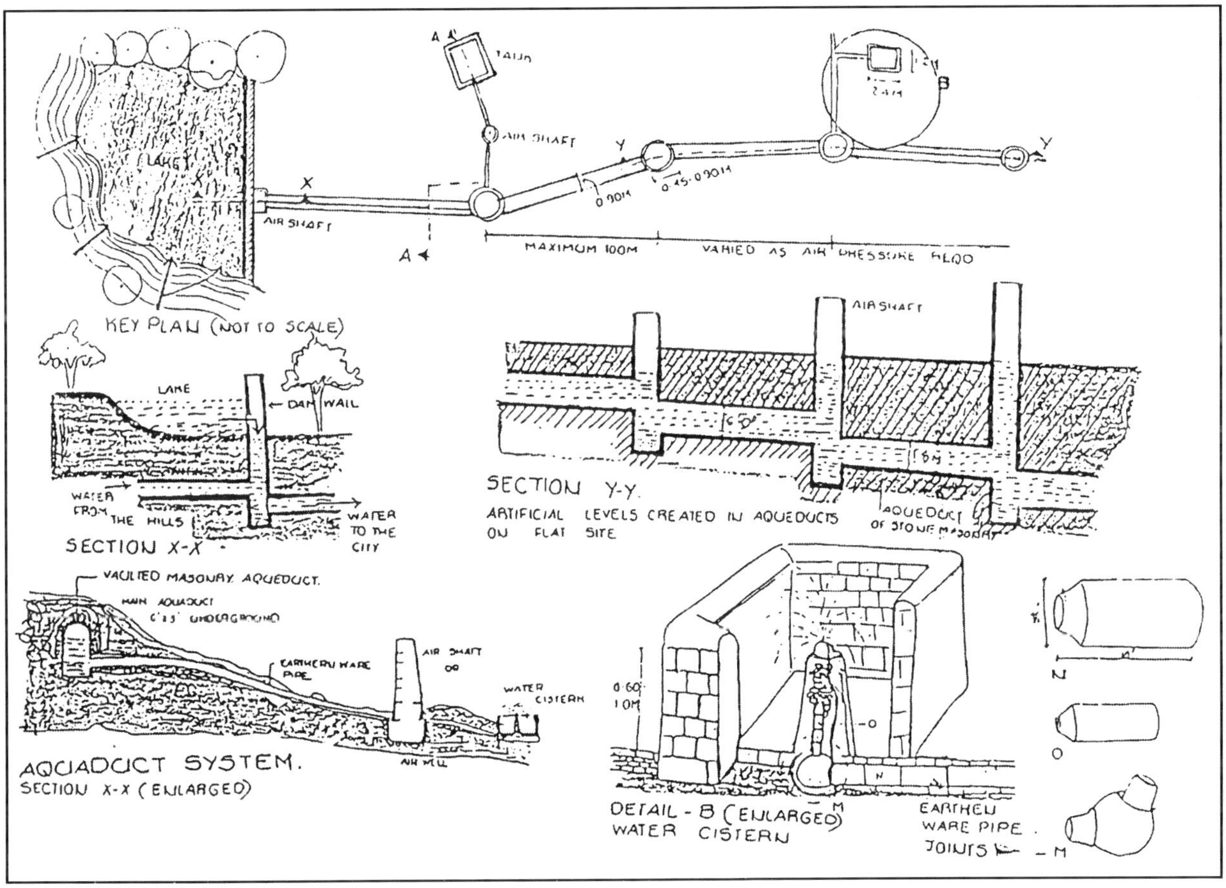

Fig. 12.2 Technicalities of the system (ref. – The Cultural Archaeology of Ahmednagar).

government centre ruled by the Peshwas who combined political authority with socio-cultural and religious dominance. The 18th century is considered to be the golden age of the Maratha empire, when a major socio-cultural, political and physical development of the city took place under the Peshwas. Pune was one of the two types of cities that began to emerge in the 18th century. This city rose to answer the needs of the emerging regional power, the structure of the city being shaped by military, socio-political and cultural needs of the rulers. Shaniwar Wada ('wada' refers to a settlement), the rulers' encampment-cum-palace (Fig. 12.1), became the focal point and the town grew rapidly in the form of 'peths' (1700-1780), characterized by different communities, namely brahmins, traders, gosavis and artisans.

The rivers and wells were the natural sources of water. Certain factors like paucity of water for the growing 'peths', the unreliable nature of the river Mula-Mutha, brackish water of wells, etc. led to a search for better alternatives for water. The Peshwas were aware of the traditional urban water supply system at Ahmednagar and its lavish use in the form of fountains, *hamams* (bathrooms), and water cisterns by the Nizamashahis (1490-1600) (Fig. 12.2). For providing continuous water supply on similar lines to the fountains, hauds, baths and wells of 'Shaniwar Wada', the Katraj aqueduct system was laid. Private connections were permitted to Sardars, who in turn built community tanks as a token of their generosity and charity. Aqueducts were constructed under Sardars like

Phadnavis, Chaudhari and Raste to provide water to their 'wadas' as well as to community tanks which lay enroute. The construction of temples later on near the tanks and planting of flowering trees like 'Parijat' made the area a community space which was an essential part of cultural ritual activities in Pune. The aqueduct system and other similar utilities, civic and monumental buildings as well as the vernacular architecture have given Pune a distinct character. Being the second largest city in Maharashtra, Pune today projects a different picture. Along with its long standing image of a socio-cultural centre, Pune was identified as an educational centre, 'Vidyeche Maherghar'. It is fast acquiring a new image, that of an industrial city. In this process, the inner parts of city are becoming a more favourable place for migrant population thus increasing the pressure on land, built heritage, open space structures, environment and infrastructure. This is affecting the quality of environment and life in the inner parts of the city.

PRESENT CONDITION OF TRADITIONAL URBAN WATER SUPPLY SYSTEM AND THE URBAN SPATIAL STRUCTURE.

Due to the lack of awareness with regard to natural and man-made heritage, the traditional water supply system is in a derelict state. The Katraj reservoir, which supplies water to the aqueduct, is under-utilized due to its overflow in the form of Ambil (Odha) stream. Its importance is reduced to an alternative source of water in case of emergency (the most recent being when the canal burst in June 1993).

The other component of the traditional urban water supply system, the tanks and urban spaces, though few in number, are also getting degraded. The inner city is becoming predominantly commercial, destroying community urban spaces by converting them into parking lots and garbage dumps. The urban spatial structure based on spatial and social pattern is not easily readable due to incongruent developments on building activity like change in land-use and road widening schemes which alter it drastically in terms of hierarchy of spaces, their scale and character.

OBJECTIVES

(i) To understand and examine the indigenous qualities of the traditional urban water supply system of Pune and to study its impact on the formation of the urban structure.

(ii) To understand the role of urban spatial structure in relation to the water supply system in order to analyse the urban spaces and assess the quality of environment through a detailed case study.

(iii) At the study area level, to identify factors contributing to the strong image of urban spatial structure and critically evaluate the effects of planning, legislation and development.

(iv) To give solutions stressing on the conservation of urban spatial structure related to water supply systems and making the water supply and the water, a positive element in it. To suggest mandatory precautions to be taken by planners and private developers while intervening with old structures, re-building activities or any development on or near the traditional urban water supply system.

13

TRADITIONAL WATER MANAGEMENT SYSTEMS IN BUNDELKHAND

Sunanda Kirtane and Krishna Gandhi

ABSTRACT

Bundelkhand region consisting of seven districts of Uttar Pradesh and six districts of Madhya Pradesh and identified as one of the dry zones of India, faces severe water problems. Low ground water resource against the hard rocks like gneiss and granite and less rainfall has made it a drought prone area. A survey undertaken at the two development blocks – Niwari of Tikamgarh (Madhya Pradesh) and Bangra of Jhansi (Uttar Pradesh) – look into traditional water harvesting structures constructed by the Chandelas, the Bundel rulers, the Marathas and the Britishers. Budelkhand being a hilly, rocky region with a steep land gradient, rainwater flows away quickly and very little is absorbed. Keeping this fact in mind, various structures such a Pukhariyan, *talab* (tanks), *bandhies, baories* and wells were constructed and maintained by the people. These water bodies not only provide water but are also sites for temples and *melas* thus assuming a cultural significance as well.

INTRODUCTION

Bundelkhand consists of seven districts of Uttar Pradesh, viz., Lalitpur, Jhansi, Jalaun, Hamirpur, Mahoba, Banda and Shahuji Maharaj Nagar, and six districts of Madhya Pradesh, viz., Datiya, Tikamgarh, Chhatarpur, Panna, Sagar and Damoh. This region is identified as one of the dry zones of India. Summers are extremely hot and temperature goes up considerably in some places like Banda. Winter is comparatively mild and of short duration. Annual rainfall is about 80 cm and is received around 35 days. All these climatic conditions make the water problem severe. In many villages, no drinking water is available during summers.

About 80 per cent of the population living in villages are dependent on agriculture for their livelihood, which is largely rain-fed. The ground water resource is very low due to presence of hard rocks like gneiss and granite which are poor aquifers. About 7.16 lakh hectares (20.45 per cent) of the net sown area in Bundelkhand region is covered under irrigation. Most of the irrigation is done through life pumps in dug wells. Several rivers, namely, Sindh, Pahuj, Betwa, Jamini, Saprar, Dhasan, Ken, Paiswini, Bagain, etc. flow through the region, but their waters are yet to be properly utilized for irrigation. Canal irrigation is confined to some parts of the northern districts like Jalaun, Hamirpur, Banda and Jhansi. In Madhya Pradesh, 16 per cent of the net sown area is under irrigation compared to 10 per cent in Uttar Pradesh. On an average, every five years, there is a draught in Northern India in 744 Hijari (AD 1366) which has also affected Bundelkhand. Records of the last 150 years show that there have been draughts in 1819, 1833 and 1898.

All these facts made us conscious of the water problem which has not been solved even 50 years after independence and it is, in fact, assuming enormous proportions. Hence, the need for a survey of traditional water harvesting structures was felt. Two development blocks – Niwari of Tikamgarh (Madhya Pradesh) and Bangra of Jhansi (Uttar Pradesh) – were undertaken for the survey, both of which are contiguous to each other. At present development activities like rainwater harvesting, afforestation, etc. are being undertaken in Bundelkhand area by our organization.

HISTORY

As far as water harvesting structures are concerned, the period from 9th century onwards assumes importance. This area was under the rule of the Chandelas from AD 831 (Nannuka, its first king) to AD 1545 (the last ruler was Kirti Varman), during which, many tanks were built by every Chandela king. Rahila (AD 885-905), the fourth king in the dynasty, built a large tank near Mahoba, Rahilya Sagar. Khajuraho inscription of AD 1059 credits Yasho Varman (AD 925-950) with the excavation of big tanks which may be identified with the tanks situated in and around the village of Khajuraho. Kirti Varman (AD 1060-1100) constructed three big lakes, Kirtisagar in Mahoba, Kirtisagar in Chanderi and Budhiya Tal in Kalanyara. Madan Varman (AD 1128-1165) too constructed many tanks. Some of these include Madansagar, Jatara and Aghara-Narayanpura in Tikamgarh district in Madhya Pradesh. Gadhadara, the prime minister of Madan Varman, also constructed a tank with broad storeys in the boundary of Deddu Village. Parmardideva (AD 1165-1203) built Parmala tank at Ajaygarh. Vira Varman's (AD 1245-1285) wife, Kalyanidevi constructed a 'Nirjara Well' and a tank at Ajaygarh, which is described in an inscription as resembling an ocean. In the Kalinjar stone inscription, Vira Varman (AD 1245-1285) is credited with the construction of many tanks and ponds. Apart from Chandela kings, their relatives and ministers also built tanks, for example Gadadhara and Kalyanidevi. Alha's (Paramardideva's warrior, who fought against Prithviraj Chauhan) father Dashraj built the Shandilya Tal. These are only some of the well known tanks built by the Chandelas, but there are hundreds of tanks scattered throughout the region of Bundelkhand whose history is largely unknown. In fact, one can find at least one tank in almost every village of Bundelkhand. Many of these tanks may have been built by village communities. Instances of construction by Banjaras/nomadic trading communities can also be found (for example, in Chachawali). Many a time, kings used to award as punishment the construction/repairs of tanks (e.g., Futera Talab, Sadikpura).

The Chandela domination started giving way to the Bundelas after Parmardi Varman (AD 1165-1202). Bundela kings also built many tanks during their period, e.g., Sindur Sagar was built by Vir Singh (who helped Jahangir by killing Abul Fazal) in 1605 and Sujan Sagar near Adjar was built by Sujan Singh in 1661. Various Bundela kingdoms merged into Indian republic after the independence.

Maratha dominance started in the region from AD 1729 (when Chhatrasal sought help from Peshwas) and continued up to 1857. However, the Maratha kings and sardars made little effort towards solving the problem of water management. After 1857 during the British period, attention was paid to canal irrigation and some canals were built or extended in the command areas of some of the bigger Chandela tanks (e.g., Pachhwara, Magarwara, Kachneo in the area under study), and some big dams like Paricha on river Betwa (1886), Pahumch on river Pahunj (1907), Lahchura on river Sukhnai (1910), etc. were built. In the period immediately after independence, many dams such as Kamala Sagar (1952), Govinda Sagar (1953), Mata Tila (1954), etc. were built. In the recent past, government agencies have built some check dam/stop dams. However, most of these check dams have a very short lifespan.

TRADITIONAL WATER HARVESTING STRUCTURES

Bundelkhand is a hill and rock region. As land gradients are quite steep, rainwater flows away very quickly and very little of it is absorbed. Moreover, high flow velocities of the rainwater cause severe soil erosion. Therefore, the need for impending the rainwater for replenishment of ground water as well as minimising soil erosion must have been felt. This was done through the construction of the following types of structures using locally available materials in very simple and cost-effective ways.

PUKHARIYAN

The only natural lake is in Sipun village of Banda district, which is quite small and shallow, and the water dries out in a few months after the rainy season. In many places, ponds of 10-12 sq. m. area can be seen. These ponds are either natural or made artificially, and are known as 'Pukhariyan'. Water in these ponds dries out a few days after the rainy season and then people harvest rice.

TALAB (TANKS)

There are many small hills encircling plain areas in this region through which countless rivulets and nullahs flow. These have been, at places, trapped by erecting earthen embankments between two hills. There are innumerable tanks made in this manner, which are being used by both human beings and animals and for fishery as well. Murary, Bhasinde, Kisurua, Kamal, Kamalgatta, Jalbhatta are also in tank water. In some tanks, where water dries out after rainy season, the tank bed itself is used for cultivation. These tanks help in increasing the water table of nearby areas. However, during the Chandela period, it seems irrigation was mostly done from wells. Large-scale direct irrigation from tanks started during the Bundela and British periods and also immediately after independence. Canals were built and sluice gates were provided in the larger Chandela tanks (Sakuli, Astari) and Bundela tanks (Sindur Sagar, Adjar, etc.). Today, on most of the bigger tanks, one can see sluice gates (Ghughsi, Pachwara, Ladpura, Kachneo, Magarpur, Magarwara, etc.). As a result of direct irrigation from these tanks, they become empty much before the onset of summer, whereas the original purpose of the tanks was to provide water throughout the year as well as to store water for use in draught years.

BANDHIES

Bandhi (Haveli Bandhi) system of cultivation is also a traditional way of water harvesting practised in the black soil areas of Bundelkhand. In this system, rainwater is impounded in bunded fields during monsoon and direct sowing of rabi crops is generally done after removing the impounded water. In this way, only single crop in a year, either rice in kharif or any rabi crop, is cultivated. Rice may be followed with wheat or other suitable rabi crops that use the residual moisture, so as to increase the cropping intensity.

However, since the advent of soya bean as a more remunerative crop, farmers have switched from rice cultivation to soya bean cultivation in the kharif season. But, whereas rice cultivation requires the impounding of rainwater in fields, soya bean requires a water-free field. Hence, the traditional bandhies have been dismantled by the farmers in the region on a large scale. This has very adversely affected the ground-water re-charging during monsoons leading to lowering of the water table year after year.

Fig. 13.1 Baory (Ber) presently in use (drinking and agriculture).

BAORIES

Baories (also called Ber), i.e., wells with steps, were also constructed extensively during the Chandela & Bundela periods. Water from these baories was used for drinking needs of humans and animals, and also for irrigation (Fig. 13.1). Many of these bers were built by Banjaras, one of them is situated in Chachawali. Some of them have beautiful architecture (Fig. 13.2) and a majority are on the verge of extinction.

WELLS

Wells are the traditional source of irrigation and drinking water. According to *Orchha State Gazetteer*, 1907 tanks irrigated 18,218 hectares and wells 41,924 hectares. Today tanks irrigate 20,371 hectares and wells 55,581 hectares.

It is clear that within 66 years (from 1907 to 1973), over 2,153 hectares were irrigated by tanks and 13,675 by the wells. But recent figures show that land irrigated by tanks has continuously dwindled after 1970. In fact, the

Fig. 13.2 A Baory (Ber) with beautiful architecture.

land irrigated by tanks is even lesser than what it used to be in 1907. In 1997, this figure has decreased to 12,674 hectares whereas the land irrigated by wells has increased to 1,60,390 hectares.

The above figures throw light on the condition of tanks today. Due to negligence from every section, the condition of these tanks is deteriorating continuously. Also, the continuous increase in well irrigation points to over-exploitation of underground water. One of the major roles of tanks in this region since Chandela Period was to increase the water table of surrounding areas. Over-exploitation of underground water and destruction of water re-charging system of tanks aggravate the water problem. In 1978, the Tube-well Engineering Department of Tikamgarh had warned that there is no further possibility of digging new tube wells or wells here.

STRUCTURE OF CHANDELA TANKS

Chandela tanks have a peculiar structure. In most of the cases, incoming rainwater in the form of rivulets/nullahs flowing between hillocks is stopped by building one or more massive earthen embankments between them. The earthen embankment has a stone pitching mostly on both the sides and sometimes only on one side (the inner side) of the embankment. It would be more appropriate to say that these stones, arranged in the form of steps, form a supporting wall for the earthen embankment. The dimensions of

Fig. 13.3 Close-up of embankment without mortar.

Fig. 13.4 An embankment constructed without the use of mortar.

these stones are approximately 2 ft. x 2 ft. x 1 ft. Use of mortar is negligible (Figs. 13.3-13.4). The breadth to height ratio of the embankments is quite large compared to the ratios prescribed as per modern engineering methods. For example, in the cases of Kagar ka Bandh at Kachneo and Begam ki Taleyan near Orchha (Figs. 13.5-13.6), this ratio is approximately 7:1. Waste-weirs are mostly natural structures like rocks. A detailed technical study of these structures is necessary so as to understand the reasons for the longevity of these tanks (which is almost a thousand years). The life of the newly built dams/check dams is not more than 25 years.

Embankments of the Chandela tanks are usually not straight, but have a sharp convex curvature into the tank somewhere in the middle of the embankment, at which point, the breadth of the embankment increases and where a small temple/chabootara is usually constructed (Ladpura ka Talab). Some of the Chandela tanks form a chain consisting of 2-3 tanks (e.g., tanks near Teharka, Kachneo, Jugiayi, etc.).

Bundela tanks are mostly bigger in size. Quite a few of them are built on the same site where the Chandela tanks existed earlier (e.g., Sindur Sagar, Fig. 13.7). This is evident from the stones used, which are of the Chandela Period, usually with the typical Chandela carvings on them. Bundela tanks have lime mortar masonry work. They are not as cost-effective or simple as Chandela tanks, but are bigger, and have *ghats*, and associated structures like *Chabootaras* (Fig. 13.8), *Kothis*, etc. designed to show off the glory of the king who built them.

Fig. 13.5 Kagar ka Bandh at Kachneo.

Fig. 13.6 Begam ki Taleyan near Orchha.

Fig. 13.7 Sindur Sagar (tank) – A Bundela Tank, constructed upon an earlier Chandela tank.

Fig. 13.8 Bundela tank with ghats and *Chabootaras*.

MAINTENANCE OF CHANDELA TANKS

It is important to know how these were maintained in the past. Some of the Chandela tanks are almost 1000 years old and yet function very well. This makes it clear that they require very little maintenance, which was done by the villagers themselves. But after independence, the scenario has completely changed. The maintenance and operation of these traditional structures were usurped from the hands of the villager and handed over to government departments. This process which had started during the British Period itself has helped in making village level water management traditions weaker. Today, the village has no powers to take decisions, due to external interference by the government departments, political parties, etc. It is no longer cohesive and does not have control over the behaviour of its residents. Many tanks and check dams require little repairing, e.g., check dam of Gidkhini needs a gate, check dam of Dhamana needs only minor repairs, but villagers do not think that they can do it at their level.

The government on its part has adopted a policy of total neglect of common property resources of villagers such as common lands, forest patches and village tanks. Many influential persons in post-independence period brought, mostly illegally, many of these resources under their personal ownership. People who are in power do not hesitate in selling pitching stones of the embankments (e.g., Asati Talab) or breaking the embankment to empty the tank so that submerged lands can be cultivated illegally (e.g., Javan where embankment was broken in 1996 (Figs. 13.9-13.10).

Fig. 13.9 Javan-where the embankment was destroyed illegally in 1996.

Fig. 13.10 Another view of Javan-where the embankment was destroyed illegally in 1996.

The successive land reforms initiated by both the state and central governments resulted in the common land resources being distributed among the poor. Legally speaking, lands falling in submergence area cannot be given on *Patta* (lease hold), but vested interests along with *Gram Pradhan* and/or *Patwari* started giving *Pattas* of this land illegally by showing the tank to be located somewhere else on the village map and revenue records. The land under submergence area is mostly fertile, hence cultivation of this land is most remunerative.

Illegal cultivation in tank submergence area has created many problems. Cultivators want to empty the tank before the *rabi* crop is sown whereas it is in the interest of Dheemar community (which traditionally cultivates fishes) that the tank remains filled as long as possible. Increasing settlements in the low-lying lands near a tank led to the tank not being fully stored with water, e.g., Sindur Sagar where people of Dheemarpura do not let the waste-weir level to be increased, even though the tank has more storage capacity.

CULTURAL IMPORTANCE OF TANKS

Almost each and evey tank, big or small, has a temple (of Shiva or Mata or Hanuman or Ghatoitan Baba) on its embankment or on the hilltop by its side. One can also see Sati temples near some tanks (Chachavali, Patharam). The idol in a Sati temple is a stone with the figures of a man, and a women, with a sun and a half-moon carved on it. Sometimes, a palm (hand) is also shown. These are characteristically Chandeli symbols. This shows that tanks have been very much a part of the religious life of the people here. In some cases, tanks are owned by temples (e.g., Ubora). *Melas* are also organized near these tanks. Traditionally, the *mela* is organized on a particular auspicious day which is different for different tanks, e.g., a *mela* is organized near Adjar tank on Dev Uthavani Gyaras, and near Sakuli tank it is organized on the day of Rakhi. At Pachwara tank, it is celebrated on Makar Sankranti. Near many tanks, weekly markets are held. Tanks have, thus, been natural centres for social interaction and need to be preserved at any cost.

14

ANCIENT WATERWORKS AS MODELS FOR LOCALIZED WATER MANAGEMENT

J. Manuel

ABSTRACT

In the backdrop of burgeoning and affluent lifestyles gnawing on water resources, also due to the increasing consumption of energy and materials, alternative methods of water management have to be searched. Thus, people perforce used common sense techniques for water management that are low on energy and material. The savings made in energy and materials in turn saved water that would have otherwise been invested on it. Simple techniques like flagstone slab lining the platforms and drains leading to tanks; temple tanks storing the overland flow of rainwater; tapping of ground water and supplying it without using energy, are only some of the numerous ancient techniques spelled out herein. Self-sustained discrete clusters of settlements, that are separated from each other by a buffer zone, where the ground water level, flora and fauna remains in a pristine state, should be strived for.

INTRODUCTION

As is well known, pre-historic man was literally close to water. This situation somewhat changed in the proto-historic period, with permanent settlements coming up and consumption of water increasing dramatically. For making pots, pans and bowls, use in agriculture and for construction purposes water was drawn up in larger volumes. With the mastering of iron technology and subsequent availability of the metal, man could establish colonies in newer areas, most often, with still higher investments in energy and water. This trend has now reached a stage, wherein consumption of water, the energy invested in it and the water, energy and materials spent to make suitable permanent structures, require a holistic review.

POWER SIPHONING OF WATER

In the pre-Neolithic cultures man went near water, but with the advent of settled lifestyle man began to draw water towards him (Fig. 14.1). This trend was showing a moderately

Fig. 14.1 Man and water: increasing distance and energy.

increasing mode, until the establishment of industrial age, when electrical machines caused water to be brought from much larger distances. The competition within urban areas is apparent when one sees new building complexes installed with more powerful pumps extracting water, out of the reach of economically less fortunate residents.

A glimpse of the future scenario could be understood from the fact that the posh parts of Ahmedabad have at least 50,000 borewells. This in effect means that a common property resource like water is going away from the reach of common man, into the hands of a decreasing percentage of populace, which can still afford the luxury of power-siphoning of water. Similarly, in the agricultural sector, wealthy ground water farmers continue to extract more water despite falling depths of the water table. Unabated deepening of wells and withdrawals cause drying of open shallow wells which usually poorer farmers depend upon for irrigation (Katyal, 1997).

CONSUMPTION TRENDS

Water problems arise from increasing demand generated by burgeoning population, urbanization, industrialization and irrigation need for additional food production. For agriculture its availability in sufficient quantity and acceptable quality determines the sustainable performance of diverse crops. At present 65 per cent of the agriculture is rainfed which contributes 44 per cent food and supports 40 per cent of the human population (Katyal, 1997). To bridge this huge gap stress has been laid on a highly efficient irrigation cropping system which alone can sustain India's expanding population (Sivanappan, 1997). However, notwithstanding the higher efficiency of irrigated agriculture, a question arises as to how much water would remain free which is not channelized or contained within man-made systems. Moreover, besides water used for irrigation, the investment of energy and materials has in many ways affected the quantity of water somewhere else.

Modern urbanization has also imposed a mind boggling impact on the availability of water. With the increasing size, affluent lifestyles and services available in the cities, per capita consumption of water is much more than in rural areas, so much so, that a city like Delhi no longer survives with water available in the Yamuna basin in which it is located (Agrawal, 1997). Besides, other than that required for routine urban life, modern construction technologies using cement, steel and bricks have further gnawed deeper into the water resources at different stages.

A quick glance on the industrial front also reveals the huge quantities of water required for the production of some modern materials. Thus, for every kilogram of aluminium, synthetic fibre, paper, glass and steel approximately 1350, 200, 170, 70 and 50 litres of water respectively, is required (Rangwala, 1992). The progress in industrialization has also increased the consumption of energy and materials and therefore by inference also of water, even in objects that are not of basic need.

WATER DISTRIBUTION SYSTEMS

As more water is being taken from reservoirs for urban areas and industry, less clean water is available for drinking purpose for villages living downstream of towns and industrial clusters (Agrawal, 1997). Obviously with the increasing gravitation of urban industrial centres all materials including water are brought from new and remote localities. Needless to say, they are brought with increasing investments in energy, materials and transit losses. Wastage of water due to leakage in pipes and unattended repairs is about 30-40 per cent (Sivanappan, 1997). Besides, in the agricultural sector, unscrupulous use of canal water has caused side effects like water-logging, soil salinity, alkalinity (Katyal, 1977), diarrhoeal pathogen, malaria and land locking (D'Souza *et al.*, 1998). The last of which leaves the farmers with little choice but to adopt the watering pattern of the dominant corp. However, unlike monoculture corps caused due to landlocking- the alternatives in cereal types resting with the farmer, would have prevented total wipe out in case of vagaries of nature, including epidemics.

WATER HARVESTING TECHNIQUES

In view of the increasing environmental costs of obtaining water, alternative methods have to be searched that are indigenous and sustainable. In areas of water scarcity people have devised indigenous methods to preserve water. In the semi-arid region of Kutch district of Gujarat, as far back as middle of 3rd millennium BC the Harappans of Dholavira came up with innovative ideas to augment the subnormal rainfall. Here, besides a series of reservoirs along with inlet channels (Bisht, 1997) a mechanism for *in situ* collection of rainwater is a unique work of the proto-historic times. The system consists of an underground drain originating from a stone-paved platform which is pierced by several manholes (Fig. 14.2) along its length of more than 150 meters. The water thus collected from the roofs and platforms of the castle used to cascade down to reach the nearby reservoir. Later, about 2nd century AD, Buddhist monks living in the Kanheri caves near Mumbai made slanting grooves in the rock face which led the rainwater to huge underground tanks (Fig. 14.3). Umpteen examples of large open tanks near ancient temples and habitation sites show the perceived importance of *in situ* rainwater storage mechanims in earlier ages (Fig. 14.4). Another interesting mechanism is the Mughal water supply system in Burhanpur town, District East Nimar (Madhya Pradesh). Here, besides overland water collected in open tanks, on the principles of intercepting the run-off in sub-soil ground water level through underground channels, water was collected in structures called *bhandaras* (Fig. 14.5) (Kambo *et al.*, 1997). The city used to get its supply of water from these *bhadaras* through a system of earthenware pipelines. Incidentally, although this ancient system taps ground water and has been brought from a distance it differs significantly from the tube-wells and other present-day systems. Herein, thus non-use of energy in withdrawal or supply of water and use of low investment earthenware pipes, are noteworthy. Another water harvesting system which deserves mention are the *tankas* of western parts of

Fig. 14.2 Dholavira, Gujarat, underground drain: Protohistoric endeavours for *insitu* collection of water.

Fig. 14.3 Kanheri, Maharashtra, grooves on the rock surface: ealry historic endeavours for *in situ* collection of water.

Fig. 14.4 Sravanbellgola, Karnataka, stone built tank for collection of rain water: A medieval endeavour.

Fig. 14.5 Burhanpur, Madhya Pradesh, air shaft of Khuni Bhandara, part of a low energy system for water collection: A Mughal endeavour.

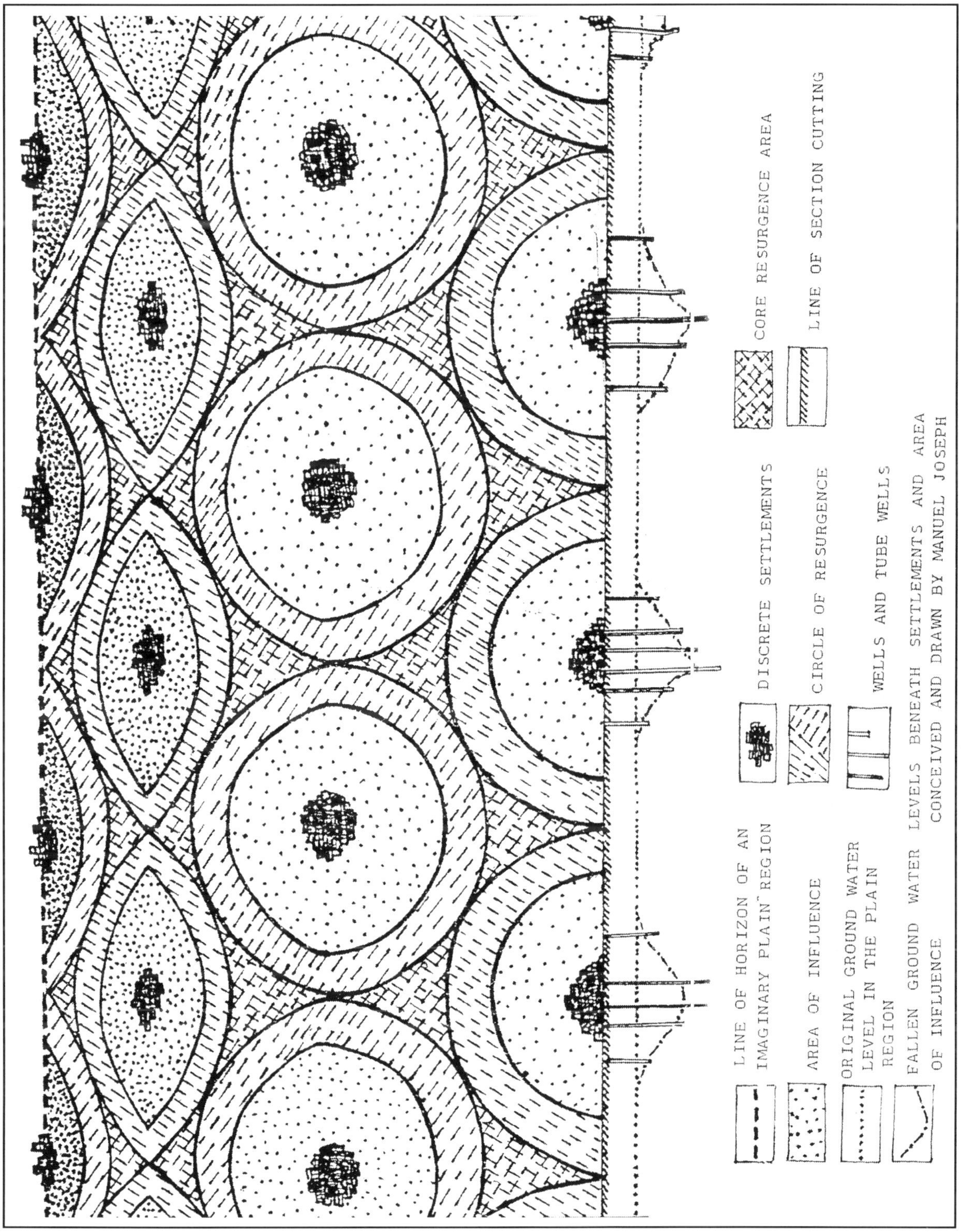

Fig. 14.6 Centrifugal planning.

Rajasthan. These are circular holes in the ground lined with fine polished lime or *chunam,* which collect rainwater. Water from *tankas* is used only when other supplies fail (Noronha, 1998). These are some of the many *in-situ,* low energy, non-invasive systems of water collection across the ages that could be put to use again. These would provide water, save energy and environmentally costly materials.

CENTRIPETAL VS CENTRIFUGAL PLANNING

The average water availability of 2000 cu m/person/year in the country is being steadily eroded by the optimum requirement of 1700 cu m/person/year (Sivanappan 1997), due to the unabated increase in population and runway consumption trends. Further, the centripetal tendencies of cities have caused water to be brought from ever increasing horizontal or vertical distances. These have caused losses in also consumed water elsewhere. On the other hand a major amount of peak demand shortage of electricity which goes upto, as much as 29% (Singh, 1996), and is likely to go up further, has to be debited to systems of water supply. Thus it is imperative that a bulk consumed material like water should be least transported. By implication the emphasis should be towards a hydrocentric planning rather than the present technocentric one, which looks for ways and means of *insitu* re-charge of aquifers using the simplest methods and technologies possible.

Besides, as suggested by many workers, the country has to take steps towards deurbanisation, decentralisation, decentralised rural electrification and other congruent measures. Further, if the settlement produces most of its requirements within a limited and well defined area of influence it will not draw on resources from far off places. This will save energy materials and water in many ways. Several such settlements (nuclei) would be separated by inner concentric circle of "area of influence" and outer "circle of resurgence" (Fig. 14.6). Within this "circle of resurgence" and in the area between three such circles (core area) ground water and all resources should be strived to be kept in its pristine state, thereby never allowing the neighbouring nuclei to coalesce. However, these individual nucleus, unlike urban centres, should strive to be self sustainable thereby preventing environmental degradations elsewhere.

ACKNOWLEDGEMENTS

I am thankful to Shri R.S. Bisht, Director, ASI for permitting the publication of the photograph of the underground drain at Dholavira. I am also thankful to Dr. Narayan Vyas and Shri G.S. Gaur for providing me valuable inputs. Thanks are also due to Shri Virendra Singh and Shri C.K. Bhanarkar both photographers, in Bhopal Circle of Archaeological Survey of India.

NOTES AND REFERENCE

Agarwal, A., 1997, Evaporating Resources, *Down to Earth,* Vol. 6, No. 12, New Dlehi, p. 6.

Bisht, R.S., 1997, Dholavira Excavations, *Indian Archaeology 1991-92 – A Review,* A.S.I., New Delhi, pp. 26-34.

D'Souza, R., P. Mukhopadhyay and A. Kothari, 1998, Re-evaluating Multi-purpose River Valley Projects: A Case Study of Hirakund, Ukai and IGNP, *Economic and Political Weekly*, Vol. 33, No. 6, Mumbai, pp. 297-302.

Kambo, D.P., J.D. Cruz and J. Ashraf, 1997, Medieval Water Supply System in Burhanpur Town, Madhya Pradesh: A Review, *Puratattava 1996-97*, No. 27, New Delhi, pp. 30-36.

Katyal, J.C., 1997, Sustainability: Relevance of Integrated Concept, *The Hindu Survey of Indian Agriculture*, Chennai, pp. 25-31.

Noronha, F. 1998, Where the water is, *Down to Earth*, Vol. 6, No. 18, New Delhi, pp. 48-49.

Rangwala, S.C., 1992, *Water Supply and Sanitary Engineering*, Charotar Publishing House, Anand, pp. 18-29.

Singh, R., 1996, Shifting Indian Paradigm, *The Hindu Survey of Indian Industry*, Chennai, pp. 53-58.

Sivanappan, R.K., 1997, Water Management: Need for Holistic Approach, *The Hindu Survey of Indian Agriculture*, Chennai, pp. 155-59.

15

NOTE ON PRACTICAL FIELD INITIATIVES

U.C. Pandey

While Himalayas are the source of major rivers of northern India the local people survive on upland rain-fed farming and are amongst the poorest in the country. In Uttarakhand, potable piped water supply is still a distant dream for a very large percentage of the villages.

It is known that of the total geographic area, 10-12 per cent is under the plough and 10-12 per cent of the cultivated area has irrigation facilities. Between 50 to 65 per cent of irrigation facilities are those that have been created by community efforts, some of which are centuries old. In spite of the very simple nature of their engineering structures, they are quite efficient and designed to meet specific needs.

In the Uttarakhand region of Uttar Pradesh and in Himachal Pradesh, indigenously built and locally owned systems are to be found in every river and drainage basin. These irrigation systems, logically linked to crop preferences, climatic factors, and norms of social behaviour, are interwoven in the fabric of rural hill society. Some examples are:

- In water shortage situation not only distribution of water is made equitable but it is ensured that crops with varying needs of irrigation water get allocated turns.
- System maintenance costs are shared, and for this purpose, adequate financial and labour resources are organized.
- Clear rules exist to discourage free riders. Those who try to tamper the system's operation related rules face quick and deterrent action.

In 1995 Vincent spoke of 'Vertical' divisions in mountain farming systems. Of these extended vertical control is seen to operate through the exchange of specialized goods. Services and labour between communities in contiguous production zones, usually underpinned by kinship and reciprocal relationship, describe Himalayan environment with fair accuracy.

There is a wide variety of irrigation systems in the Himalayan region, both amongst engineering structures and in system management and operation. In the field of agriculture too, cultural practices and rituals are to be observed. In the 'Hurkiya Bol' of Kumaon, a folk artist is a singing companion to women folk while they plant paddy. The singer, with a hand-held hour glass shaped drum, sings out impromptu verses occasionally eliciting a wise crack in inspired verse from the women. The ceremonious opening of 'Maletha Gul' in district Tehri-Garhwal is a solemn and sombre occasion. Himachal has its own religious celebrations linked to agricultural activity.

These are confined to farmer-owned systems. Government built systems are considered as impersonal articles with which the locals do not feel any empathy.

'Dying Wisdom-State of India's Environment, A Citizen's Report 4' has made a strong plea for documentation of traditional systems of irrigation. This must not be delayed any further otherwise the dying wisdom may be lost irretrievably. The two important points for consideration are:

1. Water Rights: In the Himalayan region, beneficiaries held right over water that they used for irrigation and drinking. In the 'welfare state' concept, these rights have got eroded. The earstwhile rulers of Tehri-Garhwal and British rulers in the rest of Uttarakhand made rules to protect water rights and water use systems. They recognized the importance of leaving water resources management with the people.
2. Research in management practices of traditional systems along with their socio-economic and managerial aspects and a multi-disciplinary approach is what is needed today.

Drinking water availability has always been poor in the hills. In the past, the state encouraged construction of ponds, 'bavri', 'nullah', etc. in which water was collected for drinking purposes. A variety of structures, some with excellent carvings and filigree work in stone statuettes and a certain Vaastu orientation, are to be found all over the hills of Kumaon.

DOCUMENTATION AND RESEARCH

The Himalayan region is vast in expanse and with the difficulties associated with altitude and physiography, customs vary from district to district and within small geographical territories. Three distinct geographic zones emerge and anthropological entities can be identified.

1. Inner Himalayas

Tribals with distinct ethnic and socio-cultural practices inhabit this area. Agriculture and related water resource management of this area need to be studied. The areas, very rich in information for research and documentation, could be:

Himachal Pradesh :	I)	Chamba District
	II)	Kaza and Spiti in Lahaul Spiti District
Uttarakhand :	I)	Uttarkashi

2. Middle Himalayas

People here share the culture of the plains but with a distinct local flavour. Ethnically, the area shows a mix of races. A variety of dialects are to be found. Considerable knowledge about this part of Himalayas is available which needs to be broad based. Studies related to agriculture, irrigation, water rights, local crop varieties need to be carried out. The following districts are recommended for studies:

Himachal Pradesh:	I)	Kangra
	II)	Kinnaur
Uttar Pradesh:	I)	Tehri-Garhwal

3. The Siwaliks, the Piedmont Plains and Terai

Most of this area is easily accessible and has reaped benefits of development and planning processes. Here, most of the traditional systems are extinct. Research and documentation in this area may be taken up in a later phase.

The following need to be documented

1. Practices in irrigated agriculture in remote areas and the rituals associated with these.
2. In-depth multi-disciplinary study of management practices in agriculture and irrigation.
3. Water rights and local water institutions.
4. Study of the role of women in water resources development and management.
5. Traditional cultivation and field water management practices to reduce environmental risk.
6. Initiatives for integration of both irrigated and unirrigated crops in farming systems.
7. Empowering a community for taking up management responsibilities in state-owned systems. Turn-over of operation and management responsibility of government-built systems.
8. Models for development of irrigation institutions documenting existing models.
9. Technology incorporating traditional knowledge in water resources management for drinking and irrigation purposes.

FIELD INITIATIVES

To begin with, the following initiatives may be considered:

a) Documentation of studies related to water rights, management practices in water resources, use in agriculture, socio-religious customs related to above which would involve the disciplines of law, sociology, anthropology, archaeology, history and engineering.
b) Model testing for policy formulation.
   - Turn-over to user groups of state-owned irrigation systems and other water use systems.
   - Medium to small-sized irrigation and power generation systems in place of large systems.
c) Preparation of manuals.
d) Training programmes – all these involve the disciplines of law, economics and engineering.

16

PHAD SYSTEM OF WESTERN MAHARASHTRA (A Traditional Method of Water Harvesting and Management by the Farmers)

R.K. Patil

ABSTRACT

The experience of the past hundred years or so in the management of irrigation systems has created an impression (and belief) among the policy makers that the activities related to water harvesting and management must essentially be in the public domain and the state knows how best to manage such activities. The farmers' role has been narrowed to 'decision takers'. Their needs have no voice in the management of water system.

However, judging from the experience of the past forty years or so, this policy has apparently failed. It witnessed the unutilized potential created under major and medium irrigation projects. Interest has, therefore, been revived in the extant, age-old systems, where farmers have managed the systems, albeit small ones. The Phad System in Western Maharashtra is an example of this type of water management by farmers.

The system is more than three hundred years old. Though the associations managing the system are not legal entities, their locus standi is based on centuries of efficient management and benefits to the farmers. The operation and maintenance functions, including the equitable water distribution, are performed efficiently without any state intervention.

INTRODUCTION

In North-Western Maharashtra, a community-based irrigation management system known as 'Phad System' is in practice. Though the origins of the system are shrouded in historical mist, available documents indicate that the system came into existence in the early 16th century or so.

The system is operative on three rivers in the Tapi basin, viz., Panjhra, Mosam and Aram, in the districts of Dhule and Nasik. A few salient features of the Panjhra System are discussed in this paper. The principles of operation are the same in all the three rivers.

PANJHRA RIVER BANDHARA SYSTEM

The river Panjhra originating in the Sahyadri ranges, runs from west to east for about 88 km, and meets Tapi River at Thalner. The river has a steep gradient and flows through rocky beds, suitable for construction of diversion weirs. It receives run off from the monsoon rains (June to October), but has a significant post-monsoon flow which can sustain sizeable irrigation in the winter and summer seasons.

A series of *bandharas* were built on the river to divert water for agricultural use. A graphic description of their construction is available in *The Gazetteer of Bombay Presidency*, Vol. XII, Khandesh, published by Khandesh Collectorate in 1880, which incidentally, is the first document giving these details. The relevant extract is given below:

> The weirs (*bandharas*) must at one time, have been very numerous. In the west, there is scarcely a stream of any size without traces of them. Tradition attributes their construction to the Muslim rulers and it is probable that many of them date from the time of the later Farukki Kings (1370-1600). In many places foundation holes, cut in the sheet rock are the only traces of former dams. Others are found in every stage of ruin. Many are entire and a great number are still in use, while others apparently as perfect have been abandoned from scarcity of waters, silting and other causes. Here and there huge masses of overturned masonry lying a few yards down the stream from the line of the weirs show the violence of occasional floods and excellence of the old cement. The sites of these dams were as a rule well chosen. Except a few, built straight across the stream, dams are more or less oblique, the water course issuing at the lower end. Where the rock below is not continuous their forms are most irregular. In building a dam holes were cut in the rock in the proposed line of the wall from 6 to 13 inches square, the same or more in depth and from 3 to 6 ft. apart. In the holes stone uprights, sometimes small pillars taken from the Hindu temples, were set and the dam was either built in front of these or the stones were built into the dam leaving only the backs of the uprights visible. The dams are strong, clumsy walls commonly sloping on both sides to a narrow top. The materials are commonly black basalt stone, coarse concrete mixed with small pieces of bricks and the very best cement. Occasionally large blocks are found in the face of the wall, but the inner stones are all small. Dressed stone is seldom used for either facing, quoins or copying. Except some small openings at the middle or at the base, no provision seems to have been made for removing the silt. While the dams were built with the greatest care, the water courses were laid down with the strictest economy, following the level of the ground and making long bends to avoid cuttings or aqueducts. By some, these long windings are condemned as causing waste by absorption and evaporation. But the present generation defend their ancestors on the ground of the original layout and because a gentle gradient and therefore a long course was required to regulate the flow and prevent it from being wastefully rapid. Khandesh valleys are open and level, and the smaller rivers rising in Sahyadri hills flow in shallow beds blocked here and there by rocky ledges of much service in making masonry weirs while from their flatness or very gentle cross slope large areas of land are easily commanded.

While the exact number of *bandharas* on the river is not known (as some of them are in a dilapidated condition), a study on Panjhra Project in 1964 mentions 45 *bandharas*. However, presently, only 14 *bandharas* are functioning in the upper reaches. There are a few functioning in the lower reaches, managed by traditional hereditary village functionaries rather than the community. Today, even this is not in practice because of the abolition of hereditary rights of village functionaries.

Each independent sub-system comprises a *bandhara* (a low diversion weir in stone masonry) across the river, a small canal on the bank and distributories for irrigation. The area irrigated under different *bandharas* varies from 4 ha. to 192 ha. The following table gives the number of *bandharas* on each of the three river systems and the annual area under irrigation.

Number of Bandharas and Area Irrigated

Sr. No.	Clear	Number of Bandharas	Area Under Irrigation
1.	Panjhra (1)	45	3035
2.	Mosam (2)	20	1500
3.	Aram (3)	8	275
	Total:	**73**	**4810**

Though no records are available indicating as to who built the *bandharas* and the canal system, one of the documents available with a prominent farmer in Rayawat *bandhara* suggests that his ancestors built the structure and later approached the ruler and obtained hereditary rights of village headmanship (known as 'Patilki'). He was made responsible for the maintenance and distribution of water with the help of local farmers. The present generation is the twelfth in the lineage.

THE PHAD IRRIGATION

Physical System

The Rayawat *bandhara* system, which is typical, comprises a weir across the river Panjhra near village Bhadane. A canal takes off at the right bank and after running for about 2 km through ravine land, commands an area of about 234 ha. of the village Rayawat (34 ha. of assured irrigation – Kayam Bagayat – and 100 ha. of unassured or temporary irrigation). In addition, an area of 7 ha. of village Bhadane is also commanded on the way. The inlet to the canal is without a gate and therefore the canal draws in water only when there is flow at the *bandhara*. There are no records to indicate the design capacity of the canal. However, it appears to have a uniform capacity of about 150/300 litres/second. Along its length, there are a couple of escapes (called Sandani) for diverting excess flow into the natural drains. The maximum discharge in the canal is limited by the provision of notches (without free board), in the side walls of the aqueducts. There are distributaries from this canal for feeding different sub-areas of the command and each of these distributaries can carry the full discharge of about 200 litres/second. From the distributaries, there are farm water courses (called *Sarangi*) for carrying the water to individual farms. Generally, there is a masonry structure at the head of distributary and diversion of water is controlled by putting wooden planks or earthen bunds across the canal. Even though there are escapes on the canal and distributaries, there is no planned drainage system for different fields. The soils are generally well drained, and the topography also permits speedy drainage.

The canal system is very elaborate and in some cases it runs from 10 to 12 km. There are deep cuts (excavated up to 30-40 ft. depth), a few tunnels and a number of aqueducts. Considering the technologies available then, the system is an engineering marvel. The aqueducts on the nullah crossings provide for escapes, so as to minimize damage to the channels. Wherever topography is favourable, free catchment is tapped and integrated in the system. Slopes of about 0.6 to 1.0 per cent in the farms are not uncommon, but no wasteful application of water is seen.

SITUATIONAL AND TECHNICAL ASPECTS

The command is a compact unit of a couple of hundred hectares mostly within the limits of a single village. As the area is small, communication is quick. According to the water flows available at the head of the canal, the flows in the distributaries and the number of farms under irrigation are adjusted. If any one of the irrigation staff has neglected his work, it is immediately noticed and corrective action taken. The village being the unit, social control is enough for management. All the irrigators are from the same village and they respect the authority of the village *panchas*, both at the social and formal levels.

Availability of water in relation to the irrigation requirements is another important factor as there are annual variations in the rainfall. In the Phad System, these variations are managed by demarcating the command in two categories: assured irrigation is so limited that, in most of the years, it can be irrigated without much difficulty. During years of water scarcity, irrigation is done by extending the rotation period in summer. Since the unassured area, which is always at the tail-end, gets irrigation benefits only in those years of good rainfall, perennial crops are not grown here. The large capacity of the canals is another interesting factor. The capacity of the canal is practically constant from the *bandhara* down to the distributaries. This means that the capacity factor (ratio of actual capacity of the canal to the capacity required as per crop water requirement) increases from head to the tail of the canal, providing a better flexibility of operation at the Phad level. This is comparable to the uniform capacity of canal in the Huerta of Valencia, Spain, where irrigation management is practiced successfully through the participation of irrigators.

Division of the command into *phads* (blocks) and planting of only one crop in each *phad*, helps in the management of irrigation. The share of water that the *phads* get, varies according to water requirements of different crops. Thus, a *phad* with a wheat crop can be allotted a higher share of water (per hectare) than a *phad* with a sorghum crop.

The sequence of irrigation in a *phad* runs from head to tail with the top-end farmers receiving water first and the tail-end ones last. In such a sequence, the efficiency of water application is relatively higher. When the upper farm is irrigated, any excess flow reaches the lower farm, but before the irrigation in that farm is completed. Similarly, there is no need for fine adjustment of flows in the distributaries to avoid wastage of water in the channel.

A head-to-tail irrigation sequence requires better social discipline to ensure that the tail-end farms get adequate water supply. Such a discipline has been in existence on these *bandharas*, facilitated by the age-old rule whereby no second watering of the top holding would be done until the last tail-end plot is irrigated. Within the field, especially for sugarcane crop, serpentine water courses are laid, which saves labour for water application.

CROP AND WATER MANAGEMENT

The whole command area (called 'Patasthal' or 'Thal') is divided into *phads*, their size ranging from a few hectares to 50 hectares, depending upon the topography. Only one crop would be grown in one *phad*. The choice of crops to be grown in the different *phads* is decided well before the rainy season, by the assembly of irrigators. Crops are rotated among the *phads*, such that over a period of two to three years, every *phad* gets sugarcane, the main cash crop. The meeting takes place generally on the auspicious day of 'Akshaya Tritiya', falling between about mid-April and mid-May. Usual crop rotation is as follows:

1. Sugarcane.
2. First yield of sugarcane.
3. Sorghum in rainy season followed by wheat in winter.
4. Rice in rainy season followed by wheat in winter. Vegetables are not grown in the *phads*.

The sequence of irrigation is from head to tail and is elaborately described in the 'Record of Rights'. The entire flow in the canal is diverted into the *phad*. Within the *phad*, the farms at the head are irrigated first and then the next ones and so on, till the tail farms are irrigated. Generally, there is another meeting of the irrigators and depending upon the rate of flow in the river (and in the canal), broad guidelines are laid down as to how the water should be rationed. Water distribution is done by irrigation staff. The rotational schedule is strictly followed and those infringing the discipline are fined by the committee. The actual water application on the farm is also carried out by the irrigation staff. The land owner is not authorized to supply water to the farm.

MAINTENANCE

Maintenance and repairs of the *bandhara* structure is the responsibility of the government, whereas the canal system is maintained by the irrigators themselves. They do not require much annual maintenance/repairs; they need repairs, at the most, once in 15-20 years. As these are beyond the means of the farmers, these have been entrusted to the government. Maintenance (cleaning) of the canal system is done generally twice a year – in May and October. The cleaning starts from the head of the canal and is done in stretches between escapes. The cleaning groups are generally arranged in the following sequence:

1. Cutting the bushes and weeds.
2. Removal of silt with shovels.
3. Carrying the silt in baskets.
4. Ploughing with bullocks.
5. Dozing with bullock-drawn scraper.

The stone beds in the canal indicate the levels at which the cleaning has to be done.

Immediately after the first general meeting in April-May, all the irrigators are informed through a public announcement about the maintenance requirement. Each family has to provide a pair of bullocks and three men for one day. The families which cannot provide these in kind, have to pay the charges (Rs. 30 for bullock pair and Rs. 10 for two men). The requirement of labour varies from *bandhara* to *bandhara* but the average requirement is about 100 men and 50 bullock pairs working for about 4 to 5 days. Records are maintained only by a few committees. The records of Kasare *bandhara* show that over a period of 6 years from 1960-61 to 1965-66, the labour input varied from 214 men to 440 men and 86 bullock pairs to 180 bullock pairs.

The farm water courses (for carrying water from the distributary to the farm) are maintained by the individual irrigators. The responsibility of the irrigator is to maintain the channel length between the off-take and his own farm.

WATER MANAGEMENT COMMITTEE

For the management of irrigation under the command of each *bandhara,* there is a committee (called 'panch committee') elected by the assembly of all irrigators. One cannot hold an office in the committee unless one is an irrigator in the command. The Committee appoints irrigation staff every year, hears the complaints of irrigators and irrigation staff and also takes policy decision regarding the allocation of water and maintenance of the system.

Irrigation staff (appointed by, and responsible to the Committee) comprises *Havaldars* (supervisors), *Patkaris* (watermen), and *Jagalya*s (watchmen). On the Rayawat *bandhara* (command 134 ha.), there are two supervisors, six watermen and six watchmen. It is the duty of the watermen to see that the water flows in the main canal and the distributaries. They are, therefore, actively involved in the maintenance operations. During irrigation periods, all the staff work in the same *phad* where water is applied. Application of water to individual farms is done by the watermen only. Irrigators, as noted earlier, are not permitted to apply the water. The watchmen are responsible for protecting the crops, particularly during the harvesting season. The supervisors have to oversee the work of watermen and watchmen.

Method of payment varies from wholly in kind to wholly in cash, with different forms of mixed payments in between. On the Rayawat *bandhara,* for example, payment is in cash for sugarcane and in kind for other crops. Each irrigator has to be paid according to the crop grown in the *phad.* The payment is per farm (with adjustments for variation in size). If the irrigated crop is a food crop like wheat, rice, sorghum or pearl millet, the payment is in grain per season (called 'Kadi-pendi'), or in terms of unharvesting rows of crop (called 'Chache'). In the case of sugarcane, in the old days, the payment used to be in terms of quantity of raw sugar (jaggery) but now it is in cash. In rainy season and winter, the payment for sugarcane is per farm per season and in the summer (March-June), it is per watering. The payment is to be distributed amongst the different staff but generally the supervisors get more than others. In monetary terms, the salaries are equivalent to about Rs. 2000 to Rs. 3000 per year. (On the Samode *bandhara,* the supervisors are employed on a monthly salary of Rs. 200 each or Rs. 2400 per year.) The staff is generally better off than an irrigator with a farm of half to one hectare area.

DEFAULTERS

Default generally takes the form of:

a. Unauthorized (out of turn) watering;
b. Non-maintenance of farm water course;
c. Non-participation in the maintenance of canal.

In the case of unauthorized watering, the matter is reported by the supervisor to the committee and a penalty is imposed in the form of fine. For example, the records of Kasare *bandhara* show the imposition of fines and their recovery. An entry in the records says that one irrigator took water out of turn on 11.01.1972. He was fined Rs. 51 and he paid the amount on 02.03.1972. Non-maintenance of farm water course results in the loss of turn of the irrigation. Non-participation in the maintenance of canals (either in the form of contribution of labour and bullocks or payment thereof) is also dealt with in the same manner as unauthorized watering. Such cases are very rare.

MANAGEMENT SYSTEM ON LOWER BANDHARAS

The Phad System, in its traditional form as described so far, is practised presently on the 14 upstream *bandharas*. On downstream *bandharas*, the system functioned in a somewhat diluted form, till 1960s. Some of them are now in-operative.

The Kheda *bandhara* marks off the river section from where water flow becomes uncertain. Enquiries with the present generation of irrigators revealed that so long as their memory goes, the Phad system was prevalent on the upstream. Water management was done by a committee of six officials, comprising Policy Patil (law and order official), Mulki Patil (revenue and civil official), Talathi (revenue record keeper), supervisor and two watermen. The supervisors were paid a yearly remuneration from government funds; additionally he and two watermen were paid in kind by the beneficiaries. Though there was no control on the crops grown, the committee ensured equitable distribution of water in the command and successfully resolved the conflicts in water distribution. The committee was backed by the power and influence, commanded as a result of its government positions. Even this system collapsed in about 1964 when the post of Mulki Patil was abolished and the supervisor's remuneration terminated. Since then, this *bandhara* and those downstream have been victims of power politics. Attempts to re-organize the committee on a voluntary basis have evoked a very weak response. Presumably this is the result of extreme water scarcity.

ECONOMIC AND MANAGEMENT ASPECTS

Maintenance

As noted earlier, the routine maintenance is the responsibility of the irrigators and their *panchas*. However, many a time, this was not done properly and the government had to intervene. Such a situation arose in 1862 and it is interesting to see how the then British rulers handled the situation. Below is the verbatim translation of the order issued by Mr. Roberts, then Collector of Khandesh. The original order is in Marathi and in Modi script.

In the regime of Queen-Empress, Mr. Roberts, Acting Collector, Khandesh is promulgating the following Declaration. It has been observed that farmers take waters as they want and the rest is released either on roads or nullahs, creating waterlogging and wasteful use of water. Some farmers are deprived of water. All-forgiving God has given waters to the people, despite their sins and this valuable resource is misused, thus betraying the God's largesse's. The Acting Collector is grieved over the situation and desires to bring to the public notice the following clauses of Act No. 45 of 1860:

Clause 430: Anybody who hampers the flow of water for agricultural and allied purposes knowingly, would be liable to imprisonment for a maximum of five years or a fine or both.

Clause 431: Anybody willingly hampering the road, bridge or nullah flows or diverting waters on these facilities would be liable to imprisonment for a maximum of five years or fine or both.

Clause 432: Any person who diverts the flows of water on roads or any public facility and creates public nuisance by such acts would be liable to imprisonment for five years or fine or both.

Hence in any village where there is Patsthal (i.e., Phad System), Patil and Kulkarni shall arrange to build canals in the fields on receipt of this order. To meet the expenses thereto, a cess of Annas 8 per bigha of sugarcane, and Annas 4 per bigha of wheat and paddy should be levied. If this cess is insufficient, the rates may be doubled. Whatever the expenses, canals and channels must be built. Within three months of this order, channels should be built, and Patil and Kulkarni will be held responsible for proper utilization (avoidance of defalcation) of funds and adequacy of construction. Mamaltdar should overview the operations and report to the Collector.

It should be understood that Government will not meet routine and maintenance. The above rates should be collected every season and the accounts placed before the Panchayat. Panchayat should see that the amounts collected are spent for the started purposes. If there is any surplus in any year, this should be kept either in the Treasury or with the local Sahukar with interest, so that it may be available for future use. Dated 18 January 1862.

It is clear from the above declaration that the erstwhile rulers handed over the maintenance responsibility to the farmers while laying down the guidelines on how this is to be done. As stated above, the Panchayat engages watermen, *patkaris* and vigilance staff for whom the payments are made generally in kind. It is worth noting that in 1936, some irrigators refused to pay these charges on the plea that these staff have been given Inam lands in exchange for the performance of tasks. The matter was referred to the government. After going through the papers, the Assistant Collector came to the conclusion that even though Inam lands were reserved for the staff, they were insufficient, and hence ordered that *Kadipendi* should be given on the following scale:

Havildar

1. Two or three sheaves of wheat per *bigha*
2. One sheaf of bajri & one of peas (*watana*), one *kadap* of gram per *bigha*
3. Six seers of jaggery per *bigha*
4. Groundnut crop 16 cubits lengthwise per *bigha*
5. Cotton crop 16 cubits lengthwise per *bigha*
6. Other corn 3 seers per *bigha* so also wheat and bajri 3 seers each should be taken.

Patkaris

1. 8 to 10 sheaves of wheat per *bigha*
2. Bajri 1 to 2 bundles per *bigha*

3. Peas (*watana*) and gram 1 to 2 *kadpas* per *bigha*
4. 8 seers of jaggery per *bigha*
5. Groundnut crop 22 cubits (piece) lengthwise per *bigha*
6. Cotton crop lengthwise of the field one row
7. Other corn one *kadap* of each corn

By this decision, the Phad System received a short in the arm and the system still continues.

Conflict Management

The principal conflict in irrigation arises when there is a scarcity of water. The question is, who should be denied water in such situations? In the Phad System, the area for irrigation is earmarked in relation to average annual rainfall. Some areas (unassured irrigation areas) are irrigated only in the years of good rainfall, and therefore, the farmers who cultivate this area are aware that they get water once in a few years. This area of unassured irrigation is not interspersed with the assured area. This is a very practical arrangement.

There are years when the average water flows are also not available. To some extent, this is predictable early in the season, and hence, cropping plan is suitably adjusted. When the scarcity of water is noticed late in the season, the water is rationed by extending the irrigation interval, thus ensuring equity among all the members.

In most of these systems, there is an idle length of the canal, a few kilometer between the *bandhara* and the command area, generally in the boundary of another village. There are some areas which can be commanded by the canal in this length. In the past, there were occasions when water was diverted upstream for unauthorized irrigation. In such cases, on an amicable basis, one day (or half a day) was allotted to such a village for drawing the water from the canal. This situation arose because of the topography, and a practical solution was accepted perhaps because of the threat of potential damage that could be done by these upstream farmers from other villages.

Another cause for conflict relates to the amount of water to be applied on each individual farm. This situation is dealt with in the Phad System by assigning farm water application function to the irrigation staff. As they are not interested in any particular farms nor own any land, they are expected to be fair in application of water to all the farms.

With such institutional arrangements made to avoid recurring situations of conflict, it is not difficult for the committee to deal with the occasional conflicts. Non-participation in canal maintenance and taking water out of turn are penalized by way of fine. Fines are paid expeditiously and the matter is settled.

GENERAL OBSERVATIONS

In an irrigation system, as in any man-managed system, three activities are most important: allocation of scarce resources, system maintenance and conflict management. The system would operate smoothly only when institutional and organizational elements relate to key rules, and roles of participating individuals and groups are accepted by the beneficiaries. It appears that the indigenous Phad System, as evolved over the centuries, has shouldered the responsibility for the smooth performance of these functions, through institutional safeguards.

The cohesive force binding the group is the common concern. How strongly this cohesive force operates is illustrated by the fact that despite political and local rivalries, the farmers' groups have been working harmoniously as far as water management and distribution is concerned. In a small community, social and group pressures operate successfully, as everyone knows that any infringement is likely to rebound on oneself.

Though the common concern provides the motivating force, stability to the groups is imparted through rule formulation which has to be equitable to gain acceptance of the members. Though there is little information on how these rules were framed initially, its codification and incorporation in the land revenue records in 1920s gave the needed sanctity. Further, a perusal of these documents shows that the principle of fairness to all members permeates the rules and hence its acceptability became convincing. Being a written record, it is known to all the farmers and they are conscious of their roles as well as responsibilities.

The command areas being small and the water resource being within easy accessibility of all the members, an acceptable interpretation of the key rules is easy to arrive at. The jurisdiction of the group is limited to a village; in case the topographical factors dictate inclusion of areas of the upstream village, the day-to-day management aspect is separated. A specified share of time is allocated to this area, but management is left to the group of the upstream village. This emphasizes, perhaps, the difficulty in managing two villages in the same command by one group.

Parenthetically, it may be noted that the inclusion of upstream village in the command was dictated by its nuisance value. But, the solution arrived at was more practical.

Similarly, roles of the members and the *Panchas* are clearly defined, in respect of all the three activities. To avoid conflicts among members, the task of water application was handed over to the irrigation staff, appointed by and responsible to *Panchas*, but paid by individual members. This arrangement did away with the maintenance of any salary records. Of course, there were situations when members refused to pay their shares to irrigation staff, but group pressures were normally sufficient to remedy the matters. In extreme cases, as it happened in 1940s, the matter went to the judiciary. Here too, the court judgement went in favour of the groups, and seemingly, the system derived further strength.

It appears that tradition has played an important role for the success of Phad group. However, in reality, it is the well-defined rules and roles of individuals and the *Panchas* that have kept the system going, aided by the environmental factors such as relative stability and reliability of the water source.

FUTURE

Though these farmers' organizations have functioned well, especially in the 14 upstream *bandharas*, their future is uncertain in view of two major developments in the surroundings. For utilizing the available river waters, the government has built storage reservoirs, affecting the post-monsoon flows downstream, where *bandharas* are built. Secondly, a sugar factory has come up in the area, increasing the demand for sugarcane, a water intensive crop.

On the Panjhra River, a new weir with a canal system was built at Sayyadnagar in 1952, to draw supplies from the run-of-the-river. In the 1970s, two storage dams were built upstream, Panjhra dam on the Panjhra River and Malangaon dam on its tributary, the Kan. These schemes have their own command areas, served by extensive canal system. The whole river is notified and the *bandharas* are declared as first class irrigation works.[1] However, the distribution of this allocation among the several *bandharas* and provision for implementing mechanism were not done. The inlets to the canals at the *bandharas* are still unregulated. The regulation of river flows without a matching regulation of flows into the *bandhara* canals, has affected the situation. Inter-*bandhara* conflicts have now surfaced. Even though a part of the storage is earmarked for the *bandharas* for ensuring reliability of water flows, the releases from the reservoir are now felt to be inadequate. As perceived by the farmers on the *bandharas*, the river flows now available are less reliable than in the past, and more and more rationing of water is now required in the Phad System. This is reflected in the elongated rotational intervals. This change in the water regime poses a threat to the group.

NOTES

1. In the state's irrigation parlance, once the river is notified, any person/group drawing water from the river requires the government's permission. Further irrigation works include major and medium systems and the operation and the maintenance is the responsibility of the government irrigation agency. Second class works are small (less than 100 ha.) with no storage for ensuring reliable supplies and for which it is too costly to engage separate staff on government account. Among second class works, repairs, maintenance and operation are left to beneficiaries. Consequently, the irrigation charges are considerably less compared to those on the first class works functioning. In this connection, it is interesting to note that the department has to requisition police patrols to check the tapping of waters in the sequential *bandharas*. The river supplies drinking water to Dhule town, downstream of the *bandharas*. This is considered as first priority. These waters, though regulated from the dam, can be easily tapped by the Phad who are water thirsty, hence the need for patrol.

The declaration of *bandharas* as first class works had led to considerable enhancement of irrigation rates to be paid to the government. Earlier, the rates were nominal and merged with land revenue. This extra burden, without any compensating services, plus the rising maintenance costs have made the irrigation benefits quite costly. The groups are still functioning, but there is a clamour for government support for maintenance. The argument is that the financial returns from irrigated agriculture are not commensurate with the costs to be incurred. In a way, this is a valid argument, as the reliability has been affected after the dam construction on the upstream. No rules are framed on the allocation of waters to each *bandhara* and its implementation. On an adhoc basis, some maintenance is now carried under Employment Guarantee Scheme (EGS). But the time has come to systematize the whole institutional arrangement in tune with the changing environments. This has to be done at the governmental level, as there is no federation of the *bandhara* groups to impose discipline. The second external happening is the establishment of a sugar factory in the area in the early 1970s. Consequently, there is an increasing demand for sugarcane on canal waters. The resulting conflict does not augur well for the functioning of the Phad system. The Phad groups are anxious to put as much area in their command to sugarcane crop, while the river water flows are now regulated and hence sufficient supplies are not available. In the earlier days, the shortage of waters at the *bandharas* could be blamed on nature or heavy withdrawals on the upstream *bandharas;* but now, the group blames the government. The type of information and communication system that needs to be evolved to tackle these new problems has to be studied. It appears that the changed environment is posing a threat to this age-old management system. Unless the physical system is modernized, water measurement devices introduced, and farmers trained in the new crop technologies and water-saving irrigation systems, the Phad system, at least in the Panjhra river, is likely to fade. Guidelines for dam water allocation among urban water supply, canal farmers and the Phad farmers have to be evolved and an acceptable implementation machinery set up for monitoring and control.

17

POND SYSTEMS IN PANVEL TALUKA AND THEIR CONSERVATION

(Traditional Water Harvesting in Panvel)

Makarand Pendse

ABSTRACT

Panvel *Taluka* of Maharashtra has a large number of ponds whose main source of water is rain. Most of the ponds are shallow with a less storage capacity. To make full use of pond water and also to get clean water, wells have been dug either on the periphery or within the boundary of these ponds. At some places ponds were also found excavated at some height so as to allow sedimentation of dirt. Ponds are used for other purposes like fish cultivation, lotus production, etc. Due to a number of reasons, these ponds have now fallen into disuse. An example is the Ballaleswar/Wadale pond which has been neglected to a great extent. Immediate measures need to be taken to repair and conserve these ponds.

INTRODUCTION

Traditionally, water harvesting systems are represented predominantly by tank and pond systems. Though tanks are products of a long period of evolution and adaptation, there have been no major innovations in the technology, design, etc. related to them or in the way they are managed.

In this context, our club 'Nisarga Mitra' conducted a survey of a few tanks in Panvel and its surrounding area with the following objectives:

(a) Study of floral and faunal values related to tanks and study of pond eco-system.
(b) Historical evolution of ponds and utilization of ponds in earlier days vis-á-vis present days.
(c) Present status of pond system.
(d) Understanding the pond water supply system of earlier days in comparison with prevailing water supply schemes in these areas.

This paper is based on the information collected during field visits and also on available records.

Most of the tanks in Panvel *taluka* can be classified as 'rain-fed tanks' as the main source of water is rain. All of them are community resources and were built by the communities themselves through collective efforts. As the water holding capacity of the soil and the rocks in these areas are not very good because of the basaltic formation, such ponds which have been excavated on plain terrain act as major water holding bodies.

Typically, most of the ponds are shallow water bodies with low storage capacities, the average depth not exceeding 10-12 ft. Many villages have at least one tank. Almost on every tank, a religious structure like a temple (invariably of Siva) or a mosque and in some cases crematoriums are observed. The funeral rituals are also regularly performed near these tanks.

The management of the tanks is decentralized with the village community deciding matters such as laying down rules, repair and maintenance, etc. The tanks have normally one filling during the monsoons. To ensure proper utilization of water, various steps have been taken:

1. In some cases, wells were dug on the peripheral areas of the ponds as the water from the tanks could not be used for drinking purposes. Pond water is diverted to the wells where it gets filtered through the layer of sand. The wells are generally owned by two bodies – those near the tank are owned by the public and the other wells on the periphery of the tank are privately owned.
2. At some places, wells were found within the boundary of the pond (e.g., wells in the village Kiravali in Panvel *Taluka*). The water of these wells was used for agricultural purposes.
3. In the village of Apte, the pond is situated at a certain height from the ground level so as to allow sedimentation of dirt at the bottom of the pond. The trapped water is then taken further down, through a well-built channel made of stone, to a chain of very small storage tanks. Through copper pipelines, the water is led into a comparatively bigger storage tank where it can be used by the villagers.

As regards the maintenance of ponds, the individual ponds are controlled by the local *gram panchayats* or the municipality. In Panvel and the surrounding areas, ponds are being given on quarterly lease by the municipality or the *gram panchayats* to local residents.

These ponds are being used for various purposes like fish cultivation and lotus plant production (for its roots and the fruits). The water is used by people and animals. The ponds control temperature of the surrounding areas and also have considerable social values.

CASE STUDY OF BALLALESHWAR POND (WADALE POND)

This pond is located to the north of Panvel city on the Bombay-Pune highway. It covers an area of 31 acres (earlier it was about 120 acres).

The history of the ponds in Panvel town dates back to about 250-300 years. The *Shatsanvatsarik Grantha* of Panvel mentions that during Vasai war between Peshwas and

Britishers, a confrontation took place at Panvel. Chimaji Appa, the great Maratha sardar, halted at Panvel along with his platoon with an intention to loot Panvel and collect money for the war. One Balaji Bapat, a noted citizen, made arrangements for the money. Pleased by this, Chimaji Appa constructed a pond at Panvel to cater to the needs of its residents. The Wadale pond was thus constructed about 250 years ago with the help of the Peshwas.

The Ballaleshwar pond (earlier known as Wadale pond) had a typical water management system. The pond was divided into four sections called *ghats*. The Bail Ghat was mainly used for tending cattle. Another *ghat*, Tulsi Ghat was used by the residents of Panvel for fetching drinking water. Names of the other two ghats are not known, but they were being used by other communities. This system of water management continued even in the 19th century, and the records show that provisions were made for the maintenance and repair of the ponds in years 1880-81 and 1884-85.

Water accumulating in this pond helps to maintain the ground water level in the surrounding areas and thus ensures water availability in the wells even in summers.

CONSERVATION MEASURES

Ever since water started being supplied through pipes, the residents of Panvel as well as the municipality started neglecting this pond. The threats and disturbances to the pond are described below.

1. As this pond is located near the National Highway, heavy traffic, pollution and noise disturb the pond eco-system to a large extent.
2. The privately-owned land surrounding the pond has been sold to builders, and land filling has already started. Sky-high buildings and commercial complexes will come up shortly in this area. This would no doubt disturb the pond.
3. Sewage from the surrounding areas is being led into the pond, thereby causing water pollution. Water hyacinth, which is an indicator of pollution, has spread over some areas.
4. In addition to this, the loose soil falling from the sides is slowly filling the pond and the pond is getting converted into a marshy land. The present area of the pond is almost one-fourth of its original area.
5. The pond is also being used as a dumping ground. Garbage and litter is thrown into it. This has made the pond extremely dirty.

PRESENT SCENARIO

Unfortunately, these tanks are at present in a state of neglect owing to the ever increasing population and haphazard development. The sewage water entering the tanks is causing heavy water pollution, and has posed a threat to the birds and the plant life. Besides, it has converted some ponds into marshy lands and in this way a few ponds have already vanished. Garbage and litter are being regularly dumped in the tanks inviting diseases like malaria.

Survey has revealed that the absence of trees around the tanks is causing silting and the soil which thus accumulates inside the tanks reduces the depth of the tanks thereby affecting their water-holding capacities. However, for some tanks walls have been built.

CONSERVATION ASPECTS

A strong action group is required to protect these deteriorating ponds. Experts should find ways to control the water hyacinth which is a major weed causing these ponds to die. The earlier efforts of controlling hyacinth by bacterial control named VEEVIL, need to be further augmented in order to make it more effective. Property rights have to be elaborated in the context of these water bodies so as to control encroachments. Local support groups and action groups should be formed at every *taluka* level in order to put pressure on the government authorities to look into the matter and conserve this age-old, yet important water harvesting system. Awareness campaigns can help to create public opinion which used to work effectively and efficiently in earlier days. Collective efforts for de-silting the ponds and cleaning must be made. Taking into consideration the beautiful bird life which is a part of the pond ecology, the ponds can be converted into aquatic sanctuaries.

18

CONSERVATION OF TRADITIONAL WATER SUPPLY OF BURHANPUR TOWN

S.S. Raghuwanshi

ABSTRACT

During the regime of the Mughals, emperor Shahjahan had camped for a long time in Burhanpur which was called the 'Gateway of South India'. An army of about two lakh soldiers was stationed at Burhanpur to conquer the southern territory from Maratha rulers. The Mughal ruler conceived a system of water supply for military population that would be safe from the activities of the enemies. A Persian geologist named Tabkutul Arz investigated the re-charge potential of Satpura Valley in AD 1615. Ground water flowing towards Tapti River from Satpura ranges was tapped and stored in underground tunnels having ventilating shafts to a common sump called Jali Karanj and was supplied to township and camps through earthenware and dressed stone pipes. The system still supplies nearly one million litres of water to Burhanpur town.

INTRODUCTION

In the early part of 17th century, the Mughal emperor Shahjahan constructed eight underground water supply systems near Burhanpur for military and civilian population of around two lakhs. Out of eight systems, two got destroyed after the Mughal Period, three continued to supply water to Burhanpur and the rest to the nearby village of Bahadurpur. The ground water of Satpura basin was tapped with the expert assistance of a Persian geologist named Tabkutul Arz at Bhandaras, namely, Mul Bhandara, Sukha Bhandara, Chintaharan and Khuni Bhandara on the north-west side of Burhanpur. The *bhandaras* were constructed in rectangular shapes to collect ground water which was taken to Burhanpur town through underground tunnels up to distributing sump named Jali Karanj. The connecting tunnel was provided with ventilating shafts of 1.2 to 1.8 m diameter, placed about 20 m apart and constructed out of brick masonry with lime mortar. The system is tapping ground water from 30 km distance and the depth varies from 30 m to 2 m below ground. At a common junction, water from Mul Bhandara, Chintaharan Bhandara and Khuni Bhandara was collected from where it was distributed to Burhanpur town through clay ware and dressed stone pipes. Later on, the clay ware and stone pipes were replaced by cast iron pipes with pumping arrangements by the Municipal Corporation of Burhanpur. The monumental system is still intact, though with declining discharge due to drilling of deep tube-wells in the basin and deforestation activities.

THE PROBLEM AND ANALYSIS

The system of water supply, conceived about four hundred years back, is still functioning and catering to the demand of about one million litres of water per day. There is no maintenance of *bhandaras, kundies,* conveying tunnels and traditional monumental structures by the local municipal corporation. The physical site appraisal of this system was done (Sihorwala and Raghuwanshi, 1991) and a detailed conservation plan was submitted to the State Housing & Environment Ministry. The following problems were observed:

(i) The brick masonry structures of shafts were damaged due to bullock carts plying nearby, and the arched tunnels show at places loss of lime mortar and holes in masonry due to ageing.
(ii) The parapets of *kundies* have been broken, and sewage and drainwater is entering the potable water system through ground level *kundies.*
(iii) Public toilets have been constructed adjoining the *kundies* causing pollution of ground water and accidental re-charge into the system.
(iv) The obstruction to water flow due to collapse of brick mortar, refuse dumps through *kundies,* and ingress of pollution may convert the system into a non-functional ruin, pits and drains.

At present the condition of these structures is excellent and water is being supplied to the town of Burhanpur through the same system. The system was networked through 150 sq. km catchment area of watershed in the basin having thick forest with tree roots deeply penetrating into the overburden which is conducive to re-charge. The soil beneath is composed of pebbles and boulders having good re-charge potential below 30 m to 50 m depth. In the present days, the population explosion in this region has been responsible for over-exploitation of natural resources. The commercialization of agriculture with illicit use of chemical fertilizers is another contributing factor for dwindling water resources and pollution built up as far as ground water resource is concerned. Fast pace of urbanization, industrialization and de-forestation is not commensurate with the eco-sustainable developments. Lack of peoples' input in common and public systems and the ineffectiveness of democratic system are also responsible for sustainable environment of water resources of the country.

In Madhya Pradesh, the National River Conservation Programme for the rivers like Narmada, Betwa, Wainganga, Kshipra, Khan, Chambal and Tapti near Burhanpur has been taken up by the Housing and Environment Department on the lines of Ganga River Action Plan. The government should notify the plan and line of conservation to concerned people and industries which have been responsible for pollution. It should also help to create a mass awareness about problems and traditional and conventional approaches for solutions at the grass-root level. Analogous to NRCP, national traditional systems of water supply at important public, tourism and pilgrimage centres should be identified.

In addition to giving importance to religion, history, culture, technology, education and functional utility, priority needs to be given to the conservation and preservation of national traditional systems of water supply. Apart from preservation, it is recommended that the present traditional water system in Burhanpur be declared an archaeological monument.

SUGGESTIONS

(i) State/Central Government should take decisions of conserving the traditional system in Burhanpur with the formal consent of the Municipal Corporation.

(ii) Plans of conservation, detailed survey and restoration may be finalized by a committee comprising public health engineer, architect, archaeologist, chief municipal officer, administrator of Burhanpur M.C., district collector and representatives of Housing and Environment Department.

(iii) Allocations available with the Housing and Environment department may be claimed for the conservation of Burhanpur systems.

(iv) Plan of conservation should include physical upgradation of components, environmental upgradation of basins, watershed management of catchment area, improving water withdrawal techniques and evaluation of impact assessments for review or for further updating.

NOTES AND REFERENCES

Sihorwala, T.A. & S.S. Raghuwanshi, 1991, Conservation of historic water supply of Burhanpur town from Khuni Bhandara, *Journal of Indian Water Works Association*, Mumbai, pp. 24-28.

19

TANKS OF KOHLIS IN GOND KINGDOM (Traditional Water Harvesting Systems in Bhandara District of Maharashtra)

Manish Rajankar and Yogini Dolke

ABSTRACT

This is a study of traditional water harvesting systems in Bhandara district of Maharashtra where tanks are the most ancient and major source of irrigation. Today there are about 44000 tanks irrigating about 80 per cent of the land. Most of these tanks were constructed 250 to 300 years ago. Tanks grew in number for supplementing water required for rice fields, besides for fresh water fisheries.

The tanks were built with traditional knowledge and simple techniques. These structures were need-based and within the capacity of local people to address the maintenance and repair requirements. Thus, the inhabitants were not dependent on external agencies for such works. The paper emphasizes that the traditional practices should find wider application.

INTRODUCTION

Traditional systems are specific responses to ecology and culture in which they evolved. They have benefitted from collective human experience since time immemorial and in that lies their biggest strength.

Water harvesting is an age-old concept in India. During our field visits to Bhandara district, we could observe the forest clad ridges, valley sides and cultivated valley floors interspersed with numerous tanks. Large number of tanks in this region provoked us to undertake a study of the unique traditional knowledge of lake building in this region. This paper is based on the visits to about 40 small and big tanks in the Bhandara district; the details of a few are given below.

LOCATION OF BHANDARA DISTRICT

Bhandara district of Maharashtra is situated in the Wainganga basin and lies between

20° 39′ and 21° 38′ N and 79° 27′ and 80° 42′ E. It is surrounded by Balaghat district in the north, Rajanandgaon district (both in Madhya Pradesh) in the east, Chandrapur and Gadchiroli districts in the south and Nagpur district (all in Maharashtra) in the west. The district is drained by the river Wainganga, the most important and the biggest river flowing through the district, and the Bagh (one of its principal tributaries). The area of the district is 9280 km and its population, according to the 1981 census, is 1,837,577. In terms of area, it ranks 21st and in population it ranks 17th among the 31 districts of Maharashtra. Thus, Bhandara is one of the smallest districts in the state in respect of area and population.

In its geographic setting, the district offers a marked contrast to the rest of the state. The rocks are dissimilar to those which underlie most parts of Maharashtra. The soils are highly varied and formed of the tropical sub-humid weathering of crystalline metamorphic and igneous rocks. Most of the cultivable soils belong to the morand and sihar types, both of which are light and slightly acidic in nature. The sihar is best for rice cultivation while the morand soil is suitable for growing rabi crops like wheat, linseed and kharif crops like jowar.

AGRICULTURE AND IRRIGATION

The main crops grown in the district are paddy, wheat and sugarcane. In every *tehsil* of Bhandara district, the proportion of irrigated area is considerably higher than the state average. In fact, of all the districts of Maharashtra, Bhandara has the largest proportion (approximately 410,000 ha.) of irrigated land.

Tanks are the most ancient and major source of irrigation and are found throughout the district. They were a characteristic feature of Indian agricultural economy in the past and even today their importance in the district has not diminished. There are 43,381 tanks irrigating 78 per cent of the net irrigated area in the district. The district has 238 large tanks with a size of 10 hectares and above; 3007 tanks with size between 10 to 4 hectares; 7534 tanks between 1 to 2 hectares and 19,313 tanks below 1 hectare. On an average, 10 to 50 acres of area is irrigated by a single tank.

HISTORICAL BACKGROUND

The Bhandara district falls within the boundaries of Deogarh, Mandla and Chanda kingdom of the Gonds. In order to strengthen and spread his kingdom, the Gond king Hirshah (16th century) released a *farman* which said,

> A person who clears a patch of forest for colonizing will become a Sardar and Zamindar of that area. A person who shall construct a tank will be awarded the land irrigated by such tank as a reward.

Such *farmans* encouraged the colonizing of villages and construction of tanks in this region.

A few Marathi castes of cultivators are found in the Wainganga Valley. The Kohli is an important caste which enjoys the credit of having constructed a large number of irrigation reservoirs/tanks. The water is used for irrigating rice and sugarcane, the latter being the favourite crop of the Kohlis. Kohlis respected a person who owned maximum number of tanks.

IMPORTANCE OF TANKS

Most of the tanks in the district were constructed more than 300 years ago. In certain cases, forest areas were allotted to people for habitation and cultivation through an enterprising person (agent) known as 'Patil' (*malguzar*), whose duty was to colonize villages by bringing families from various places. These villagers cultivated rice crop which failed frequently because of lack of timely rains. Tanks were therefore built as a supplementary source for irrigating rice fields. The need of expanding cultivation over the years led to the construction of more and more tanks. Besides irrigation, these tanks are also being extensively used for fresh water fisheries which is a source of livelihood for fishermen community residing in the area.

TYPES OF TANKS

THE TANKS ARE OF TWO TYPES:

1. Large tanks which are constructed on the hills, particularly in the Gaikhuri range of Navegaon and Palasgaon hills, belong to the first category. The catchment area of these tanks ranges from 1 to 40 km. These tanks have been constructed by the Kohli caste without any sophisticated technical and engineering knowledge.

Village Name	Number of Tanks	Name of the Tank	Area of the Tank	Area Irrigated
1. Navegaon	One	Navegaonbandh	20 sq. km.	10,000 acres
2. Shivnibandh	One	Shivnibandh	5 sq. km.	4,630 acres
3. Shiregaon	One	Shiregaonbandh	340 acres	560 acres
4. Chandpur	One	Chandpurtalao	N.A.	N.A.

2. The tanks of the second type are more in number and of a much smaller size. These are generally constructed at the foothill or on the slope of the valley by raising an earthen embankment of a few meter height at its lower end. They do not carry water during summers or in the years of low rainfall. Nevertheless, they are an important source of irrigation in the Bhandara district. Besides irrigation, these tanks are used for fresh water fisheries.

Village Name	Number of Tanks	Name of the Tank	Area of the Tank	Area Irrigated
1. Sakoli	Two	Navtalao	40 acres Gaotalao	Total 227 acres 100 acres
2. Khandala	One	Gaotalao	196 acres	310 acres
3. Kosbi	One	Gaotalao	104 acres	400 acres

Village Name	Number of Tanks	Name of the Tank	Area of the Tank	Area Irrigated
4. Parsodisadak	One		32 acres	150 acres
5. Koharitola	Four	Mothatalao	70 acres Navtalao Khunitalao Kutantalao	Total 450 acres 40 acres 40 acres 22 acres
6. Khadipar	Two	Mothatalao	N.A. Lahantalao	Total 634 acres
7. Chictola	One	Gaontalao	97 acres	301 acres
8. Kohlirengepar	Three	Mothatalao	85 acres Navtalao Chichtalao	300 acres 30 acres 175 acres 30 acres 100 acres
9. Baradkinhi	One	Gaotalao	80 acres	310 acres
10. Pavni	Two	Gaotalao	42 acres Kanaharibodi	Total 250 acres 32 acre
11. Seloti	One	Gaotalao	25 acres	250 acres
12. Murpar	One	Rantalao	100 acres	247 acres
13. Sonegaon	One	Gaotalao	60 acres	215 acres
14. Chikhla	Five	Bazartalao	9 acres Pashsatalao Hivratalao Gaontalao Rantalao	Total 470 acres 12 acres 13.5 acres 7 acres 10 acres
15. Rajapur	One	Gaontalao	40 acres	150 acres
16. Nakadongri	Three	Futkyatalao	N.A. Rantalao Gaontalao	Total 305 acres N.A. N.A.
17. Aashti	Four talao	— Forty-six boris	—	Total 1000 acres
18. Gangazari	Two	Gangazari Tank	22 acres Majitpurtalao	Total 350 acres 41 acres

It is interesting to note that the temple of Bhuraji Deo is found on the bund of many of these tanks, for example the temple on Shregaon bund. This god is believed to protect the bund from natural calamities and enemies. The temple of Bhimsen is also found on some of the bunds, for instance, Navegaon bund and Parsodisadak tank. During drought and delayed monsoons, people apply cowdung on this god because it is believed that this would annoy the god and to get rid of the cowdung, the god would order the clouds to shower upon him.

The Navegaon bund, which is built between two hillocks, is 330 ft. in length while the area of its reservoir is 15 sq. km. As the area is bowl-shaped, water has little space to escape. It is said that Kolu Patel, who built the great tank of Navegaon bund, selected the site by observing the level of dust and grass particles on trees and the surrounding hills.

TECHNIQUES

The bund was raised in stages using black cotton soil (*Kankar mati*) which is hard and has a remarkable water holding capacity. Initially, a small bund was constructed. The water trapped in this small bund not only hardened the bund but also provided strength to it. This process also decided the height of bund to be raised in the consequent years. The eventual height of the bund was finalized only after careful observations for years. At some places, where water pressure on the bund was high, the foundation was made by using stones and a mixture of soil, stones, lime and jaggery.

The mechanism used for drawing water from the reservoir for irrigation is called 'Tudum' or 'Monga'. Different mechanisms are employed depending on the size of the tank. For a small tank or a *bodi*, a straight tunnel across the base of the bund is constructed using stones. A log is placed at the mouth of this tunnel and plastered with clay. It is removed whenever water is required. For medium and large tanks, a straight tunnel is constructed across the base of the bund using stones over which a stair-like (*monghad*) structure is constructed with a hole (*daccha*) in each step. The size of the tank usually determines the number of steps to be constructed. The holes are blocked with either a stone slab or a wooden log and carefully plastered with clay. Water could be drawn by removing the stone slab or the wooden log. In another method, a hollow tree trunk is placed across the base of the tank, connected by a vertically planted hollow tree trunk having holes at regular distance. These holes are plugged using wooden logs which are removed when water is to be sucked from the tank. This method requires frequent repairs as the tree trunk gets decayed very soon. Very few *tudum* of this kind are found these days because of the stringent forest laws. It is observed that this technique is still used, but bricks have now replaced the earlier hollow tree trunks.

Plenty of care was taken while constructing a tank and related structures. If water is let out through the *tudum* directly, the canal would be destroyed due to the force of water. *Kutans* were constructed adjoining big tanks to minimize the force of water released from tanks.

All the nullahs and streams in the catchment area were diverted towards the bund to increase the amount of water coming into the tanks. In case of excess water flow, one more tank was constructed downstream in which the water coming from the *pharas* or *pohar*, i.e., waste wier was trapped to optimize the utilization of the available water.

MALGUZARI SYSTEM

There were 16 anna Malguzari systems in the Bhandara district. A *malguzar* was a person appointed by the king to collect revenue and to look into the overall administration of an area. He had to deposit the entire revenue (fixed by the king himself) with the king. In case of surplus revenue, *malguzar* would make profit. On the contrary, during bad seasons, he had to bear the loss. To ensure that loss is not incurred, he used to supervise personally the maintenance of tanks and related activities which minimised the failure of crops resulting from water shortage.

Any damage to the tanks, canals or the outlets was repaired by the villagers under the supervision of the *malguzar*. The distribution of water was handled by a committee of *malguzars* along with some respected people from the village. The committee decided on the distribution of water as per its availability, which was to be obeyed by all the cultivators. In addition, the committee appointed a person called *pankar* whose duty was to release water and ensure that the decision taken by the committee was implemented properly. The *pankar* was preferably a landless labourer having no interest in using water for his own benefit. Every cultivator had to give his share of crop to the *pankar*, and in case of default, the *pankar* would contact the cultivators and recover his share of crop from them. When found unfaithful, the *pankar* was removed from his post and denied all his rights and privileges. Anybody found guilty of damaging the canal or the tank was denied his share of water for that year. In case he availed his turn of water, he was fined in cash or kind. If he failed to pay the fine, he was denied his share of water next year also.

Those cultivators who laboured in the construction, maintenance and de-silting of tanks/canals were provided water for their crops free of cost. The silt (*pakan*) dug out of the tank bed was utilized as a fertilizer in the fields. The *malguzar* used to decide the de-silting exercise which would take place once in 3 or 4 years. However, any cultivator was free to dig up silt as and when required with the permission of the *malguzar*.

The tanks were formally maintained and repaired by the beneficiaries whose efforts were co-ordinated by the *malguzars*. Thus, services of all sections of the village were solicited in the construction, repair and maintenance of the tanks and canals. These efforts were compensated by allotting land and free water to these people in the command area. Systematic rules were laid down regarding the utilization of water. The people living in the surrounding areas shouldered the entire responsibility of taking care of the tank as the tanks were the essential life-support structures. Tanks were not just structures but a living system in itself.

ABOLITION OF PROPRIETARY RIGHTS ACT 1950

Abolition of Proprietary Rights Act was enacted in 1950 as a result of which rights over the tanks were transformed to the Irrigation Department and the Zila Parishad. These government departments were entrusted with the responsibility of repairs and maintenance of the tanks. They were not equipped to address the task of managing such a large number of tanks. Consequently, the local people had to suffer.

In late 1960s, the government machinery took up the task of adopting modern techniques, and replaced most of the traditional local structures of these tanks to enhance the water holding capacities and to improve the water distribution system. Somehow, because of the shortage of man-power in the government machinery, the new structures could not be maintained properly. Moreover, the villagers lost the traditional bonds with these structures since they were not associated with the people in the government machinery in charge of maintaining these tanks. Prior to the Malguzari Abolition Act, the *malguzars* supervized the repairs and maintenance of the structures and the water distribution system. With the abolition of Malguzari system, the involvement of local people in the maintenance and repair works and water management came to an end.

The alienation of people from tank and related activities has resulted in the deterioration of the condition of these tanks throughout the district. People find themselves helpless in the maintenance of the complicated structures constructed by the government machinery. At many places, new structures have become non-functional, and people have resorted to the old traditional technique of water harvesting and distribution. In some pockets, people have realized the importance of old structures and have started installing the locally known techniques of water harvesting and have reduced their dependence on external agency.

PRESENT SITUATION

Official figures indicate that 78 per cent of the land under cultivation is being irrigated by tanks. Before the Malguzari Abolition Act, these tanks were under the control of *malguzars*. Majority of the agricultural lands were then owned by the *malguzars*. But, now with the Land Ceiling Act, the *malguzars* have lost proprietary rights on tanks and also most of their agricultural fields. The present situation is such that the majority of the benefit of irrigation is enjoyed by the *malguzars* and the small farmer and the landless labourers have been deprived of these benefits. Thus, two distinct classes of people have emerged, one of the *malguzars* having wealth and power, and the other is of their dependents, i.e., landless labourers and small farmers living in abject poverty.

CONCLUSION

Tanks in Bhandara district were built using the traditional knowledge and techniques. The expertise required to build such tanks and distribution systems were available locally and any kind of emergency was addressed immediately to minimize the loss. Moreover, these structures were need-based and within the capacities of the local people to address the maintenance and repair requirements of related structures. Therefore, the technologies adopted were simple and could be utilized by local inhabitants. That is how the local community was not dependent on external agencies for tank building, repairs and maintenance.

Traditional practices ought to find wider promotion, acceptance and application. In the area of water management and agriculture, one of our greatest drawbacks has been the devaluation of traditional knowledge and practices, which was an outcome of centuries of experiments and experience.

20

STRATEGIES TO PROTECT THE DWINDLING DOMESTIC WATER SUPPLY : KUTCH DISTRICT

K.C.B. Raju

ABSTRACT

Kutch district, accounting for one-fourth of the geographical area and sixty per cent of the drought prone area of Gujarat, is facing acute drinking water supply problem. The resource of the district is entirely dependent on the precipitation which is low and erratic. Water supply to many townships and villages located in Banni and in the border area is being met from the tube-wells located at far away places. In the central part, water is supplied to some villages in tankers. Over-exploitation of ground water resources in many *talukas* and recurring droughts have resulted in the decline of water levels and deterioration of water quality. The only way to protect these drinking water supply sources is to re-charge these depleted aquifers by harvesting the rainwater. A brief summary of rainwater harvesting for re-charging the Manchar aquifers in the coastal area of Mandvi and Mundra *talukas* by Shree Vivekananda Research and Training Institute is given in this paper.

INTRODUCTION

Kutch district of Gujarat is entirely an independent entity regarding its water resources as both its surface and ground resources depend on the precipitation it receives over the area. It has a geographical area of 45,652 sq. km and forms a crescent-shaped peninsula between the Rann of Kutch and Gulf of Kutch and has a coastline of 313 km. It has a semi-arid type of climate and accounts for nearly 60 per cent of the drought prone area of the state. It has 10 towns and 912 villages.

The district receives an average annual rainfall of about 330 mm from the south-west monsoons. The average rainy days are about 15 with high coefficient of variation. Droughts are a common feature and they extend continuously for 3 to 5 years. In the recent past, the year 1987 was worse with almost no rainfall followed by the year 1993. During 1994 it received more than 1000 mm rainfall in many *talukas* with a maximum of 1200 mm in Abodesa.

There are 97 river systems originating from the central flanks and flowing towards north to the Rann or south to the Gulf of Kutch. The rivers are ephemeral carrying water for a few hours in a day or a few days in a year during the south-west monsoon. The area is underlain by the rocks of both marine and non-marine origin and volcanic rocks.

WATER RESOURCES

It is estimated that the available surface water resource is of the order 390 MCM, of which, 330 MCM (85 per cent), as estimated in 1991, by NWRD is utilized allowing another 60 MCM for further harvesting.

There are 20 medium irrigation projects with live storage capacity of 281 MCM. The total irrigation potential of these projects is 40, 366 ha. (CCA) and the irrigable command is 20824 ha. However, the average is only about 16.2 per cent of the CCA as these schemes have only 37 per cent filling of the designed capacity.

One hundred and sixty-two minor irrigation schemes had been completed till 1993 with a live storage capacity of 252 MCM with CCA of 32989 ha. and the averge was 25.6 per cent of the CCA due to average filling of 50 per cent.

GROUND WATER

The total ground water resource estimated in 1991 is of the order of 517.07 MCM and utilizable ground water resource is 439.50 MCM. The gross draft is 346.50 MCM, i.e., 67 per cent has been developed. However, at the *taluka* level, thc estimated development level shows substantial variations. Of the nine *talukas*, official estimates show that ground water resources are over-exploited in two *talukas*, Bhachau (109 per cent) and Anjar (113 per cent), fully exploited in Mandvi *taluka*, and full exploitation is approaching in three *talukas*, namely, Rapar, Mundra and Nakhatrana.

There are about 30,000 wells, dug-cum-bores and about 200 tube-wells in the district. More than 85 per cent of the irrigated agriculture is under well irrigation. Even in the worst drought years of 1987 and 1993, cropped area under well irrigation was substantial thus leading to dwindling of the ground water resources.

Majority of the drinking water supply schemes are drawn from ground water resources. There are only three surface water sources in the district.

DEMAND

The GWRDC has estimated the requirement of water supply, as 13,855 MCM of which, 40 LPCD is needed for a rural population of 9,456 lakhs and 19,699 MCM & 140 LPCD for an urban population of 3,855 lakh. This is the figure projected by them for AD 2001*, considerimg a 15 per cent increase in the population.

The above assumption of 40 LPCD for the rural population and 151 decennial increase does not appear to be logical. In Kutch, the livestock population is more than the human population. During 1981 to 1991, the increase in human population was about 20 per cent. Similarly, the demand estimated for industrial requirement was very low. A large population of the rural areas of Kutch stay abroad with very good business and their

* By now the figure has changed.

– Editors

village houses have all the amenities of a modern urban house and some have even swimming pools. So, the demand of water for the rural population is much higher than that of the assumed 40 LPCD. It is, therefore, better to assume the national standards of 70 LPCD including the cattle population and the rural population. Since many posh hotels have come up and the floating population is also quite heavy, the urban requirement may be taken as 180 LPCD.

Taking the above into consideration the requirement of water supply for domestic purposes will be as follows:

Rural Population in Lakhs	LPCD	MCM
9.456	70	24.16
3.855	180	25.32
Industries	5.00	54.48

Presently, only 5.5 MCM is available from the surface water sources like Tapar, Shinaya, etc. The remaining requirement is met through the ground water resources, either through open wells, dug-cum-borewells or tube-wells.

It is interesting to note that major portion of the domestic water supply is being met from the aquifer of the Bhuj Series (Cretaceous Sandstone) which occur over an area of about 2700 sq. km. Some of the tube-wells located in Nakhtrana and Bhuj *taluka* supply water to Abadasa, Lakhapat and Banni villages. The same aquifer supports more than 15000 wells for irrigation. These aquifers are over-exploited as a result of which water level in these areas has fallen down by more than 30 m during the last 30 years. For example, the wells at Mou (N) in Mandvi *taluka* were overflowing earlier, but today, the water level stands 40 m below the land surface. Similarly in the Viri area, water level in the wells was within 3 m from the land surface, but today, it is more than 30 m. The GWSCB has schemes for supplying water to villages in Abdasa *taluka*, Kandla and Gandhidham townships. In coastal areas, due to the decline in water levels, sea water has intruded into the fresh water aquifers.

There are two major organizations in the Gujarat state, namely, the GWRDC and GWSSB, the former being responsible for the assessment of ground water resources and tube-well irrigation schemes whereas the latter handles domestic and industrial water supply schemes. Another major consumer is the farming community. These government organizations have concentrated only on fulfilling water supply demand, but no projects have so far been taken up by them. The GWSSB schemes have not been able to meet the demands.

As mentioned earlier, the water resources of the Kutch district are dependent entirely on the rainfall which is very low and erratic. It is, therefore, essential that rainfall is harnessed properly to re-charge the aquifers.

The present domestic and industrial water requirement is of the order of 55 MCM and by 2001* it may go up to 66 MCM taking into account the population growth during last three decades, which is more than 20 per cent per decade. The government policy is to provide safe drinking water to one and all, for which lot of funds are made available both by Central and State Governments. The Prime Minister of India made a statement

* By now the figure must have gone up considerably.
– Editors

in Parliament on 19th May 1995 that adequate funds will be made available to the State Governments to implement the drinking water supply schemes in view of the fall of water levels. It is high time the government organizations take immediate measures to augment the ground water resources through re-charge projects wherever it is feasible. Some of the voluntary organizations are playing a very important role in this regard. However, since the resources are limited and the demand is great, they ought to be supported by the concerned governmental organizations.

RAINWATER HARVESTING BY VRTI

Shree Vivekanand Research and Training Institute is engaged in rainwater harvesting with a view to re-charging the depleted aquifers of the Kutch district since 1989 and to arrest the declining water levels as well as deterioration of ground water quality. It is constructing check dams, percolation tanks and sub-surface dykes for this purpose. It has developed certain designs, by changing the existing designs of re-charge tube-wells and sub-surface dykes to suit the local conditions, for harvesting the flood water for re-charging purpose. These structures have functioned effectively and the results achieved are quite significant. There is improvement both in water levels and ground water quality due to re-charge.

A. Re-charge Tube-Well

The flood water which is to be mixed with ground water occurring at a great depth should be potable and free from suspended solids. To achieve this, a filter bed is provided on top of the re-charge tube-well which is drilled in the area of the dam or percolation tank. The diameter of the boreholes is 50 cm and the PVC pipe used is 6 kg having a diameter of 20 cm. The annular space between the borehole and the pipe is filled with Sivalia gravel and developed with the compressor till it gives clear water. On top a 6 m x 6 m x 6 m dimension pit is dug out keeping the tube-well at the centre and the section is filled with small rounded boulders, chips and sand. The slotted section at the top is wrapped with coir. A 10 cm gravel pack and sand layers are provided around the slotted pipe up to the filter bed. The top 1 m is filled with sand. Air vents of 7.5 cm diameter are provided for letting out the air trapped in the tube-well as well as in the upper sand zone.

When the flood water passes through the top sand, much of the suspended material will get filtered out. The second filter around the slotted section holds back the remaining suspended material. If some fine sand passes through, the coir filter will prevent it from entering the tube-well. Even when some very fine silt passes through and gets accumulated in the re-charge tube-wells, it can be cleaned by pumping the tube-well with compressor after rainy season so that it is clear for the next season. The water thus purified passes through the filter bed on the top and the gravel section and comes out from the pumping well. This re-charge tube-well can also be pumped out at the time of emergency during severe drought to supply water to animals and human beings. Every year 20 to 30 cm of sand should be removed from the top of the filter bed and replaced with clean sand. Re-charge tube-well with compressor/pump should be installed in every monsoon to prolong its effectiveness.

B. CHECK DAM (Figs. 20.1-20.2)

Normally, the check dam in the drainage courses of narrow streams was designed to be masonry. The height of the check dam is generally half the height of the bank. When the bank is at considerable height, the dam height can be designed in such a way that flood water does not spill over the bank during high floods. The distance between the two check dams will be such that the dam in the upstream is beyond the water spread of the dam on the downstream. The surface storage reservoirs are earthen dams including the percolation tanks with masonry spillway.

C. SUB-SURFACE DYKE

In the streams which are wider and carry sufficient water, sub-surface dams are designed. Here, the entire width of the river is excavated down to the water level or at least 15 to 20 m if it is quite deep. The downstream well is made impervious by providing polythene sheet. In case water levels are deep, re-charge tube-wells are constructed in the dyke section and the entire excavated structure is filled with pervious sand and a sand bag barrier is provided if the velocity is low and flow is less. If the flow is great and the velocity is high, a masonry structure of suitable height is provided on the downstream to impound the flood water to harness for re-charge. With this, the best flow will be available for re-charge which considerably depends on the length and the width of the river and the thickness of the pervious material available along its length. The

Fig. 20.1 Masonry check dam full of rain water.

Fig. 20.2 Masonry check dam.

number of re-charge wells depends on the volume of water available and the size of the impounding structure.

It has also been shown that even in the low rainfall years, there is a good possibility of harvesting the rainwater as there will be a couple of floods occurring when the daily precipitation is over 20 mm. The results of the Rayan Project have shown that during 1989, when rainfall was 310 mm and storage capacity was 44715 m^3, the re-charge was 66469 m^3 resulting rise of water levels from 1.2 m to 3.65 m and reduction of TDS from 10 ppm to 420 ppm in the wells spread over an area of 750 ha. In 1990, the rainfall in Rayan was 181 mm and the storage capacity was increased to 1,27,020 m^3 and the re-charge was 203967 m^3. This led to the rise of water level by maximum 6 mm and reduction of TDS by 920 ppm against 3.65 m and 420 ppm in 1989. In 1994, when the rainfall was over 1000 mm, the structures received nearly five filling and the re-charge was about 344664 m^3. The average raise of water levels was 15 m and the average improvement in quality was more than 800 ppm.

In 1994, two sub-surface dykes were constructed, one at Bhujpur and the other at Kandagara. The Bhujpur sub-surface dyke which has a storage capacity of 0.21 MCM (7.5 Mcft) with three re-charge tube-wells, has re-charged about 1.19 MCM. There is an average raise of water levels of 20 m in the area. In many dug-cum-bore wells where water was standing at 40 m depth and never seen above, the bore is now having 10 m to 15 m water column in the open wells.

Similarly at Kandagara, where the sub-surface dyke is provided with three re-charge wells having a capacity of 0.33 MCM, the total re-charge occurred is of the order of 1.05 MCM resulting in raise of water level by 15 m to 20 m.

Till the end of June 1994, 64 check dams, 25 percolation ponds, 4 subsurface dykes, 58 re-charge tube-wells and 46 storage tanks have been constructed creating a storage capacity of 6.47 MCM. This re-charge structure has a storage capacity of 2.9 MCM which can re-charge about 8.7 MCM in a good rainfall year. During 1994, rainfall re-charge through this re-charge structure was more than 10 MCM.

By the end of March 1995, the total rainwater harvesting structures constructed were 166 and 72 re-charge tube-wells and the storage capacity created was 13.85 MCM at a cost of Rs. 5.15 crores, financed by CAPART, SPWD, SDC and DRDA; and work of local people on 20 structures is in progress.

In order to strengthen the border village water supply schemes, re-charge projects at 12 places, spread over the entire Kutch, were taken up costing about 83 lakh rupees which was financed by the Department of Narmada and Water Resources and the government of Gujarat.

RECOMMENDATIONS

Knowing fully well the scarcity of water resource in the Kutch district, it is high time that the concerned governmental organizations take immediate measures to protect the dwindling drinking water resources by adopting suitable measures to harness the rainfall over the area for re-charging the depleting aquifers. The rural technology developed and executed by Shree Vivekanand Research and Training Institute has given positive results and has a very good scope for replicating them in other parts for re-charging the depleted aquifers. The immediate priority has to be given to re-charging the Bhuj and Manchar aquifers which have been over-exploited, and many water supply schemes tap these aquifers.

Industrial units at Kandla which get the water supply from far away places, should adopt recycling of water for industrial uses. Similarly, waste water in the townships could be recycled for non-domestic purposes.

The success of the re-charge schemes depends on the active participation of all the governmental organizations dealing with water resources of government.

TALUKA	ST	PT	CD	SSD	RT	COST (Rs.)	STORAGE (Cum)
MANDVI	27	23	50	2	46	28196707	3530015
MUNDRA	12	5	11	2	13	11277230	2033767
ABDASA	12	-	4	1	1	8340727	1819121
ANJAR	-	1	2	-	4	3324165	205283
BHUJ	3	1	4	-	6	3616458	11181459
NANHATRANA	-	3	1	-	2	1925555	420118
LAKHPAT	6	-	-	-	-	1945813	851150
BHACHAU	2	3	-	-	4	1908940	449687
RAPAR	1	-	2	-	-	1667166	629326
TOTAL	63	36	74	5	76	62196761	11119926

Summary of the Structures Constructed by V.R.T.I. tillI March 1996

S. No.	Type of Structure	No.	Cost (Rs.)	Storage Capacity Created (CU.M.)	No. of R.T. Wells in (STR.)	Area Vrt Cenef. (acres).
1.	Storage Tank (S.T.)	63	15, 986, 817	6, 640, 669	-	4, 284
2.	Percolation Tank (P.T.)	36	19, 391, 310	1, 981, 565	36	3, 665
3.	Check Dam (C.D.)	74	22, 987, 192	2, 352, 180	29	7, 849
4.	Sub-Surface Dyke (S.S.D.)	5	3, 423, 562	273, 712	11	
5.	Farmer Well Re-charge (F.W.R.)	205	656, 793	-	-	1, 025
6.	R.T. Wells in Existing STRS	17	1885165			2, 100
7.	Gully Plugs (G.P.)	18	67, 099	72, 000		
8.	Farm Ponds (F.P.)	24	872,910	64, 800		240
	Total:	**442**	**65,270,848**	**11,384,926**	**76**	**19,163**

GROSS STORAGE CAPACITY = 6, 640, 669 + 72, 000 + 64, 800 + 2 X (1, 981, 565 + 2, 352, 180 + 273, 712) = 15, 992, 383 Cu. M.

AREA BENEFITTED = 19163 ACRES COST PER MCM OF WATER HARVESTED IN FIRST NORMAL MONSOON YEAR = Rs. 4,081,979

COST PER Mcft. OF WATER HARVESTED

IN FIRST NORMAL MONSOON YEAR = Rs. 115,588

Stamina	Normal Annual Rainfall (mm)	SS (mm)	CY (%)	()	Annual year	— average Rainfall in 14 hrs.
BHUJ	342.4	224.6	65.6	1311.4	1959	468 15.7.59
ANJAR	343.5	192.6	56.1	982.0	1979	326 23.7.81
RAHAPAR	365.4	223.3	61.1	1139.6	1975	198 02.9.84
BHACHAU	383.0	253.4	66.1	989.0	1979	-
MUNDRA	439.7	247.7	56.3	957.5	1959	-
KANDLA	433.2	226.9	52.4	893.2	1967	-
NALAYA	451.9	364.8	80.7	1372.6	1959	263 15.7.59
MANDVI	401.8	283.9	70.7	949.2	1967	276 12.7.81
NAKHATRANA	381.6	234.6	61.5	864.7	1979	-
LAKHPAT	338.4	266.5	78.8	956.9	1959	-
KHAVDA	345.5	245.5	71.1	988.2	1961	-
MANDVI	433.0	269.2	62.1	1671.0	1884	-
KHADIR	381.4	211.5	55.5	853.0	1959	-
Average:	**387.75**	**249.52**	**64.46**			

Table showing the T.D.S. variation of Group projects in 1994 monsoon

Name of Group of projects	Premonsoon max/min T.D.S. in ppm	Postmonsoon max/min T.D.S. in ppm	Improvement max/min T.D.S. in ppm
Rayan	3360/1230	2720/870	1520/10
Kandagara	2320/900	2000/860	280/10
Bhujpar	3300/1240	2100/820	1620/40
Dumra	5410/1360	4860/1000	700/360
Bharundi	6660/1220	6250/1080	1220/10
Bidada	6000/1100	2000/920	4170/160
Moti Khakhar	3380/1160	2000/860	1340/30
Sang	4200/1450	3800/1260	1390/20

21

PONDS IN BHANDARA DISTRICT AND WATER MANAGEMENT

Manish Rajankar and Yogini Dolke

ABSTRACT

This article studies the ponds in the Bhandara district and suggests that the existence of about 50,000 ponds is due to the district's geographical features and the efforts of the local people in pond building. The ponds are about 300 years old having been built during the time of the Gond kings, by Kohlis, Pawars and Gonds. The water distribution system and the role of government vis-à-vis ponds are also discussed.

INTRODUCTION

The Bhandara district in the state of Maharashtra is renowned for its ponds. Of 43,381 ponds, some are less than 1 ha. in size while some are over 10 ha. or even larger. The existence of water bodies on such a large-scale is due to the peculiar geographical features such as undulating terrain, water retaining capacity of the soil as well as to the successful efforts of the local people in pond building.

A BRIEF HISTORY

These ponds, which are approximately 300 years old, were built during the period of Gond kings. This period also saw the development of the region from the Wainganga river basin to the Kanhan River, a region which was largely forested. The Gonds offered rewards of *jagirs* and titles of 'sardar' to those who would clear the jungle and build a settlement there. Similarly, anyone who constructed a pond would be gifted with the land irrigated by the pond. The construction of the ponds was thus undertaken by various castes like Kohlis, Pawars and Gonds.

Once the site of the pond was selected, local tribes were involved in the process of construction. After the completion of the pond, these tribes were given lands lying within the irrigation limits of the pond for cultivation. The canals were de-silted every year before the monsoons and repaired, when required, by all the residents of the village. The pond too was de-silted and the silt was either spread in the fields as fertilizers or piled on the edge of the pond. The *malguzars* would either supervise these works themselves or appoint a committee of village elders for the same purpose. *Pankars* were appointed to implement the decision of the *malguzar* or the committee. Their main duties were to clean the canals and the pond and to ensure proper distribution of water.

In the past, water was released through wooden or stone gates called *tudum* made by the local people using simple technology. At some places, water was simply released by making a temporary breach (called *Khand*) in the mud embankment. Even though there are no documentary records of these techniques and practices, the *tudum* are still found in many villages and some of them are still in use.

The people were given water free of charge for cultivation and, in turn, they had to help in the cleaning and maintenance of canals and ponds. Individual water use was calculated on the basis of the amount of water available. The normal practice was to begin the distribution of the water from the head of the canal, in which, the farmer who had lands at a higher level, would receive the water first. When sufficient water was available, crops were grown in summer also. Normally, the water distribution was fair, but in case of injustice, the accused was punished.

THE SITUATION TODAY

The existence of ponds points to the efficacy of traditional water management, but in recent times there has been a gradual change. The abolition of Proprietary Rights Act of 1950 put an end to the Zamindari System, and with it, the water management system also collapsed. The government took away possession of the ponds; the role of people in the water management was disregarded; the *malguzars* were no longer responsible for water distribution. Those ponds which measured and less than 200 ha. command area were handed over to the Zila Panchayats, while those above 250 ha. to the Irrigation Department. Allocation of insufficient funds for managing such vast and numerous water bodies only helped to make matters worse.

At about this time, the original stone *tudum* gates were replaced by iron ones and most of them were stolen. In case of repairs, by the time the application was granted, the problem was inspected and action taken, a lot of water had been wasted. In the past, the residents themselves were responsible for the repairs which meant immediate action and less wastage of water.

Following the Maharashtra Irrigation Act of 1976, water committees were set up in several villages under the Gram Panchayats. But these committees had no jurisdiction over matters other than water distribution. The government ordered the formation of Water Users Groups, but not a single exists today in entire Bhandara district. The government officials have been unable to motivate the people to form such groups because they say that the people harass them with all sorts of problems. It is obvious that the government officials have not understood the spirit of the Act.

GOSEKHURD PROJECT AND DEVELOPMENT

The Gosekhurd Project is coming up on the Wainganga River, in the south-western corner of the Bhandara district. Thousands of hectares of forest and agricultural land, several villages and water reservoirs fall under the submergence zone of this project. The benefits of the project are meagre in comparison to the losses. Can this be called development of the district?

Various types of soil like *Kankar, Sihar, Moran, Khardi* and *Bhardi* are found in the district. The region around Adyal is covered with *Kankar* soil, which is more fertile than the other types and easily yields two harvests a year. The maximum amount of land to be submerged by the project is in the fertile region. Obviously, the district will be deprived of its more fertile lands – this will lead to a decrease in productivity and a lowering in the standard of living. Can this be called development?

Along with the fertile land will be submerged innumerable water bodies which serve not only agricultural purpose but are also natural havens for migratory birds. For centuries, these birds have a symbiotic relationship with the farmers. Dams are not known to attract birds because of the large volumes of water in them having a small, shallow strip periphery. Compared to the direct and indirect costs that the people of Bhandara district will have to pay for this project, the benefits are negligible.

No funds are available with the Irrigation Department and the Zila Parishad for water management. As a result, repairs are carried out in spurts, owing to which the condition of the ponds is deteriorating rapidly. The real development of the district lies not in constructing large dams, but in reviving, operating and maintaining the existing ponds with active participation of the local people. The timely maintenance and repairs of ponds will increase farmers' output, benefit the agricultural labourers and improve their standard of living. And all this can be achieved with no major changes in the existing ponds, jungles and peoples' lives.

In conclusion, we wish to reiterate our belief that the true development of the Bhandara district can be achieved by paying greater attention to the existing ponds rather than by destroying fertile farm lands and natural resources through destructive projects like the Gosekhurd.

22

REVIVING TRADITIONAL WATER RESOURCE DEVELOPMENT AND MANAGEMENT IN RAMANATHPURAM DISTRICT, TAMILNADU

G. Vasudeo

ABSTRACT

Natural Resources Development Project is a part of the service activities carried out by Vivekananda Kendra, Kanyakumari. Traditional water source development for drinking water is one of the thrust areas of activity which are being implemented at the instance of CAPART, New Delhi. Ramanathpuram district in Tamilnadu is known for frequent droughts, water scarcity and salinity problem. The implementation of various water supply schemes in the last 50 years of Independence has partly tackled the problems. The government has attempted various measures to provide assured and safe drinking water but the situation remains pathetic in many pockets. Madukulattur Block is one such area with brackish water sources where the Kendra has involved the local people in developing the traditional *Oorani*, a surface water pond, for providing drinking water source to them. The fenced and protected surface water source, re-charge tube-wells in new *Oorani* to improve the water quality of existing tube-well source and the mass awareness campaign are the activities which proved successful in solving long-awaited water supply problems. This unique experiment needs attention of governmental agencies and other voluntary organizations for implementation in similar poor water quality and scarcity areas in the country.

INTRODUCTION

Ramanathpuram district in Tamilnadu is one of the drought prone areas of the country. "Acute shortage of drinking water – Rs 40 lakhs per day for drought relief work" may be the headlines in the newspapers again and again over years. Rajiv Gandhi Drinking Water Mission, under which Ramanathpuram was one of the 'Mini mission areas', was implemented by the government of India. Many sources were created for rural water supply including the de-salination plants. However, even after working on various schemes, the water supply in many pockets of the district is either inadequate and not sustainable or having high salinity. A number of piped water supply schemes from Vagai river-bed have been implemented in the last few years by the government. Kulandurai and Rajagambiram schemes envisage transporting water from the infiltration wells to several villages covering a length of over 40 km. These schemes, implemented with crores of rupees, have failed miserably due to shortage of water in the river in summer months. The government has installed 14 de-salination plants to convert brackish water into potable water which is also not successful due to the problems in feed water source, suitable high quality membranes to treat water of very high salinity, high-tech maintenance required and lack of trained persons in these remote villages. The government, voluntary organizations and the public have realized that the development of traditional sources like *Oorani* (pond) and rainwater harvesting are the realistic and viable solutions to the chronic scarcity and salinity problem in this district.

VIVEKANANDA KENDRA IN SERVICE ACTIVITY

Vivekananda Kendra is one of the voluntary organizations engaged in a number of service activities in the country and its contributions in various fields of services are well known. Under the Natural Resources Development Project (NARDEP), the Kendra carried out extensive surveys on water scarcity in Ramanathpuram district and interacted with people to know their problems and preferences. It selected a village in Mudukulattur block where the drinking water supply is very poor and the participation of people in planning and execution was assured.

PROFILE OF MUDUKULATTUR AREA

Mudukulattur town is a *taluk* headquarter in Ramanathpuram district, located 40 km away from Ramanathpuram. The nearest town is Paramakudi, 30 km north of Mudukulattur, which is well connected by NH-49 and Rameswaram-Madurai section of Southern Railways. The block is having a geographical area of 338 sq. km with 155 hamlets under 48 Gram Panchayats. There are 36 revenue villages with a population of 85,329 (1991 census). There are 61 minor irrigation tanks, 42 PWD tanks connected with the Vaigai River by a network of supply channels. The rainfall in the area is around 650 mm per year and the river carries flash flood water for a certain period in the year and many years have dry spells.

The area is covered by sedimentary rocks and the water is brackish in most of the villages. Raju & Varadaraj (1987) of CGWB have presented a detailed account of hydro-geological zones. They have also indicated the water quality inferred down to a depth of 1000 m and provided the feasibility report for creation of sources for the problem villages taken up under Technology Mission. The development of traditional sources for some remote areas was indicated as the solution.

The water supply position of the Mudukulattur Block is only partial even after the completion of Technology Mission. There are 24 power pumps and 241 hand pumps in the block but only saline water is available. Many pumping schemes introduced in the sporadic and shallow fresh water pockets have resulted in rapid upward movement of saline water. These problems and the absence of deep-seated fresh water aquifers have curtailed the ground water development in the area.

TRADITIONAL SOURCES

Ooranis are the most common traditional drinking water sources in the Ramanathpuram district. They are the dug-out ponds which collect surface run-off and also sub-soil fresh water lenses at places. Now-a-days, these ponds are not used due to certain factors. They can be made functional by enhancing the storage capacity through deepening them; by constructing simple inlet and outlet structures; by providing bunds and drains to divert run-off water towards the inlet of the pond; by having a filter trench connected to a draw-well outside the pond to get clean water; by laying grass turf to prevent soil erosion as well as to protect the slopes, etc.

CONSTRAINT

Inspite of the vast scope for repair and maintenance, there are also few constraints which are given below:

(i) Sub-soil water level and brackish ground water do not allow any appreciable deepening.
(ii) High rate of evaporation in summer which necessitates deepening rather than increasing the surface area of the pond.
(iii) *Ooranis* fed by the irrigation supply channel network of Vaigai River have poor inflow into them due to reduced supply in the tanks.
(iv) Lack of active participation of local people in the construction and maintenance of *Ooranis* in all places.

RE-MODELLING OF *OORANIS*

Inspite of all these limitations, the Kendra workers inspired the local people in Mudukulattur union through constant interaction for 6 years, and by involving them and also with the help of CAPART, New Delhi, they re-modelled the *Ooranis* at the following places – Thattankudiyiruppu, 1991; Sambakulam, 1991; Kottakudi, 1994; Mattiyerandel, 1994; Kannichen, 1995; and Selvanayagapuram, 1995.

The pitching of concrete blocks at Thattan Kudiyeruppu and Sambakulam *Ooranis* prevented soil erosion on the sides. Other works done include the grass turfing above the pitching area, fencing with *Prosopis julieflora* plants, periodic cleaning of draw well and cleaning of sand filter bed.

ROOF WATER HARVESTING

Another way of improving water sources in remote villages refers to the collection and storage of rainwater, falling on roofs, for use in lean period. Roof harvesting was planned in areas where i) no *Ooranis* were existing, ii) ground water was saline, and iii) there were no adequate or sustainable water sources within reasonable distance.

The roof harvesting structure at Thattankudiyeruppu has the following features:

I) The type of roof selected is tiled, not thatched, and it is not flat.
II) Water is collected from every roof and pooled at a place through an underground pipe system.
III) The pipe is connected to a tank where the water received is filtered and stored.
IV) A hand pump is fitted for taking out water from the underground storage tank.

HIGHLIGHTS OF THE PROJECT

The highlights of the project, which has been successfully implemented, are listed below:

1. Villagers were motivated to assess the problem as well as the role they had to play in the project through films and group discussions.
2. Villagers actively participated in de-silting work as a part of local contribution.
3. Weekly meetings were organized to discuss and sort out the problems.
4. Remodelled *Oorani* was inaugurated at Thattankudiyeruppu by Shri. A. Prasad, Deputy Director General, CAPART, New Delhi.
5. Check list for periodic reporting regarding the maintenance of *Ooranis* was given to the villagers for monitoring.
6. A village level co-operative society was formed in both the villages with a corpus fund for maintaining the *Ooranis.*
7. They also further resolved to mobilise funds on a quarterly basis to augment the deposits.
8. Nearby villagers have come forward to take up water harvesting work on similar terms.
9. Availability of drinking water has enabled them to utilize their spare time and energy for income-generating activities.

RE-CHARGE STRUCTURE IN *OORANI*

After the successful remodelling of *Ooranis,* the Kendra decided to go one step further in improving the drinking water sources by way of combining the *Oorani* with re-charge tube-wells. At the instances of CAPART, New Delhi, and in consultation with Central Ground water Board officials of Chennai and Trivandrum, the Kendra carried out detailed study, and selected Selvanayagapuram and Merku kottakudi villages in Mudukulattur Panchayat union of Ramanathpuram district.

RE-CHARGE STRUCTURE AT SELVANAYAGAPURAM

The village has a number of tube-wells and a big irrigation tank but the water is brackish. The villagers had a long-standing dream of having water harvesting structure which was taken up and accomplished by the Kendra in a short period of time, of course with the involvement of the villagers. A land of 2.1 acres, adjoining a streamlet, was purchased by the villagers for the construction of *Oorani.* Each family rendered physical service,

Shramadan, by digging parts of the *Oorani* worth Rs 50,000. The amount was reimbursed and kept as fixed deposit to be used for welfare measures. The pit dug by the villagers was deepened further using earth movers to expedite the construction before the onset of monsoon in June 1997. The average length of the pond is 83 m, width 70 m and depth 1.3 m. Two re-charge tube-wells were installed to facilitate the flow of rainwater collected in the pond into the sand layer situated at a depth of 5 m from the surface. Also, a draw well of 1.8 m diameter and 7.9 m with concrete rings was constructed in order to collect water for drinking needs. This project envisages that the re-charged water will get natural flow towards draw well in dip downside and give fresh water. The pond was filled in September 1997 and inflow into the tube-wells could be visualized by lowering water level in ponds.

RE-CHARGE TUBE-WELL AT MERKU KOTTAKUDI

Since the tube-well in this village has brackish water, people collect drinking water from far away sources. The water quality improvement in the existing tube-well was planned by executing a re-charge structure. The small depression in the upstream side of the tube-well is covered into a pond of 50 m length, 30 m width and 1.5 m depth. A tube-well of 200 mm diameter and 45.45 m depth is constructed and the rainwater filled in the pond has effective ground water re-charge into the same aquifer tapped by the production well. The water quality of the tube-well has considerably improved in the first year itself and further improvement in quality is anticipated. Another tube-well constructed downstream, about 200 m away, will allow more extraction and induce re-charge in the system.

CONCLUSIONS

The project of traditional water resource development undertaken by the Vivekananda Kendra, with the support of the local people, in Mudukuluttur area of Ramanathpuram, has proved successful. The piped water supply which comes from a distant source does not reach the designed population due to technical and social problems. However, flash flood surface water collection and roof harvesting have provided a fresh water source to the village. In addition, the re-charge tube-wells installed in the pond not only facilitate underground storing of rainwater but also provide for an easy extraction. With the scientific understanding of sub-surface flow pattern, and with the active participation of people, more and more useful schemes can be implemented by voluntary organizations in such problematic areas.

NOTES AND REFERENCE

Raju, K.C.B and N. Varadaraj, 1987, 'Identification of Microlevel Hydrogeological Zones and its Precise Quantification for Successful Formulation of Water Supply Schemes', paper presented in the *Regional Seminar on Tech. Mission*, Gandhigram, pp. 18-25.

Shri R. Sreenivasan while commenting on the water scarcity in Ramanathpuram district, Tamilnadu writes:

"Ramanathpuram district is situated in the state of Tamilnadu and is known for drought and water scarcity round the year. Water has been a saleable commodity in the district. As the landscape is plain with hard clayey soils and no major river flowing through it, modern engineering technology may find it very difficult to construct efficient water harvesting structures. But the people of Ramanathpuram (Ramnad) have changed their landscape by constructing 4000 tanks and ponds through collective effort and the philanthrophy of the landlords and the chieftains. These ponds and tanks have been the main source of water in this district, and some of the villages of Ramanathpuram have been named after them.

Tanks are earthen bounded reservoirs constructed across the slope. They are connected by a chain of canals and diversions and store running water. The ponds too have earthen bunds. They receive water from the monsoon run-off and carry water throughout the year. Strengthening of the bunds and de-silting of the tank beds are done every year. The black silt which is the most valued manure is removed from the tank beds and sprayed into the fields.

It is interesting to note that in this difficult terrain, where there is scarcity of water the major crop is paddy, the cultivation of which requires 45 cm of rainfall. However, this fact has not yet found a place in written documents. Similarly, people continue to live here inspite of the fact that the ponds are not a safe source of drinking water. Added to this is the fact that the bore-hole pumps and the wells cannot work here properly because of the salinity of water below the ground. All this goes to show that the farmers somehow make their living by primitive technology and produce more and more, year after year, inspite of the overall water scarcity."

Editors

SECTION III

SHORT COMMUNICATIONS, SUGGESTIONS AND RECOMMENDATIONS

23

WATER MANAGEMENT IN THE HIMALAYA-GANGA: RECONCILING INTERVENTIONS AND COMPLEXITY

Ajay Dixit

Water of the rivers of the Himalaya-Ganga are both boon and bane to the humankind living in the regions that depend on them. The Himalaya-Ganga is a generic name given to the highland-lowland interactive system of South Asia. It is undergoing transformations in its three inter-linked and interacting sub-systems consisting of the physical environment, the human built environment and the symbolic environment. The stress of change has led to the crisis related with data, inefficiency, inequity and impurity in managing water. These crises have resulted, among others, due to the fact that the responses of achieving water security have been perceived primarily as the challenge of making technological choice within narrow disciplinary lines. Transparency, efficiency, equity and ecology must form core of the guiding principles to tackle the emerging challenges of achieving water security within complexity of the region. Harmonious changes will come from approaches that put 'people first' than 'technology first' by re-conceptualizing water management as the response to scarcity not plentitude, to rehabilitation not new development and to institutions not technology.

24

SUGGESTIONS ON TRADITIONAL WATER HARVESTING STRUCTURES

Kamal Saxena, S. Ramanuja and Lavesh Kansal

The authors outline some of the suggestions for improving the traditional harvesting structures.

1) Proper documentation of all the traditional water harvesting structures and technologies should be made. This would include the collection of photographs, drawings, slides of such structures from different parts of the country with the help of NGOs and other institutions working in this field.
2) Study should also be made to establish the role of traditional water harvesting structures in the process of socio-economic and cultural development.
3) Large size models of complete water harvesting systems should be prepared in the premises of IGRMS utillsing its topography and locally available material with technical expertise of various experts who have done pioneering work on these systems and achieved successful results.
4) A special mention should be made to depict the chronology of these water harvesting structures and how the climatic conditions, socio-economic and political developments in the history of mankind forced him to evolve new techniques.
5) An exhibition/display should be prepared to present a comparative picture of traditional water harvesting structures with modern techniques of water harvesting elements in the modern technologies of water management.
6) These traditional water harvesting structures should also be studied in broad ecological perspective of the particular area to establish the role of these structures in soil conservation, conservation of flora, fauna and in agricultural developments.

25

INDIVIDUAL WELL RE-CHARGE TECHNIQUES

K.C.B. Raju

PRECAUTIONS

In order to prevent clogging of the aquifer (water yielding strata and pollutions of ground water), the following precautions have to be taken when individual pumping wells are re-charged by diverting flood waters into the well system.

i) If an abandoned well is available nearby, priority may be given to use this well for re-charging purpose. Nearly half the depth of abandoned well may be filled with good sand to create a filter bed. In order to maintain its re-charging efficiency the top one meter of sand is replaced after every rainy season, as in this top layer the suspended material of flood water gets accmulated.

ii) When pumping wells are used for re-charge purpose a filter well may be constructed adjoining the well and flood water should be allowed to go through this filter well.

iii) When re-charging with flood water coming from the agriculture fields including farmers' own fields, it is better not to use the first flood water for re-charging, because it not only carries heavy sediment load but also carries injurious organic matter and toxic chemical constituents derived from the organic fertilizers. Chemical fertilizers are used during the crop season. When amenables are used like gypsum to improve the soil condition the precipitates left over are sodium and other chemical constituents which are injurious both for agriculture, domestic and drinking purposes.

iv) It is better to harvest the rainwater for re-charging the individual farmers' well after the first heavy rain which will carry away many of the injurious chemical and organic constituents and subsequent floods will have less sediment load.

TECHNIQUES

1) The filter bed required depends upon the volume of water available from the run-off from farmer's own field and its extent and on the run-off going to be intercepted from the drainage courses near the fields where wells are located.

A filter pit of 2 m x 2 m x 3 m dimension is suggested if the run-off to be tapped is low to moderate. If the run-off from the *Dallas* carry greater quantity and for shorter duration the size of the filter pit may be increased depending on the volumes of water available and size and depth of well to be re-charged. The filter pit is filled by placing rounded pebbles at bottom for 0.5 m depth followed by 0.30 m thick stone chip and the top 1.5 m is provided with medium to coarse sand. The remaining top portion is kept blank for the flood water to enter and to accumulate.

2) If the source is from the field run-off, the run-off water is allowed to collect in a corner of the field in a depression and from this it is diverted to the filter pit by providing a channel or a pipe from the top of the depression (which will act as a silt trap) and then diverted to the well.

The bottom of the pit is connected to the settling pit of 1.5 m x 1.5 m x 3 m. From this pit, water is allowed to enter the re-charge well through a pipe laid about 1.5 m from the top of the small pit.

In the above design, the flood water passes through the sand bed of the filter pit where most of the suspended materials settle, and water percolates down through the filter media and enters into the small pit and better water enters into the re-charge well (Drg - I).

3) If the run-off is tapped from a drainage course nearby, a small obstruction is provided in the drainage course about 1 m to 2 m downstream from where the water is diverted into the filter pit. Here also the pipe or channel is kept about 30 m above the bed of the channel (Drg - II).
4) If the flood water is tapped from the bigger stream having good thickness of pervious material, a trench may be dug in the stream to a depth of 1 m and a slotted pipe is placed by providing a gravel pack around the pipe. This pipe is connected to a settling pit and to the well to be re-charged. This water coming from the river-bed through the slotted pipe is much clear and this also has the advantage of tapping the paseflow in the river-bed after cessation of the surface flood. The pipe laid in the river-bed should be sloping towards the settling pit or the re-charge pit to facilitate water flow into the re-charge well (Drg - III).
5) When re-charge is to be undertaken in an abandoned dug-cum-bore well the borehole pipe must be extented up to the ground surface by providing a slotted section. The slotted section has to be provided with gravel pack. Then the open dug well portion which is dry has to be filled with medium to coarse sand up to a depth of 1.5 m below the top of the well. To this, flood water is diverted from the source through a pipe. Silt traps have to be provided by constructing pits of sufficient size for settling the silt (Drg - IV).
6) In case re-charge has to be done on an operational deep tube-well, the filter mechanism suggested for re-charging the operating dug wells has to be followed and the water has to be allowed to pass through the gravel patch around the tube-well and not directly into the tube-well. In this, it is to be noted that only stream or *nalla* water should be used for re-charging an operational tube-well (Drg - V).

MAINTENANCE

Between the floods if there is large gap, the silt settled on the top of the filter bed and also in the small pit may be removed. Under no circumstances the filter bed is disturbed when the flood water infilteration gets reduced with time. Due to settling of the silt on the top if the infilteration rate is observed to decrease, this agitation of the sand bed will make the silt to go down into the underlying coarse filter bed and thereby the open spaces are filled up with silt thus spoiling the entire system.

The top sand bed should be replaced every year after the rainy season. In order to clean the sediments accumulated in the voids of coarse material, fresh water from the tanker or from the pumping well is allowed to spread on the filter bed. This water which percolates downward and comes out in the smaller pit, will bring out all the settled silt and this can be removed out from the pit, manually through buckets or through small pumps if available. This procedure will keep the entire system clean to receive the flood water in the next rainy season. This filter mechanism will not only provide good water for re-charge but also give a longer life to the filter system.

SUGGESTIONS

The re-charge should be taken on a co-operative basis, on continuous area so that it becomes more scientific and beneficial. If the farmers of 50 ha. to 100 ha. group jointly tap more flood water on the techniques mentioned above, it will be safe because sediments loaded and chemical concentration in flood water will get much diluted.

26

TRADITIONAL DRINKING WATER RESOURCE MANAGEMENT AS SOLUTION TOWARDS SUSTAINABLE SYSTEMS IN HILLS

Vijay Kumar

In many hilly areas in different parts of India, although the coverage of population on safe drinking water sources has been impressive, a considerable number of small and scattered habitants continue to rely on traditional sources.

The majority of these traditional sources are almost certainly unsafe in their present state. The so-called impressive coverage on 'safe drinking water' is of great concern to both national and international bodies who are responsible for the 'Drinking Water Decade' programme on rural water supply and on water quality monitoring and surveillance in rural areas. There are many known cases of sub-standard water quality problems, mainly associated with excessive iron content in water from hand pumps, non-functioning of hand pumps due to mechanical or hydrogeological (depletion in water table) reasons, bad taste/colour/staining/unplesant odour, etc. This in turn leads to a situation where population

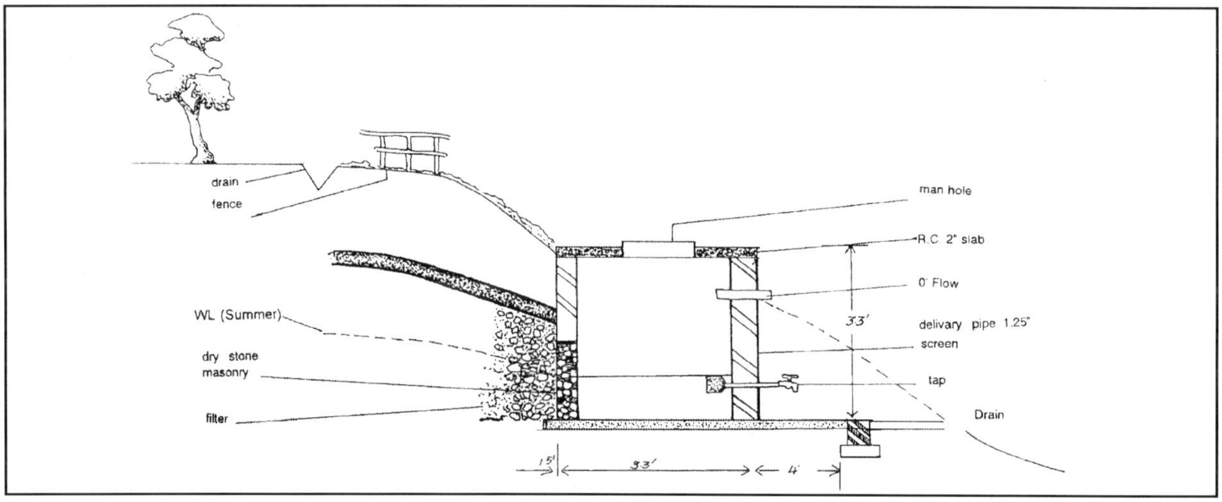

Fig. 26.1 Spring box, AFPRO design adopted.

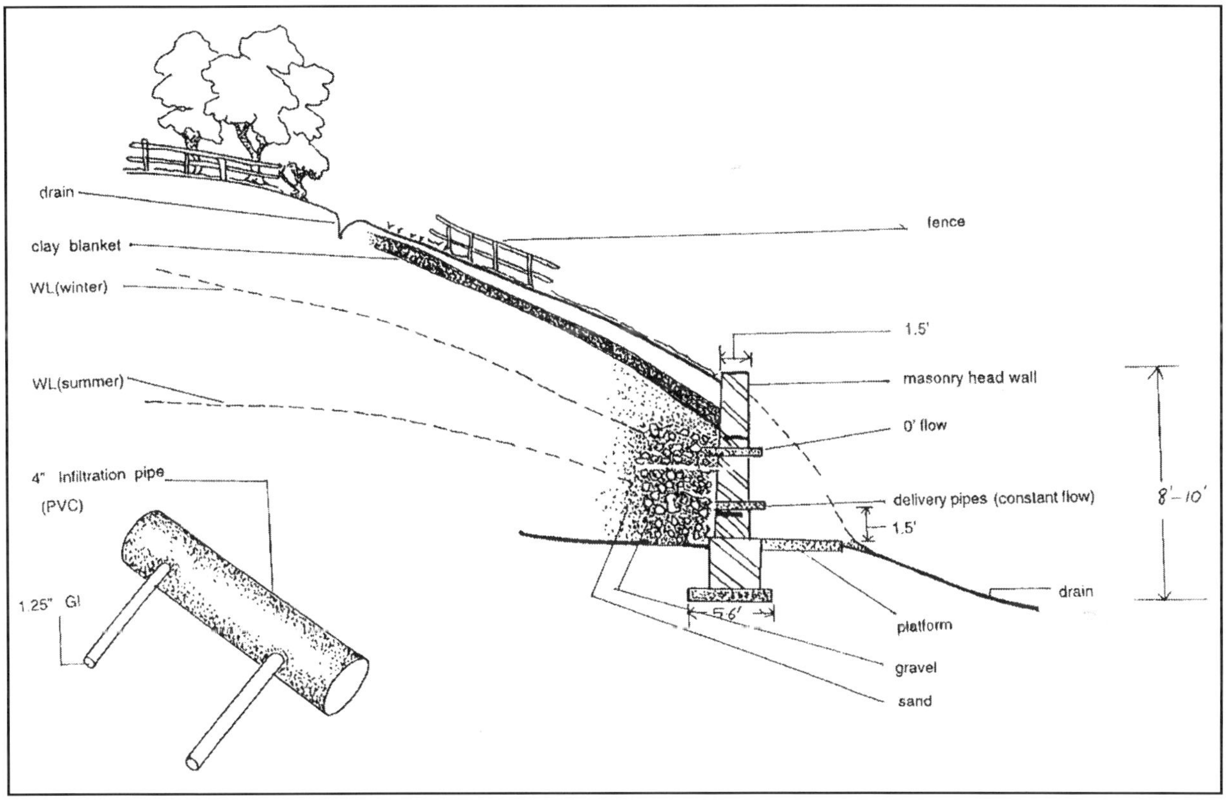

Fig. 26.2 Spring wall, AFPRO design adopted.

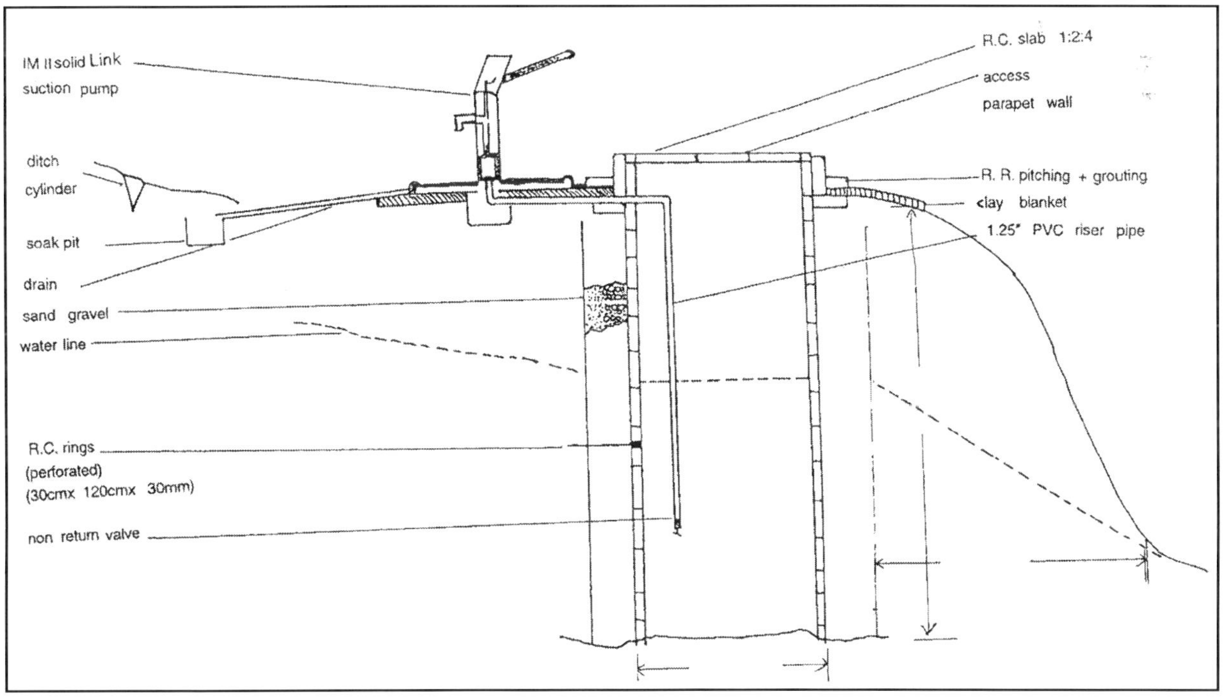

Fig. 26.3 Filter well, AFPRO design adopted.

which are deemed to have access to 'safe drinking water sources' actually reject them and fall back on traditional sources which are typically spring flows of one kind or another or shallow open wells or potholes.

Because of such scant coverage and/or rejection of safe sources, there are frequent cases of water-borne, water-based, water-scarce diseases, occasionally leading to significant loss of human life.

Anyone thinking of implementing a water project must clearly understand the water quality and quantity requirement of inhabitants. There are many uses of water and the quantity and quality requirements thus vary. Drinking water requirements are usually the most stringent.

In hilly regions, the scattered habitants continue to use traditional sources even though there is a good water supply. Are these sources safe from hygienic point of view? As such there are many issues which can be classified according to specific source type and location (See Figs. 26.1-26.3).

1. Potholes/water seepage spots.
2. Spring wall/spring box.
3. Filter wells
    (a) In conjunction with pond.
    (b) In conjunction with stream/river.

There is a need to discuss how these numerous sources can be made safe and hygienic specially with reference to the environmental drainage conditions.

27

TRADITIONAL WATER MANAGEMENT PRACTICES

Raman Patel

Different practices being adopted by the farmers of Barauch, Surendranagar and Junagadh districts of Gujarat are summarised here. The Agakhan Rural Support Programme has supported the development and management of natural resources available in these districts. Field data were also collected by interviewing the relevant people.

Modern irrigation systems like big multi-purpose dams, medium and minor canals and lift irrigation schemes, irrigation tanks, check dams etc. have certain geological and geohydrological parameters upon which they are designed.

Locally managed irrigation system is an age-old practice in the rural India. Several farmers irrigated their small pieces of land by using traditional methods like Persian Wheel, hand pumps, leather buckets with blocks etc. Some of the classical water management systems had already developed during ancient times. Over the whole of Western and Southern India, traditional farm irrigation is effected from open wells powered by two oxen- a technique existing in Baluchistan about 6000 years ago from where it diffused over much of India. Such a device can lift water from a depth of about 15-20 m and irrigate 2 acres of land. However, this methodology is being slowly replaced by pump system.

The Arthasashtra of the Mauryan period refers to check dams in Gujarat built for agricultural purposes which were renovated under king Ashoka in the 3rd century BC.

There are examples of tank irrigation from all over the country where four million hectares of land are irrigated by small tanks. The farmers of Tamilnadu, Karnataka, Maharashtra, Andhra Pradesh, Gujarat and Himachal Pradesh practice this methodology in one form or the other.

The farmers of Barauch, Surendranagar and Junagadh have adopted water harvesting techniques like peddle-pumbs and roof-rain water collection since last two years. In our efforts to identify a small scale irrigation system, the peddle-pump was introduced in 1996. Peddle-pump is a simple, manually operated, mechanical device working on the principle of balance. Two wooden peddles are connected with a peddle axle and later PVC pipes. For lifting water the person has to put his legs on the peddles and with up-down movement, water is sucked in and comes through the pipe for final delivery. Of course peddling has to be a continuous process. Some farmers have installed this pump with encouraging results.

The roof-rain water harvesting system (RRWHS) comprises an underground water tank with a storage capacity of 10,000 to 68,000 litres. The run-off from the roof is collected by semi circular PVC pipes running along the margins of the roofs and finally emptying in a storage tank through a vertical pipe. Basically, RRWHS is designed to store the rain water in monsoon for use in hot weather. After the initial experimentation, 32 and 52 RRWHS were constructed in different villages in the year 1996 -97 with encouraging results. Both these techniques are being used on a large scale.

28

FARMER ORGANIZATIONS AND ORGANIZATIONAL AND PROCEDURAL CHANGES
(Experiences from Maharashtra)

Vijay Paranjpye

FARMER-MANAGED IRRIGATION SYSTEMS (FMIS)

The irrigation systems being managed by the farmers can be broadly divided into groups of traditional systems and non-traditional systems.

TRADITIONAL SYSTEMS

Traditional systems are those which were constructed, funded and maintained by the people at their own initiative. Community Phad systems and *malgujari* tanks belong to this category of FMIS.

COMMUNITY PHAD SYSTEM IN NASIK AND DHULE DISTRICTS

Phad system of irrigation consists of dividing the entire command into a number of blocks, locally called *phads* (cultivating crops), and irrigating them in a manner pre-determined by the farmers' organizations (FO). The system is followed traditionally in Nasik and Dhule districts of the state of Maharashtra on the wiers (*bandharas*) which were constructed more than 200 years ago. The command area of Phad Schemes varies from 8 ha to 50 ha. There are 66 such schemes which command an area of 5500 ha. The system is entirely managed by the farmers themselves in regard to operation and maintenance of the canal and distribution below the outlets. The maintenance of head work and sluice is also done by the farmers. These systems are termed second class irrigation works. Special provisions exist for these works in the Irrigation Act. Though extremely useful at that point of time, the system is declining because of upstream water withdrawals both by the government and the private users.

MALGUJARI TANKS IN CHANDRAPUR AND BHANDARA DISTRICTS

These tanks in Vidarbha area were primarily constructed by landlords (*malgujars*) in the olden days for providing life-saving irrigation for paddy crops in latter half of September and October, during prolonged drought periods. A committee of eight to ten farmers managed the operation and maintenance of the tanks. All these tanks have since been acquired by the government and farmers' committee has been withdrawn.

1) Joint inspection of the distribution system can enhance the confidence of farmers, but delay in action of repairs can reduce their enthusiasm.

If the objective of delivering water up to the last *chak* is to be critically adhered to, the repairs of outlet gates are absolutely essential. Other repairs can be gradually undertaken with a phased-out but definite programme. In the Sangvi-Shirwal case, both the extremes were evident, extensive and costly repairs on the one hand and no repairs at all on the other. To maintain the basic confidence of farmers about the working condition of the canal, basic repairs can be short-listed and carried out by the FO on payment at an economic price as compared to the estimate offered by the government.

2) The farmers can be pursuaded to bear a part of the cost, if the government explains the paucity of funds.

The government's policy to encourage farmers' organizations needs to be conveyed in letter and spirit to all the rank and file of the Irrigation Department. The allocation of budget for repairs should not be tossed from one section to the other. The estimate of repairs needs to be discussed by the ID with the informal TMC in a planned way.

The farmers, on the other hand, have to assume the responsibility of at least supervising the repairs when conducted. This can be achieved by pursuading farmers to share a part of the repairs cost. Further maintenance of a repaired canal may become easier if this level of participation of farmers is achieved.

After a proper perspective was given by the NGO to the farmers about the non-availability of sufficient funds with the government, some chairmen showed preparedness to share part of the repairs cost and supervise the work personally.

The motivation of farmers to come together for undertaking the responsibility of water distribution function is to be viewed in the overall perspective of the socio-political situation in the state. The over-dependence on state machinery for any welfare measure is the outcome of traditional system and the irrigation policy made thereafter.

3) The tail-enders, if motivated, can serve as the prime movers of the FO. In majority of the Minor Irrigation (MI) schemes in Maharashtra, the initial *chaks* at the head of the canal are getting water and the tail reach farmers are deprived of the same. A measure such as 'Dakshata Samiti' may prove to be useful to expedite the process of formation of an FO.
4) The NGO can be perceived as contractors of forming FO, if the NGO is not properly introduced to the ID officials. The relationship between the ID and the NGO could be different if the intervention of the NGO is properly projected. Being perceived as partners of the ID rather than contractors, they will help in a meaningful joint action of both.

At the outset, it was assumed by us that as the previous experience of joint working with the local line agency was quite encouraging, it will be easier for 'Prabodh Sampada' to seek co-operation of irrigation officers. However, we now feel that the line agency should take initiative to seek help of the concerned NGO. It proves counter-productive if the NGO takes initiative and approaches the ID through external donor agency.

5) Proper dissimination of government's policy about FO can expedite the registration process. The Assitant Registrars in the non-CADA area need to be appraised properly of the governmental policy regarding registration of water co-operatives on MI tanks. The paper work needs further simplification. Substantial effort has been made in this regard by the DIRD, Pune.
6) The informal TMC can be trained to undertake the responsibility of water distribution and management, provided it is made aware of specific functions.

Issues of concern to be brought out include motivational problems, leadership limitations, financial difficulties, management disorders, technical short-comings, government interaction, capital raising abilities, legal implications and socio-political confrontations.

7) The draft MoU needs to be introduced to the farmers in such a way that it can highlight the mutual rights and responsibilities.

It is observed that the draft MoU is highly inclined in favour of the line agency. There are hardly any provisions to fix the responsibility of the ID and to suggest action in the event of non-compliance.

As regards the responsibilities vested with the FO, a timely planning of cropping pattern is solicited, well in advance of the operative season, to make optimum use of the available water. There is a qualitative difference in the planning of the utilization of water in the MI tanks as again a quota sanctioned under the MoU between the government and an FO was registered on a project.

After the turn-over, if the operation of the canal is to be handled by the society, it will need active support from the ID. As a characteristic of a MI tank, i.e., it is secluded in pockets geographically, there is every possibility that the ID will completely neglect the turned-over MI tanks.

In case of a MI tank, the responsibilities are felt to be as follows:

A) Line Agency

i) Help the TMC in calculating total crop-water requirement for the complete season.
ii) Conduct a performance test of the canal at the beginning of every irrigation year.
iii) After every rotation, help the TMC to calculate the water consumption and suggest economy measures.
iv) To explain the meteorological parameters from time to time to the *chak* chairmen at least, with the help of the station erected on the dam site.

B) Farmers' Organization (FO)

i) Prepare a PIP.
ii) Prepare *chak*-wise irrigation schedule under intimation to the chairmen who will, in turn, inform their respective farmers.

iii) Distribution of water, conflict resolution.
iv) Assesment and preparation of bills to individual farmers, recovery and payment to the government.
v) Record-keeping and communication with the members about quantitative and qualitative aspects of the water usage in every season.

c) Mechanism of Interaction

There will have to be a meaningful interaction between the ID & FO after the formal turn-over. Even if the ID representative is an ex-officio member of the TMC, he should be invited by the TMC invariably. The initial meetings, prior to every season, can be kept on some auspicious days so that a habit will be formed as a routine. The chairman of the TMC should be invited to the meetings of ID held at the divisional level. There should be a joint walk-through in the main canal before the commencement of hot season.

8) Training of farmers at various stages can expedite the preparedness of assuming responsibility as an FO. Training of *chak* chairmen and members of informal TMC is essential to equip the society in the water distribution system. It is useful to arrange the training in three parts, viz., in their village, at another running society and at a training institute. All the three have got distinct advantages. Designing the syllabus and engaging faculty which can communicate with the farmers effectively will play a vital role in the training process. Insistence on discipline, punctuality and making notes helps in increasing the overall impact of the course.
9) There is a qualitative difference in the motivation pattern of MI tank beneficiaries. It is normally argued that once you motivate and train people to organise themselves, this will generate continued interest. This will happen every year with the Minor Irrigation Schemes as water is required mostly during summer season.
10) The successful perpetuation of an FO largely depends on a committed leadership. The success of a farmers' organization largely depends on the quality of local leadership that you are able to develop, for example, Chairman of Tank Committee, who can be a leader of good understanding. Also, it would be beneficial to develop second command in the form of a Deputy Chairman.
11) Formation of an FO is yet an external compulsion rather than a part of job description of the line staff of ID in case of MI sector.

The efforts made by the government officials during the project assisted by an external funding agency shall come to a halt if the extraneous support is withdrawn.

The bureaucratic machinery of the Irrigation Department that was geared up to serve the function of formulating the FOs can retard if the work of promoting FOs is not made a part of the job description of the field officers and given due importance at the top regional level.

29

SUGGESTIONS FOR OVERALL IMPROVEMENT OF ANCIENT WATER MANAGEMENT ON GOVERNMENT AND TECHNICAL LEVELS

Vijay Paranjpye

A few suggestions including conservation, fund allocation, water quality, etc. have been listed below:

1. A separate authority be appointed by the Ministry of Water Resources to look after the ancient and traditional systems of water harvesting surviving today. This includes documentations, preparation of inventories of physical structures, archaeological evidences, inscriptional evidences, literary and scientific treatises, anecdotal/oral history and social systems of organizations appropriate for harnessing and utilization of water resources.
2. User societies of the kind prevalent during the period of the Gond Rajas should be re-established so that the local community can increase its stakes in the maintenance of these traditional structures. A locally elected person should be made a trustee (*Vishwasta*) for performing the functions of the erstwhile *malgujars*.
3. The Gram Panchayat should be permitted to levy a maintenance and revitalization tax. The amount of tax collected from users be supplemented by a matching grant by the state government.
4. A special Act should be promulgated by the government of Maharashtra to hand over the tanks of the Bhandara district to the local Panchayats. The district of Bhandara on the north-east border of Maharashtra may be declared as a tank district as it has a total of 43381 tanks irrigating 78 per cent of the net irrigated area of the district. All these tanks have been built about 250 to 300 years ago by the Kohli community specially commissioned by the Gond king Hirshah of the 16th century. In view of the 74th amendment of constitutions, it is recommended that an administrative and organizational mechanism be worked out for enabling the management and ownership of these tanks back to the local communities.
5. Each state government should commission a special gazetteer for documenting and recording all the information related to sources, structures and institutions of traditional water management. The special volumes must not only take form of

compendium, but should record interpretative observations and make useful recommendations which can not only avoid the unnecessary dereliction but also lead to a utilitarian revitalization of such heritage.

6. The participation of the local communities must be an important condition for taking on the task of documentation or revitalization of traditional systems, since such communities have a direct knowledge and experience of constructing, managing and using such systems.
7. The historical references and the surviving tanks and water harnessing cisterns, etc. are an excellent example of the use of simple technology for harnessing rainwater on the hill slopes of the Sahyadri and the remote locations on mountain forts. The Maharashtra State Department of Archaeology should make a detailed documentation of such water sources because they can still provide drinking water to villagers living on the forts in the vicinity.
8. Information about all the systems which are alive, relevant and in full use should be converted into models of exhibits, audio-visual presentations, simplified versions translated into regional languages, so that they become amenable for mass communication and dissemination.
9. The members of the Kohli community (and such other communities in Maharashtra) who are still practising this ancient art of dam construction should be given additional training which would add to their skills, and enable them to continue with their hereditary profession.
10. Different structures like village ponds, temple tanks, community canals, dams and *bhandaras*, community wells and other such traditional structures of water harnessing which have the main intact and are still in use must be repaired, de-silted, renovated and contemporized so as to maximise the benefits accruing to local communities.
11. All the natural springs emanating west of the Sahyadri ranges should be given immediate attention, and the traditional systems of excavating tanks and channels on such springs should be replicated on a large-scale. The catchment areas upstream of such natural streams must be afforested on a priority basis so that natural springs continue to provide water right through the year.
12. The ancient system of reclaiming coastline lands for rice cultivation by constructing embankment with one-way gates (which open out only towards the sea), should be replicated wherever possible. This system of cultivating in 'Khazan lands' (as commonly designated in Goa) has considerable potential in the Konkan coast.
13. Restoration of such systems will require relatively small amounts of money, but will permanently solve the problem of drinking water in these remote areas. For other similar areas on the Western Ghats, the techniques used on these forts could be replicated at a relatively small cost. In any case, these systems need to be documented and preserved.
14. Wherever an important technique/structure/literary reference has deteriorated to the point of extinction or wherever it may have lost its validity or relevance, effort must be made to preserve a few selected and technological representative entities so that they are not permanently lost to humankind.
15. Just as monuments are being preserved as cultural heritage sites, important representatives must be preserved as living heritage sites. This would require a deeper

analysis so that different systems can be prioritised for renovation and use, replication and expansion and archival preservation.

16. The government should make full efforts to restore the ancient water supply systems established by Mughal emperors in the cities of the Deccan, namely, Aurangabad, Nagar, Bijapur, Burhanpur and Pune. This is important because these are the only examples of ancient urban water supply systems and they have tapped sources of water which are different from the sources being used currently by the modern water supply systems. It may be noted that the water of the ancient Katraj Talav in Pune, along with other tanks was used as the measure of the lost resort immediately after the Panshet floods of the 1961 which resulted after the collapse of the Panshet and Khadakwasala dams.
17. After restoration, these ancient water supply sites should be included in the list of urban heritage sites of the concerned city. Such sites would also become important sites for tourism, which could yield future income for their upkeep.
18. Atleast five per cent of the financial allocation for the water resource development sector should be allocated and dedicated to the operation and maintenance of traditional structures which can be used as public utilities. Over the next ten years this financial allocation should increase to 10 per cent of the total allocation year marked for water resources. This recommendation assumes that it is cheaper and more economical to invest in revitalising and maintaining the old assets than to create new ones.
19. Wherever there are possibilities of replicating the traditional systems, all efforts should be made to raise the necessary finances for increasing the distribution and frequency of traditional structures in remote areas which are patently unsuitable for the modern, centralized and capital-intensive techniques.
20. In case of tanks, ponds, wells, etc. which do not have water purification and water affluent disposal systems, investments in water purification plants and disposal systems should be established in villages and towns wherever necessary. Since this would be an enormous task, the creation and addition of such complementary systems must be planned and scheduled over time.
21. All possible efforts must be made to solicit the involvement of local communities in cash or kind, in the management of water resources, so that their sense of ownership and confidence is enhanced.
22. Each state government should assign the responsibility of maintaining the traditional structures through the existing departments of water conservation/irrigation so that such assets become a conscious part of the department's inventory.
23. The traditional and modern systems must not be treated as competitive or exclusive systems, but as mutually complementary and essential parts of a scientific and historical continuum. It is assumed here that modern science has a great role to play in revitalising the traditional systems without disturbing or negating the fundamental principles of long term sustainability. Revitalising will need to be done on a prioritised basis considering the vast number of structures. It is recognized that it may be necessary at times to modify and adopt the old systems so that they can respond to the modern challenges of population explosion and unplanned urbanization.

30

RECOMMENDATIONS
(With Emphasis on the Water Management Systems in Maharashtra)

Vijay Paranjpye

As we turn to the 21st century the status of water resource development in India stands at a cross-road. It may become necessary, nay inevitable, to shed-off a good part of the over-enthusiasm related to large, centralized dam and canal systems which have proved to be financially unviable, socially unjust and environmentally disastrous during the last few decades. Simultaneously, it has become necessary to resurrect and revitalise the traditional principles, techniques and systems of water management. The next century will have to have a judicious and equal mix of tradition and modern science, so that the demands and aspirations of the forest and mountain dwellers, the desert and wetland dwellers and all others living in the rural areas get as much importance as the urban populations and the agriculturists enjoying intensive irrigation:

1. A separate authority should be appointed by the Ministry of Water Resources to look after the ancient and traditional systems of water harnessing, surviving today. This includes documentation, preparing of inventories of physical structures, archaeological evidences, inscriptional evidences, literary and scientific treatises, anecdotal/oral history and social systems of organization appropriate for harnessing and utilization of water resources.
2. User societies of the kind prevalent during the period of the Gond Rajas should be re-established so that the local community can increase its stakes in the maintenance of these traditional structures. A locally elected person should be made a trustee (*vishwasta*) for performing the functions of the erstwhile 'Malgujars'.
3. The Gram Panchayat should be permitted to levy a maintenance and revitalization tax. The amount of tax collected from users should be supplemented by a matching grant by the State Government.
4. A special Act should be promulgated by the Government of Maharashtra to hand over the tanks of the Bhandara district to the local Panchayats.

The district of Bhandara on the north-east border of Maharashtra may be declared as a special tank district as it has a total of 43,381 tanks irrigating 78 per cent of the net irrigated area of the district. All these tanks have been built about 250 to 300 years ago by the Kohli community specially commissioned by the Gond king Hirshah of the 16th century. In view of the 74th amendment of constitutions, it is recommended that an administrative and organizational mechanism be worked out for enabling the management and ownership of these tanks back to the local communities.

5. Each State Government should commission a special gazetteer for documenting and recording all the information related to sources, structures and institutions concerning traditional water management. The special volumes must not only take form of compendiums, but should record interpretative observations and make useful recommendations which can not only avoid the unnecessary dereliction but also lead to a utilitarian revitalization of such heritage.
6. The participation of the local communities must be an important condition for taking up the task of documentation or revitalization of traditional systems, since such communities have a direct knowledge and experience of constructing, managing and using such systems.
7. The historical references and the surviving tanks and water-harnessing cisterns, etc. are an excellent example of the use of simple technology for harnessing rainwater on the high slopes of the Sahyadri and the remote locations on mountain forts. The Maharashtra State Department of Archaeology should make a detailed documentation of such water sources because they can still provide drinking water to villagers living on the forts and in the vicinity.
8. Information about all the systems which are alive, relevant and in full use should be converted into models of exhibits, audio-visual presentations, simplified versions translated into regional languages, so that they may become amenable for mass communication and dissemination.
9. The members of the Kohli community (and such other communities in Maharashtra) who are still practising this ancient art of dam construction should be given additional training which would add to their skills, and enable them to continue with their hereditary profession.

CONSERVATION

10. Different structures like village ponds, temple tanks, community canals, dams and *bhandaras*, community wells and other such traditional structures of water harnessing which have remained intact and are still in use must be repaired, de-silted, renovated and contemporized so as to maximise the benefits accruing to local communities.
11. All the natural springs emanating west of the Sahyadri ranges should be given immediate attention, and the traditional system of excavating tanks and channels on such springs should be replicated on a large scale. The catchment areas upstream of such natural streams must be afforested on a priority basis so that the natural springs continue to provide water round the year.
12. The ancient system of reclaiming coastline lands for rice cultivation by constructing embankment with one way gates (which open out only towards the sea), should be

replicated wherever possible. This system of cultivating in 'Khazan lands' (as commonly designated in Goa) still has considerable potential in the Konkan coast.

13. Restoration of such systems will require relatively small amounts of money, but will permanently solve the problem of drinking water in these remote areas. For other similar areas on the Western Ghats, the techniques used on these forts could be replicated at a relatively small cost. In any case, these systems need to be documented and preserved.
14. Wherever an important technique/structure/literary reference has deteriorated to the point of extinction or wherever it may have lost its validity or relevance, efforts must be made to preserve a few selected and typologically representative entities so that they are not permanently lost to human kind.
15. Just as monuments are being preserved as cultural heritage sites, important representatives must be preserved as living heritage sites. This would require a deeper analysis so that different systems can be prioritised for a) renovation and use; b) replication and expansion; and c) archival preservation.
16. The government should make all efforts to restore the ancient water supply systems established by Mughal emperors in the cities of the Deccan, namely, Aurangabad, Nagar, Bijapur, Burhanpur and Pune. This is important because these are the only examples of ancient urban water supply systems and they have tapped sources of water which are different from the sources being used currently by the modern water supply systems. It may be noted that the water of the ancient Katraj Talav in Pune, along with other tanks was used as the measure of the lost resort immediately after the Panshet floods of the 1961 which resulted after the collapse of the Panshet and Khadakwasala dams.
17. After restoration, these ancient water supply sites should be included in the list of urban heritage sites of the concerned city. Such sites would also become important sites for tourism, which could yield further income for their upkeep.

FUNDS ALLOCATION

18. At least 5 per cent of the financial allocation for the water resource development sector must be allocated and dedicated to the operation and maintenance of traditional structures which can be used as public utilities. Over the next ten years this financial allocation should increase to 10 per cent of the total allocation earmarked for water resources. This recommendation assumes that it is cheaper and more economic to invest in revitalising and maintaining the old assets than to create new ones.
19. Wherever there are possibilities of replicating the traditional systems, all efforts should be made to raise the necessary finances for increasing the distribution and frequency of traditional structures in remote areas which are patently unsuitable for the modern, centralized and capital intensive techniques.

WATER QUALITY

20. In case of tanks, ponds/wells, etc. which do not have water purification and water affluent disposal systems, investments in water purification plants and disposal

systems should be established in villages and towns wherever necessary. Since this would be an enormous task, the creation and addition of such complementary systems must be planned and scheduled over time.

GENERAL RECOMMENDATIONS

21. All possible efforts must be made to solicit the involvement of local communities in cash or kind, in the management of water resources, so that their sense of ownership and confidence is enhanced.
22. Each State Government should assign the responsibility of maintaining the traditional structures either through the existing departments of water conservation/irrigation so that such assets become a conscious part of the department's inventory.
23. The traditional and modern systems must not be treated as competitive or exclusive systems, but as mutually complementary and essential parts of a scientific and historical continuum. It is assumed here that the modern science has a great role to play in revitalising the traditional systems without disturbing or negating the fundamental principle of long term sustainability. Revitalising will need to be done on a prioritised basis considering the vast number of structures. It is recognized however, that it may be necessary at times to modify and adapt the old systems so that they can respond to the modern challenges of population explosion and unplanned urbanization.

31

WHAT OTHERS SAID*

Gyani Lal Badam

During the course of the deliberations, a number of presentations were made, which evoked a lot of interest and discussion on both traditional and contemporary water management systems.

In his introductory address, Dr. K.K. Chakravarty (Bhopal) suggested that "the Workshop is not intended to be an end in itself but an instrument for working out follow-up action in the field. A few individuals, Institutions and NGOs are working in the field for documentation and revitalisation of traditional water management strategies. We hope that this workshop will help them in comparing notes. By the end of the seminar, we should be able to partially locate the managerial, legal or financial problems which stand in the way of recycling of local water harvesting structures. The biggest problem may be the problem of understanding the need of establishing the validity and feasibility of these structures as eco-specific and cost-effective alternatives to mega structures. The Museum would like to build an indoor and outdoor exhibition, with a travelling component, to spread understanding about these structures. It would also like to explore the possibility of promoting traditional solutions as valid alternatives, and of acting as bridge between different communities, Institutions and the Government for removing administrative difficulties in doing so. We hope that this workshop will inaugurate a phase of long term, mutually reinforcive and fruitful collaboration between the participants and the museum." This introductory note was followed by the presentation of papers, which included discussions on both traditional and contemporary water management systems. These have been summarised below.

Dr. Arun Sud (New Delhi) emphasised the use of rain water re-charge and management, ponds and sunken type water harvesting devices and need of water for irrigation techniques. He concluded that the present approach and technology is so fragmented and departmentalised that we begin and end with drinking water, and other departments manage irrigation with their visions limited to crop requirements only. This is the reason that holistic approach is necessary for management of total water needs.

* Comments of scholars and water managers, who made presentations but could not submit their papers.

Dr. Sud reaffirmed that the indigenous system is holistic and composite. Rainwater management starts from the village and not from drainage lines where modern technology lays its total emphasis. He was of the opinion that projects that are leased on traditional technologies should be given priority.

Prof. K.C. Malhotra (Calcutta, now in Noida) said that it is better to make smaller dams for more meaningful discharge of water and its various applications. He traced the evolutionary trends of water management from prehistoric to modern times and stressed that the ancient system of water management had been made available to the humankind by passing through various stages of experience and even today, it is worthwhile to take note of the applied expertise and collective wisdom.

Late Sri Jagdish Godbole (Pune) speaking on the traditional water management solutions with regard to Pauna Dam, stressed the need for making small 'Kacha' and 'Pucca' dams, small tanks and ponds. Sri Sharad Shinde suggested that priority for making dams should be given to drought prone areas. Sri Sunil Waman spoke on the need of documentation of NGOs work, giving an account of use of water in Western Ghats.

Shri Subhash Despande (Pune) speaking on farmer managed irrigation system talked about terrace cultivation and diversion and emphasised the use of traditional wisdom. He brought out the problems relating to traditional methods applied in larger medium sized dams. He discarded the encroachment by bureaucratic machinery in the traditional system and emphasised the need for peoples' participation in Non-Governmental Organisations. According to him the NGOs should be allowed to handle the budgetary provisions meant for a project as the Government can not activate the people for participatory programmes. He stressed the need for "Shramdan" on the part of the people for better results.

Dr. G.K. Dev Burman (Bhopal) gave an audio visual presentation on Santhal Huts. Emphasising that whatever structures are available for water management (may be deepwells, borewells etc.) should fit in the prevailing eco-system. He stressed the need for organising more workshops and seminars at regional and zonal levels for educating the general public. He was of the view that Govt. should act as a catalytic agent in this exercise. He appreciated the schemes so successfully initiated in Maharashtra which other states could emulate.

Shri Rajendra Singh (Alwar, Rajasthan) spoke on traditional water management system in Rajasthan (Khandav Desh), and was of the opinion that the ancient monument of water management system should be preserved as far as possible. Shri A.K. Pathak, (Mirzapur, U.P.) giving examples of traditional water harvesting systems in U.P., suggested that there was no need for making water harvesting programmes wherever irrigation is a problem.

Shri Anil Joshi (Dehradun) speaking on Traditional Water System in Uttarakhand with reference to Ganga-Yamuna, made a plea that traditional knowledge systems should be used while constructing dams and subsequently in developmental plans. Dr. Girija Pande and Shri Ashutosh Upadhyay (Nainital) spoke on "Uttarakhand : A big reservoir of water" and stressed the need for using traditional water harvesting system in the area.

Shri Anil Yadav (Ganj Basoda, Vidisha) gave an account of management of different water resources in Siruanj (M.P.) and stressed the need for declaring ancient wells and tanks as archaeological sites. He was of the opinion that saints staying in the vicinity of tanks and other water sources helped to maintain them. He, however, regretted that this tradition had almost died. His concern was about the loss of fisheries, crop system and water-borne vegetation. He invited the attention of audience to the Bhopal Gas Tragedy and maintained that fishing in the water had to be abandoned within the area of 2 km from Bhopal.

Shri Rajendra Kumar (Jhansi) gave an account of the work done by Rajiv Gandhi Mission in the Bundelkhand region stressing the need for peoples' participation in such programmes. Shri A. Jeyaram (Nagpur) gave an account of work done by ISRO Remote Sensing Department on watershed programme in Chandrapur Distt. of Maharashtra using various satellite facilities.

Ms. M.S. Vani (New Delhi) brought out the importance of law and policy with regard to traditional water system and stressed that power of managing water should be given to local people.

Dr. G. Bhaskar Rao (New Delhi) spoke on Percolation Tanks in Anantpur District of Andhra Pradesh, giving an account of effect of population density, technical know how and social systems in relation to the tanks. He emphasised that utility of tanks can be enhanced by converting them into percolation tanks. Shri V.N. Sharma (Vidisha) discussed the loss due to overflow of Percolation tanks.

Shri Vinayak Potnis (Bhopal) discussed the religious approach of the river ecosystem and questioned the utility of making big dams notwithstanding the positive aspects of these dams. Shri Dinesh Mishra (Jamshedpur) spoke on floods drawing heavily on their written accounts and considered the big dams as one of the major causes of floods. Shri Uma Gani spoke on watershed and emphasised the importance of land use map, water use map and hydrological soil map for making water harvesting strategies.

Dr. B.R. Sharma (now late) (Shimla) spoke on traditional water system in Himachal Pradesh giving an account of the importance of the religious life of the people. He stressed the need for saving water mills (Gharat).

Dr. D.V. Devraj (Mysore) gave historical background of tanks and lakes in Karnataka expressing great concern for saving them. He gave examples of some archaeological excavations in Karnataka which have preserved ancient water storage system (e.g., ring wells).

Shri Ravindra Shukla (Indore) while speaking on river pollution, said that Madhya Pradesh, upto 20 years back, was known for its clean water rivers, but now the situation is quite alarming since all the river and stream banks are over-polluted. The Narmada river, from where 10 to 15 lakh people are getting water, is polluted to the extent that it has become a health hazard for the beneficiaries. Elaborating his point, he said that Narmada has become both a centre of attraction and cause of concern for the environmentalists all over the country. Even Bhopal is also under stress of drinking polluted water due to contamination. Mr. Shukla showed some slide projections of Beladila project, Bastar Habitation Project, Sampri and Dahini river projects, Bodh ghat Pariyojana, Indravati river and Nanadeshwari temple, stressing that Beladila project is responsible for polluting the water system.

Shri P. Swami (Madurai) referred to the availability of quality water minor irrigation tanks and traditional water systems in the distt. of Ramanathapuram in Tamilnadu. He also referred to *Kanmai* – a traditional system prevalent some 2 or 3 hundred year ago. He reaffirmed that taking up of local water resources including water tanks would not solve the problem of sanitation, irrigation by gravity flow and fishing rights by the local people. He said that desilting of masonry has been a great success. Referring to typical water lifting system in the area he told that the local systems help the farmer in getting water resources even when they are located at the lower level than in the agricultural land. Dr. G. Paran (Kanya Kumari) speaking on acute water shortage of Tamilnadu, highlighted the water related programmes of Vivekanand Memorial Trust. He dwelt on motivation of people in eastern states, J&K and other states of Tamilnadu and invited the attention of scholars to the problems of disposal of night soil and its effect on eco-system. He further referred to *Oorani*, *Kanmai* and other systems of local inhabitants applied in purification of water.

Mr. Arun Kumar Kodre (Pune) referred to Vanrai Bunds and their usefulness. His main thrust was on community based participatory programme. He also said that Vanrai Bunds were getting popular in the area as soil can be conserved for a long time with these types of bunds and suggested that traditional methods and modern systems are required to be combined in this effort. Shri Kodre thought that within an expenditure of Rs. 3000/- only, the system is viable and enduring even though during the first year of commissioning of such bunds the beneficiaries may not get enough water.

Dr. Jai Nagra (Khandwa) said that people speak of "forest mafia" but not of "jal mafia". He cited an example of "jal mafia" which is manipulating the sale of land through which water supply is made to Khandwa. Discussing the whole problem in detail he raised the question as to whether catchment area of water supply should be treated a wasteland or a useful patch of land.

Shri Ramesh Billorey (Khandwa) stressed upon eliciting the traditional knowledge of the people and suggested that a series of workshops at smaller places other than the urban areas need to be arranged. He made some suggestions on sustainable alternatives which included use of traditional wisdom and of the people, alternative agriculture practices, avoidance of crops needing more water, solutions to energy problems such as water wells. He recommended the maintenance of sacred grooves, tree worship, water spring worship and arrangement of "Nadi Utsav". He further cautioned about industrial pollution, municipal waste and misuse of energy and suggested the application of consumer culture, recycling of water etc.

Shri G.T. Bhimte (Bhopal) said that people benefit from constructing dams to allow less flow of water and retention of surplus water to be utilised during successive floods. He also screened a video film on a dam constructed near Bhopal.

Shri Rajnikant Yadav (Jabalpur) referred to an urban system of water management about 500 years back around Narmade river. He informed about various tanks which were built around settlements for healthy use.

Mr. Madhav Pandit (Pune) spoke on the traditional water management systems in Konkan and explained the importance of 'Pat' system – which consists of small perennial canals – in the household water supply system of this region.

In the concluding remarks, Prof. K. Karunakaran (Chitrakoot) appreciated the points raised especially about Gujarat, Tamilnadu and Maharashtra and referred to border areas of Tamilnadu, Kerala and Karnataka in which about ten years back, the people were poverty stricken, but which are now prosperous with the help of missionaries and NGOs. He referred to the traditional system of *Kudimaramah* and *Kundrakudi* and suggested that the IGRMS may evolve a policy plan on the subject and take steps to form panchayat clusters as is done under "Gandhi Gram Yojana". He was appreciative of the work of the NGOs and the institutions, Museums and Universities in the water management solutions and thanked the IGRMS for taking the lead in this direction.

In the last session, concrete recommendations were invited from the participants, followed by a discussion. Amongst the principle recommendations were the documentation, research and analysis of traditional water systems and their restoration, the need for the allocation of Government resources for such work, and the necessity of a change in the official policies regarding water. Dr. Vijay Paranjpye (Pune) stressed the need for combining academic research with practical implementation of the recommendations through a constant interaction between such public interest groups, Government departments and the people. As an immediate step in this direction, a committee of some of the senior participants was formed, to ensure a follow-up action and lobbying with the Government and also a sustained communication within the group of interested people.

Finally, the objective of this workshop was to provide a forum to all individuals who have worked on this subject, and to arrive at a set of policy recommendations which would enable reinstatement and revitalisation of those traditional systems which are relevant today. It was also proposed that all this scientific information be converted into simplified and lucid information for the benefit of the community at large. The translations of resource material into regional language, publishing it through regional press and other media, and putting together a small mobile exhibition would be the means of documenting and compiling all traditional concepts, epigraphs, documents, photographs, anecdotes, techniques, structural evidences, plans/designs and information available in Classical or Modern literature. Such work would help in identifying the elements that can be restored, reinstated or practised with benefit in the modern times. The workshop also aimed at identifying elements which can be integrated into the so called modern systems being established today. Besides this, through this workshop it was intended to simplify the concepts and to make them available for the common man through newspapers and magazines.

32

CONCLUDING REMARKS

Gyani Lal Badam and Ashwani Wanganeo

India experiences various climatic zones — both longitudinal as well as latitudinal. This variation results in unequal distribution of rainwater resulting in periodical water crisis. Even in the places of excess rain drought spells have been observed, e.g., Cherrapunji with excessive precipitation also suffers periodically from drought. Sometimes the rainwater lasts for a few hours in a day or a few days in a year in some places, causing spate in ephemeral rivers and channels. On the other hand, the over-exploitation of resources together with drought spells has resulted in the decline of water levels and its quality.

Looking back towards the early period, the migration of early man was also on account of his preference to settle down near water sources like rivers, ponds and natural springs. In order to settle down at a specific place, people of various places devised innovative methods of water harvesting and conservation techniques. Though since time immemorial rivers have been used for irrigation purposes, in the Harappan Period, deliberate attempts were made to control water course by raising structures, like the Great Bath at Mohenjo-daro (c. 2500 BC) and create artificial irrigation canals.

Historic records also reveal that water was harnessed and distributed on a large scale through the construction of dams and canals. As far as religious establishments in rock-cut caves are concerned, water reservoirs were dug to store the natural spring water. During early medieval times, efforts were made to store water close to religious establishments like temple complexes by constructing specific structures such as *kunda* or *pushkarani* (tank, well, step-well).

Arthashastra refers to the concept of *khayas* (irrigation canals) and *bandhya* (bunds) constructed through cooperative efforts. The works of Patanjali and Panini also refer to water channels, while the *Arthashastra* refers to the construction of check dams and reservoirs. The canals were maintained and the water supply was regulated through monitored sluices.

During the time of Emperor Ashoka (273-232 BC) the Yavana governor Tushaspa added conduits to the dam constructed by Pushyamitra, during the time of Chandragupta Maurya. This feat of Mauryan engineering skill lasted for nearly eight hundred years with periodic renovations and additions. Further, the traditional sources consisted of wells, step-wells and a few ponds adjoining Hindu and Jain temples.

In Gujarat and Rajasthan where the rainwater is available for a very brief period, step-wells were constructed. These step-wells were meant not only to make access to water easy but were also luxurious and cool resorts. They were bedecked with considerable amount of sculpture and ornate galleries, as such they are important architectural monuments as well. Besides this, the local harvesting device known as *kundis* (huge concrete saucers) existed in the Thar Desert. The concept of step-well continued even upto the Mughal Period and can be seen at Delhi, Agra and Fatehpur Sikri.

In Bundelkhand, traditional water harvesting structures were *pukharian* (natural or man-made ponds), *talab, bandhies* (water is impounded in bunded fields during monsoon and direct sowing of rabi crops is generally done; rice cultivation may be followed with wheat or other suitable rabi crops that use residual moisture*), baories* (similar to wells with steps) and wells. In Burhanpur traditional water supply conservation invited attention towards investigating the re-charge potential of Satpura Valley in AD 1615. Ground water flowing towards Tapti river from Satpura ranges was tapped and stored in underground tunnels having ventilating shafts to a common sump called *Jali Karanj* and was being supplied to township and camps through earthenware and dressed stone pipes. The system of water supply conceived about hundred years back is still functioning and catering to the demand of about one million litres of water per day.

The surviving tanks and water harnessing cisterns are an excellent example of the use of simple technology for harnessing rainwater on high slopes of the Sahyadri and other remote locations on the foothills of Maharashtra. Four thousand four hundred tanks irrigating about 80 per cent of the land have been constructed 250 to 3000 years ago. The *Phad system* (community based irrigation) developed in Maharashtra is an excellent example of water conservation. The proto-historic irrigation system of Inamgoan in Pune revealed how the floodwater was diverted and stored for subsequent use.

In Kalahandi district, Orissa, also rainwater with seasonal *nullah's* were diverted to fill *kata* (a big reservoir, usually located at the end of the village) and *munda* (small embankments constructed at the top of the village). Apart from having utilitarian values, these ponds and reservoirs of *pushkaras,* etc. served religious purpose too like purification, ritualistic bath and the water of these was used for consecration of kings. Very often a pond was dedicated to mother goddess or fertility deity.

A surface water pond (*Oorani*) constructed for providing drinking water to the area with predominant brackish water in Madukulattur block in Ramanathpuram in Dist. Tamilnadu, has not only improved the quality of existing tube well source but has also solved the long awaited water supply problems. Ownership of 1/10th of the area of land was given to the person who irrigated the land by the tank constructed and maintained by him on his own expenses. Thus, village tanks were dug in practically every conceivable place within the Krishna and Cauvery river basins of south Indian peninsula. There are examples of tank irrigation from all over the country where four million hectares of land are irrigated by small tanks. The farmers of Tamilnadu, Karnataka, Maharashtra, Andhra Pradesh, Gujarat and Himachal Pradesh practice this methodology in one form or the other.

The farmers of Barauch, Sorandranagar and Junagadh have adopted water-harvesting techniques like peddle-pumps and roof-rainwater collection since last two years while in Mizoram harvesting of rainwater from corrugated iron sheets was developed long back as a better management and conservation strategy.

However, among traditional water sources, ponds and lakes are not given much importance in Himachal Pradesh because of pollution due to stagnation, while emphasis is laid on springs, snow-fed streams, rivers and infiltration galleries. On the other hand, in other hilly regions, the scattered inhabitants continue to use traditional sources even though there is a good water supply.

The proceedings of the seminar on 'Traditional Water Management Systems' have focused on various problems and solutions in the management of different water bodies. A critical examination of the problems associated with water management has shown that the system differs from region to region depending on geohydrological situation and the availability or otherwise of water sources. The system is more eco-specific than general in terms of usages and utilities.

As water is an integral part of human life, management of water bodies has been taken on a priority basis since time immemorial. In this context, we have discussed some of the examples in ancient times and shown as to how water system was managed with the utmost care and responsibility for different sources including those of temples and forts.

The workshop has helped us to recapitulate and revisit the eco-specific models of water management. Arising out of the proceedings, some important aspects were discussed. For example, it is necessary to involve people at every level about the awareness of the traditional water management solutions. This can be done is schools, at Panchayat level, through audio-visual aids and with the help of small booklets in regional languages which can be distributed free of charge. More voluntary organizations, non-governmental organizations and environmentalists may be encouraged to take up this venture.

The papers touched upon aspects from archaeological sites like Inamgaon, heritage points like temples, forts and the inscriptional evidences. Examples of contemporary water management from site-specific areas like Kutch, Tamilnadu, Himachal Pradesh, Uttar Pradesh hills, Maharashtra and other areas have been discussed bringing out the gradual development of water management and its lacunae. Finally, suggestions and recommendations that emerged out of the deliberations have been put in black and white for a follow up action.

It was stressed that small and big bunds and the medium-sized dams should be constructed with the help of local technologies and efforts should be made to introduce measures in order to avoid soil erosion as far as possible. In this respect, the example of Vanrai Bunds in Maharashtra was cited as worth emulating. In addition, this is a very inexpensive method to conserve and filter water.

It was perhaps for the first time that people and scholars were made aware of various 'mafias' operating in several areas like 'forest mafia' and 'jal mafia'. The latter manipulates the sale of land through which water supply is given. A strong plea was made for tackling this problem at various levels and if necessary involve also government authorities. If this 'jal mafia' is not curbed, the whole exercise of the water management system will lose its meaning. It was also agreed that there should be a proper ban on leasing out of catchment area of water supply for cent percent results.

The participants were of the view that the problem of water system should not be treated in isolation but should form part of the culture of the country, since the basic development of a nation including the generation of energy, the fauna and flora, irrigation patterns, etc. depends on the supply of water. It is also not to be forgotten that though lot of technological advancement has come up in recent years, application of traditional wisdom in technical and non-technical water management should not be overlooked. It was agreed that the indigenous local systems, for example, *'Haveli'*, *'Kanmai'*, *'Oorani'*, *'Kudimaramah'* and *'Kundrakudi'* should be revitalised for providing an efficient background to the users of water management by advanced technology. Also, these traditional methods will be useful in controlling the flow and diversion of water, and finally, will also partly contribute to controlling floods.

To keep our tradition alive, steps should be taken to maintain sacred groves, worship trees and also water springs, and periodically organize water festivals like 'Nadi Utsav'.

Keeping in view the above water harvesting and conservation technology, it can safely be concluded that the time-tested technologies devised need to be strengthened besides renovating the existing structures for the betterment of Indian public at large.